"The theme of love, sacred and secular, in the Middle Ages has long interested scholars and intellectual historians, but few have had the competence and wide knowledge to do justice to both and to show how they are related. Fr. Parmisano's beautiful book accomplishes this difficult task and puts to rest the stereotype that medieval society knew only a theological Manicheanism horrified of sex and a profane cult of extramarital "romance." Joyful and passionate love within marriage has finally found a place in our understanding of medieval Christian culture."

Fr. Augustine Thompson, O.P., S.T.M.
Professor of History
DSPT and Graduate Theological Union, Berkeley.

*****

"According to many scholars, the medieval period saw the rise of romantic love, separated from any relation to marriage and opposed to the Church's teaching. Father Stan Parmisano shows how very wrong this picture is. Treating the reader to a delightful exposition of medieval moral manuals, the Church's nuptial rite, the teachings of medieval theologians such as Thomas Aquinas and Alexander of Hales, and the poetry of Geoffrey Chaucer, John Gower, and John Lydgate, Parmisano reveals the rich and salutary teaching on love and marriage that characterized the medieval Church and that the Christians today continues to uphold. This splendid tour de force lays to rest the hoary myths promulgated even by many Catholic theologians today.

Matthew Levering
Professor of Theology, University of Dayton.
Co-editor: *Nova et Vetera*
Author: *Jewish-Christian Dialogue and the Life of Wisdom*

*****

The Craft of Love should prove informative, appealing and helpful to clergy laymen and professors alike. Through an informed and fascinating treatment of the theology of Augustine and Aquinas and the poetry of Chaucer, Gower, Lydgate and others, Father Parmisano demonstrates that the Catholic Church has always had a healthy appreciation of human sexuality as a gift from a loving God. This book reminds us that we are all called by our Creator to practice the craft of love. It also shows us that when it comes to love and intimacy, the Church's position makes the most sense.

John F. Millard, Ph.D.
John A. McNeice, Jr., Chair
Blessed John XXIII National Seminary

*****

As some wag put it, "Nothing is so unpredictable as the past!" Logically, this is so because one can only predict the future. Of course, there's also "retrodiction." That is, one can give an explanation of what has happened, pointing to the conditions which led to the phenomenon of interest. But the wag's chief point is that often we don't know what's happened, or why, or why what's happened is misunderstood. Such is the case with regard to the curious career of love's craft. Stan Parmisano's welcome study gives us a start in putting things right by bringing them to light.

Prof. James Hanink
Department of Philosophy
Loyola Marymount University
Editor: *New Oxford Review*

*****

The Craft of Love

Love and Intimacy in Christian Marriage

Stan Parmisano

Solas Press
Antioch
2010

© 2009 Stan Parmisano O.P.

All rights reserved.

No part of this book may be reproduced, stored in a retrieval system, or transmitted in any form, or by any means, electronic, mechanical, photocopying or otherwise, without prior written permission of the publisher, except by a reviewer who may quote brief passages in a review.

Permissions Dept
SOLAS Press
P.O. Box 4066
Antioch CA 94531
USA

Library of Congress Cataloging-in-Publication Data

Parmisano, Stan.

The craft of love: love and intimacy in Christian marriage / Stan Parmisano.

p. cm.

Includes bibliographical references (p.   ) and index.

ISBN 978-1-893426-03-0

1. Marriage--Religious aspects--Christianity--History of doctrines. 2. Love--Religious aspects--Christianity--History of doctrines. I. Title.

BT706.P37 2010

234'.165094209023--dc22

2010038131

Inspiration

Set me as a seal upon your heart,
as a seal upon your arm;
for love is strong as death,
jealousy is cruel as the grave.
Its flashes are flashes of fire,
a most vehement flame.

Many waters cannot quench love,
neither can floods drown it.
If a man offered for love
all the wealth of his house,
it would be utterly scorned.

Song of Songs (8, 6-7)

Table of Contents

Forward xi

Chapter 1
PROLOGUE 1

Chapter 2
PRIESTS AND POETS 13

Chapter 3
ARISTOTELIAN THOMISM 33

Chapter 4
FRANCISCAN AUGUSTINIANISM 63

Chapter 5
THE MIND OF CHRISTENDOM 91

Chapter 6
PRAYING AND BELIEVING 97

Chapter 7
THE MORAL MANUAL 119

Chapter 8
LOVE IN SECULAR MANUALS AND POETRY ... 141

Chapter 9
CHAUCER'S CRAFT OF LOVE 155

Chapter 10
GOWER'S CONFESSION OF A LOVER 199

Chapter 11
LYDGATE—LOVE-GOOD, LOVE-BAD 225

Chapter 12
OTHER POETS OF THE 14TH CENTURY 245

Chapter 13
CONCLUSION 257

Notes 263

Bibliography 287

Index 295

Acknowledgements

Since the completed work has been long in coming before the public those to whom I most owe thanks for it are no longer here to receive them: Kenelm Foster, O.P., Thomas Gilby, O.P. and, especially, Jack A. W. Bennett, all of whom helped in the initial research and writing that has been reduced and expanded to the present volume, though they are in no way responsible for its limitations. I also owe a debt of gratitude to the then editors of *New Blackfriars* who back in 1969 published two articles of mine culled from my research and which off and on through the years have brought me requests to get the whole of it into print. To my Dominican brothers of the Western Dominican Province I am grateful for more than need be expressed here, but particularly for the long and fruitful Cambridge sabbatical that made it all possible. My thanks to Don and Helen Wood and the Christian Brothers of St. Mary's College, California, for a room of my own and all the peace and quiet needed for the task of revision, and for the hospitality they offered me as relief from it... Finally, I thank my sister, Corinne, who through dark times and light learned well the craft of love, taught it to her children and (though she will be surprised to hear it) helped teach it to me.

Stan Parmisano 2007

Fabian Stanley Parmisano (1926-2009) was proud of his Italian roots and was delighted to recall his family's involvement in fishing and fish marketing in San Francisco California. He would laugh as he told the tale of how he didn't last long in his first job—as a bartender in the family speak-easy.

Stan joined the Dominican Order and was soon sent to Cambridge University to study for a Ph.D. in English Literature. At Cambridge he studied the best English writers, old and new, and he knew well, and often by heart, many of the classics from Beowulf to the poems of T. S. Eliot.

His work on Chaucer and 14th century English literature revealed a pre-modern appreciation of marital love. He recognized clearly that, no matter what our particular vocation was, married or widowed, single or celibate, a deliberate "craft of love" was needed for each of our human pilgrimages. He was truly that contemplative who shared the fruits of contemplation in teaching, writing, and preaching.

Editor's Note

In 2007 Fr. Parmisano hoped to publish the results of his intensive study. We worked to draw together various papers to unify them within the framework of his manuscript on spousal love. The aim was to provide a broad review addressing theology, liturgy, lay teaching, and poetry dealing with fourteenth century marriage practices in England.

Why fourteenth century England? Parmisano could see that the rude facts of a 2000-year Church history could be marshaled to any ideological point of view and that a broad view of a one period would better show the truth. In a polemic, unique to him, he says, "While present-day historians and theologians have found ample evidence for criticisms and censures [of Christian practices] in the past ... It will surely be found that the critical views are not untrue so much as incomplete and untrue only when they are offered as the whole story."

He approved of what was done. To quote him: "I find you've done what I feared was impossible ... making it inviting to and readable by the non-scholar ordinary intelligent reader while respecting its scholarship ... Once again, thanks for not only reading my text but CREATIVELY reading it. It's still a work for the scholar but now for just about everyone interested in, concerned about, love, which, of course, is EVERYONE."

Unfortunately his final illness did not permit further work, and infelicities in construction and references will be seen by specialists. However, 'EVERYONE' can read with profit his subtle understanding of romance and spousal love.

EDITOR

ABBREVIATIONS

Some abbreviations used in Chaucer References

****

BD: *The Book of the Duchess.*
CT: *The Clerk's Tale.*
GP: *The General Prologue.*
KnT: *The Knight's Tale.*
MT: *The Monk's Tale.*
MLT: *The Man of Law's Tale.*
Pars: *The Parson's Tale.*
PF: *The Parliament of Fowls.*
WBP: *The Wife of Bath's Prologue.*
WBT: *The Wife of Bath's Tale.*

Foreword

In order to illustrate the importance of this text I need to situate it into the larger theological conversation concerning the good of marriage in the past hundred years. In defining marriage, the 1917 *Code of Canon Law*, following terminology made prominent by Aquinas six centuries earlier in his *Commentary on the Sentences*,[1] taught: "The primary end of matrimony is the procreation and raising of offspring; the secondary, mutual help and the remedy for concupiscence."[2] The language of hierarchy—primary and secondary—is not repeated in the 1983 Code. The revised formulation says instead that marriage "is by its nature ordered toward the good of the spouses [*bonum coniugum*] and the procreation and education of offspring.[3] To an untrained eye, this might appear as merely a shift in rhetoric introducing no significant change in meaning. But the shift is rather more significant.

Centuries of theological interpretation, going back to at least Augustine (d. 430), considered the spousal relationship—the *marriage*—as an instrumental good, a means, albeit a necessary means, to ends beyond itself, most principally procreation.[4] Was this also Aquinas's meaning? This is debatable. Aquinas did not use "primary" and "secondary" in a strictly evaluative sense. He did not mean that the mutual relationship of the spouses was less important than procreation. He meant that procreation was metaphysically prior to the

---

[1] *Commentary on the Sentences*, 4, d. 26, q. 1, a. 1; *Summa Theologiae*, Sup., q. 41, a. 1.

[2] CIC 1917, c. 1013, §1.

[3] Can. 1055, §1; see also Vatican II, *Gaudium et Spes*, no. 48.

[4] In *De Bono Conjugali*, no. 9, Augustine states that just as learning is not sought for its own sake but for the sake of wisdom, so marriage (he includes intercourse) is not sought for its own sake but *for the sake of* friendship.

spousal friendship insofar as procreation pertains to man and woman in respect to the generic nature they share with all animals. Their mutual relationship is "secondary" because interpersonal relationships and the duties they give rise to—principally of rendering to one another what is due (*ius*—from *iustitia*, or justice)—pertain to man and woman in respect to their properly human nature. Nevertheless, the instrumentalist interpretation of marriage dominated Catholic thought until the 20th century.

The 1983 code rules out an instrumentalist rendering. Marriage it says is "ordered toward" *procreation* and the *good of the spouses* [*bonum coniugum*]. Both pertain to marriage's very intelligibility. Procreation is not set forth as primary and marital unity (the perfection or fulfillment of the spouses as persons and as a couple) as secondary. Both rather are set forth—and this is the great contribution of Vatican II theology of which the '83 Code is a juridical expression—as what marriage *is*. Marriage, sought for its own sake, *is* a procreative and unitive type of human communion. This in no way devalues the procreative goodness of marriage. It rather embeds it side by side with the *bonum coniugum* into marriage's very nature. So marriage's defining goods, that is those intrinsic benefits I choose precisely in choosing marriage, are the good of the spouses and the procreation and education of children.

This is not different from or more than what is taught in Sacred Scripture. The two creation narratives in the Book of Genesis emphasize respectively these two intrinsic goods. In Genesis 1 (the so-called "Priestly account") we see an emphasis placed on procreation—"be fruitful and multiply", and in Genesis 2 (the "Yahwist account"), on the unity of the spouses—"a man... cleaves to his wife and the two become one flesh." But the mature formulation in which both are defined as inseparably connected, as mutually defining of this unique type of human community, waited until the period of the Council. We legitimately can refer to this as a development in the Church's articulation of its doctrine of marriage.

How should we understand then the *bonum coniugum*? What is this spousal good sought in and through marriage? It is a one-flesh good, a fulfillment of human communion precisely of the one-flesh type, an actualization of a possibility for a unique form of human community. Said in another way, marital unity, unlike other forms of human community, is a one-flesh unity, a communion of person's entailing the mutual gift of the bodily-personal self in its masculinity and femininity.

Both reason and revelation affirm that this communion is *per se aptus ad prolis generationem* (Canon 1061, §1), that is, *procreative in type* (although not always actually functionally fertile). In realizing their one-fleshness through the marital act, spouses unite in a procreative type of communion. Marital intercourse then is a paradigmatic expression of an act that is at once unitive and procreative. It is a unique expression of what Vatican II refers to as "conjugal love" (*Gaudium et Spes*, no. 50).

Some say that at Vatican II the Church finally discovered sex and love—before it only saw babies. This is a gross caricature. But caricatures are only recognizable because they exaggerate existing features. Admittedly, Catholic thought until recently articulated the centrality of procreation in marriage at the expense of the basic goodness, and, in sacramental marriage, the holiness, of shared marital love. But an apocryphal story has evolved in the last hundred years as resilient as a.cockroach. It says that the Catholic Church until recently not only viewed marriage as little more than a procreating contract, but that it effectively forbad marital love altogether, or at least any expression that might include romance and the enjoyment of sex.

Fr. Parmisano, well aware of the great contribution of Vatican II to the Church's theology of marriage, challenges this caricature, what he calls "the popular view." He faces squarely the limitations of Catholic thought, not dodging flawed expressions of attitudes towards love, sex and marriage in the historical corpus. But he argues persuasively that those expressions express neither a rooted ignorance of the centrality of love in marriage nor a monolithic opposition to it.

His thesis was first put forward in two influential articles published in the theological journal *New Blackfriars* in August and September 1969.[5] There he argued that during the Middle Ages the bond of love and unity—referred to by the Latin term *sacramentum*—came to be seen as having a defining significance for marriage: "Of the marriage goods distinguished by medieval theologians—fidelity, progeny, the

---

[5] Fabian Stanley Parmisano, "Love and Marriage in the Middle Ages I" and "II," in *New Blackfriars*, vol. 50, no. 591 (August 1969), 599-608 and vol. 50, no. 592 (September 1969), 649-660.

sacramentum—it was the last which was commonly given the edge over the other two: fidelity and progeny were what marriage intended, but the sacramentum, which was defined as the indissoluble bond between husband and wife... was what marriage is" (p. 604). Parmisano points to the works of the 14th century, University of Paris theologian, Nicholas Oresme, who, he says, in discussing *sacramentum*, presents an "integrated doctrine of marriage" as a *relationship of love and friendship* between a husband and wife. If marriage is an image of Jesus' love for the Church, then the most significant feature of marriage is this bond of love imaging Christ's love. This understanding of marriage, Parmisano says, is found in the writings of Albert the Great, Aquinas, Bonaventure, Scotus and Alexander of Hales:

> That they were thinking of the bond precisely as a love bond is evident from their linking it with the love of Christ for the Church... But they are likewise clear as to their appreciation of the natural, carnal element in the bond (p. 604).

This bond of love begins with natural human love, which includes "carnal" love (purged of lust) and is "perfected by the spiritual love toward which it disposes" (p. 604-5). Yes, procreation is an end of marriage, a defining end; but marriage "has purposes beyond generation: it preserves fidelity and deepens and intensifies the love between husband and wife" (p. 603).

The present text represents Parmisano's most extensive elaboration of this basic thesis. He marshals for support a wide range of texts in medieval theology and philosophy, poetry and prose, from popular preaching, especially wedding sermons, and, perhaps most importantly, from the prayers used by almost all faithful Christians in England in that realm's common marriage liturgies. Throughout these texts we find the union of spousal affection and friendship extolled, and rightly ordered sexual desire, bodily beauty and conjugal intercourse judged to be good. The most important theological image for marriage of the period, as august in its terms as inspirational in its expression, was (and still is) the undying love of Christ for his bride, the Church.

Parmisano does not attempt to argue that the centrality of spousal love received its due during the period, nor does he endeavor to exonerate Catholic pastoral practice of criticisms for the way it often considered married persons to be second class citizens in the Church compared with clerics and other consecrated Christians. He means rather to refute the myth that marital love was forgotten, or worse, disdained during in the Middle Ages. In the conclusion he writes:

> In all of the doctrine considered, whether of poetry or theology, the desirability of a full, courteous, physically and spiritually romantic and joyous love between husband and wife is amply in evidence, as is also the undesirability of bestial or extra—or contra-marital love and a love that grows old and dies. There was, therefore, no conflict between the ecclesiastical teaching on human love as it appears in the Church's liturgy and the best of its theologians, and the love themes of the greatest English poetry of our period.[6]

With the publication of Fr. Parmisano's *The Craft of Love*, a more complete and so truer story can now be told of the Catholic commitment to marriage and the love that realizes it. He aids us in seeing that marital love—constituted of the dual goods of unity and procreation, of the *bonum coniugum* and the *bonum prolis*—was seminally understood and taught for centuries, nurtured at the heart of Catholic thought waiting for its full flower in the mature articulation of the theology of Vatican II.

E. Christian Brugger, D.Phil.
Cardinal Stafford Chair of Moral Theology
Saint John Vianney Theological Seminary Denver, Colorado

---

[6] See p. 260.

The Craft of Love

Love and Intimacy in Christian Marriage

CHAPTER 1

PROLOGUE

In the recent past, the belief that love was born in the poetry of the High Middle Ages remains commonplace. By love is meant here, of course, not just sexual or familial love, nor that of friendship, nor the love of God or the Christian *caritas* that has roots in the eternal as well as temporal good of one's neighbor; but that refinement and exaltation of the erotic passion since known as *romance*.

Popular notions of romance and sexual fulfillment

The love that is romantic, the theory goes, had little enough to do with God and less with marriage and society as a whole: it involved lover and beloved exclusively. It bled the man and divinized the woman. It was sexual but never brutal, having the innate quality of *courtoisie*. It could bide its time in patience, but the longing for fulfillment, indeed sexual fulfillment, was always there and would eventually assert itself, whatever the laws of Church or State dictated to the contrary. One thinks of the myth of Tristram and Isolde, sprung full-grown and vibrantly alive in the twelfth century, but also of tales of other contemporary star-crossed lovers like Launcelot and Guinevere, Troilus and Criseyde, Paolo and Francesca, and a host of others who fed the medieval imagination and still fascinate, and dominate us.

While this scrutiny of romance and marriage may seem both remote and academic the very opposite is true. Even if we confine ourselves to concern for civic society, neglecting entirely the eschatological, we must still conclude that the intimate relations of the sexes is of the utmost importance. The primordial community of an individual man and woman is the cornerstone of the larger communities in which life is lived. Thus family, village, city, state are all in part determined by the nuances of sexual relationships and so affect our ability to lead happy, peaceful and productive lives.

THE CRAFT OF LOVE

Living as we do in an age which desires to alter the relationship of the sexes, and thereby to topple a foundational pillar of Western civic society, it would be wise to discover the true nature of what is slated for destruction. The loss of respect for the 'primordial community' has surely contributed to the increase in divorce, cohabitation, and single mother families. In turn there is anecdotal and scholarly evidence that the dysfunctional family is in some measure responsible for the declining fertility and social disorder in Western societies—what Francis Fukuyama has labeled the "Great Disruption."

The term *amour courtois*, or 'courtly love' is of modern origin, having been coined in 1883 by the French medievalist Gaston Paris to designate "this new form of love which makes such a decided break with previous forms and which appears for the first time in Europe among the Troubadours of twelfth-century Provence." Andreas Capellanus says it is "a love which both as a literary theme and as a social ideal is something entirely new on the European scene, and from which our modern notions of romantic love derive in large measure."[1]

Henri Davenson will not allow that the particular kind of love the troubadours celebrated was a new "creation"—'only God can bring something out of nothing; we humans always work with materials already at hand,' but he does find it novel. It was a love "*tout autre chose que la pure sexualité*" and "*tel amour n'a pas toujours existé.*" There was something else new about it. Hitherto, in the earlier medieval literature, it was the woman who loved and languished, and was off somewhere to the side. But "*un beau jour, tout est change: c'est 1 l'homme maintenant d'aimer et de languir,*" and the woman was now center stage. The "bright day" was when William IX of Aquitaine, the first of the celebrated troubadours, began to write his love poems.[2]

In the popular mind and indeed in the minds of many specialists the medieval Church opposed any and all manifestations of such love even within the marriage bond. The critics say in the doctrine and preachment of the Church romance was disdainfully ignored; the love play of passion forbidden outside of marriage and barely tolerated within it; and the use of sex "excused" only when conjugal procreation was the intention. As St. Paul had put it, it was better to marry than to burn. All "burning" before marriage was evil, and afterwards,

PROLOGUE

hopefully, the marriage would by its very nature extinguish it altogether!

It was generally agreed that so deeply rooted was this teaching that it endured till the last ecumenical council when the Church *almost* finally caught up with the rest of the world and acknowledged that there is more to love and marriage than the begetting and rearing of children. Of course, the more extreme of these views entertained a certain cognitive dissonance since wedding ceremonies and exchange of vows only signaled a true Christian marriage where the couple later achieved consensual sexual union.

In addition to explicit criticisms the fundamental basis of Christian marriage has been a conundrum in the popular mind and to many scholars. The widespread dualistic view of the human person was put forward by Rene Descartes whose sobriquet is 'father of modernity.' In this understanding: of persons, "there is nothing entirely in our power but our thoughts," thus the body is an instrument of the mind. This made the teaching of Jesus—a man and woman that became "not two but one flesh"—difficult to grasp. A union of the flesh is impossible for ethereal minds and hardly necessary for the Cartesian mechanico-chemical bodies that were seen as mere instruments.[3]

The popular Catholic historian, Thomas Cahill, epitomizes the negative views of Christian love, sex, and marriage. In his analysis he does not point a finger at Christian theory in itself. Rather he suggests that the spirit of classical civilization was defeated when the Latin Church adopted Saint Augustine's 'abhorrence of the feminine and fear of the sexual function.'[4] Although Cahill's work drew adjectives such as exuberance, freewheeling, playful—not words for a *summa cum laude* in history—from the reviewers; nevertheless his book became a notable popular success. Earlier a Catholic scholar, John Noonan, who was to become well known for his views, appears to indict ancient Christian attitudes. He proposes that not until the late fifteenth century did Martin le Maistre—a layman theologian at the University of Paris—make the 'modern' breakthrough to the role of love and sex in marriage. Being a layman is an important aspect of the censure since deficiencies attributed to Christian theory in this regard are often laid to the door of celibate divines. Noonan concedes a case can be made that late medieval theologians were 'somewhat in advance of their society in their declarations on the ideal of married love' but he emphasizes, they failed 'to incorporate love into the purposes of marital intercourse.'[5]

The purpose here is not to determine what the root causes might be for these commonplace or popular views. Obviously the more extreme views will have fewer adherents and individuals could be influenced by lack of knowledge, Enlightenment theories, the 'sexual revolution,' and on and on. In what follows right minded persons can form more complete and truthful ideas of the Christian concepts of love and sex in marriage, the relation of poets and priests, and the practice of these Christian virtues.

Difficulties with the popular view

One reviewer, while trying to be fair in her critique of a Uta Ranke-Heinemann book, raises questions about the internal dynamics of her study. She asks, "How do these negative instances relate to and compare with more positive pronouncements by other members of the Church at other times? Were all these incredibly negative statements never contradicted and criticized, or to some extent balanced by teachings on marriage, sexuality and celibacy which show us a Church more understanding and caring, a Church which can be loved rather than hated?"[6]

Such critiques could be applied over and over again. One of the flaws of the scholarship devoted to the history of Christian love, romance, and sex is that too much is treated in too little space. Long periods of time—centuries, even millennia—and many theologians and poets are indiscriminately considered.

Clearly, in two thousand years of history one could find endless scholarly quotes to support almost any thesis. Often, in consequence, little if any attention is paid to context. Texts quoted or referred to are selected according to the conscious or unconscious bias of the historian, while those from other sources are simply ignored; and today's authorities are uncritically summoned.

PROLOGUE

This critique is not, of course, to be applied indiscriminately. Peter Lamont Brown's study, The Body and Society, though it traverses four centuries of the early Church's teaching on sexuality is one of the exceptions. Its detail along with its respect for the context of the lives, as well as teachings, of the Fathers is satisfying. As for the poetry: L. T. Topsfield's Troubadours and Love is a splendid example of the variety rather than sameness that is revealed when individual poets are given their whole say and critiqued accordingly.

But how in the space of a few pages can any sort of justice be done to a mind and temper and life as vast and complex and deep as that of an Augustine, an Aquinas, a Dante or a Chaucer? Especially when the matter is itself as vast and complex and deep as love. And how with any kind of assurance evaluate the teaching of the Church *as a whole* when so much of it is thus distorted and so much else simply ignored?

Thomas Cahill's quote of Saint Augustine to describe Christian attitudes to love, sex and marriage, is a case in point of ignoring the broader context. Cahill recounts the story of Saint Augustine's debate with a certain Bishop Julian, "Julian informs Augustine that he had sex with his wife whenever and wherever he felt like it." Cahill says, "Augustine explodes: 'Really, really: is that your experience? So you would not have married couples restrain that evil—I refer of course to your favorite good? So you would have them jump into bed whenever they like, whenever they feel tickled by desire. Far be it from them to postpone this itch till bedtime: let's have your 'legitimate union of bodies' whenever your 'natural good' is excited. If this is the married life you lead, don't drag up your experience in debate!"[7]

If this exchange was all that was known of Saint Augustine it would lead to some tentative conclusions. First, Augustine might be taking issue with Bishop Julian for introducing such a private matter into a *debate*. Second, since Bishop Julian in saying, "he had sex with his wife *whenever and wherever he felt like it*" he appears to deny the mutuality of the marriage act and Saint Augustine may be led to think he was promoting lust instead of love. However, there is a clear imputation that Saint Augustine, a Father of the Church, thought as the Manicheans did—that the marriage act was evil.

THE CRAFT OF LOVE

Outside of Cahill's work Augustine's opposition to the Manicheans is well known and in another place he says, "What does the madness of foulest impiety say to this? What do you say to this, you Manicheans, you who attempt to bring forward to us, indeed as from the apostolic Epistles, two natures without beginning, one of good and the other of evil; and the apostolic Epistles, which correct you from that sacrilegious perversity of yours, you do not want to hear. Just as you read: 'the flesh lusts against the spirit,' and: 'In my flesh no good dwells,' so also read: 'No one ever hateth his own flesh, but nourishes and cherishes it, as also Christ does the Church.' And as you read: 'I see another law in my members warring against the law of my mind,' so also you read this: 'As Christ loved the Church so also ought men to love their wives as their own bodies.' Do not be crafty in using the one group of testimonies of Sacred Scripture and deaf to the other, and you will be corrected in both. For if you accept these latter as they deserve, you will try to understand the former, also, in their truth."[8]

Twentieth-century scholarly indictments

Authors abound who when treating of the Church directly with little if any reference to the poetry, find the early and medieval Church narrow and limited in its teaching on love and sex in marriage. There are the early indictments of H. C. Lea which are still regarded as respectable if not definitive.[9] E. Westermarck, another older but still respected authority in the historical area of human sexuality, is equally severe with the early and medieval Church. Speaking of that Church's exaltation of virginity as springing from "the most perfect indifference to all earthly matters" and, in particular, from contempt for anything sexual, he claims that for the Church, "far from being a benefit to the Kingdom of God by propagating the species, sexual intercourse was on the contrary detrimental to it by being the great transmitter of the sin of our first parents."[10] In its extreme (and uncomfortable!) form, the same indictment appears in Stuart Alfred Queen: "... it is plain to see that the early Church viewed sex as vile. It condemned not only fornication, adultery, pederasty, masturbation, and bestiality, but also contraception, abortion, the reading of 'lascivious' books, singing 'wanton' songs, dancing 'suggestive' dances .... A sterner code would be harder to envisage."[11]

PROLOGUE

Philip Sherrard writes that for Saint Augustine, as for all medieval theologians, marriage may be good but copulation is "sinful and shameful." All marriage could do, says Augustine (as read by Sherrard), "is to make it possible for those who engage in the act of coition to engage in it not to satisfy their lust but as a distasteful duty unavoidable in the begetting of children .... By such an argument, then, Augustine and his theological successors (who include practically every medieval theologian in the western Christian tradition) separated the idea of marriage from that of sexual relationship.... They [the medieval theologians] had to conclude that the act of coition is necessary to marriage so long as its motive is to produce children; but even this motive did not in their eyes exonerate the act from impurity and shame"[12].

Carrying the same criticism into the 1980's and 1990's are writers like Uta Ranke-Heinemann where she presents texts from antiquity to beyond the Middle Ages that demonstrate, to her thinking, a Church that was, and remains, morbidly anti-sexual.[13] An example of cursory scholarship Uta Ranke-Heinemann proceeds with patent and *angry* bias against the Church's past and present teaching on love, marriage and celibacy; she heaps negative text upon negative text from the Fathers, theologians, councils, and canon law.[14] Her best selling, impassioned broadside, attack on the Catholic Church comes up with as bleak a picture of the subject as the staunchest of the Manichees might have invented.

Eric Fuchs, though less immoderate, is essentially of the same mind, and adds that it was the reformers of the sixteenth century who finally extricated marriage from procreation as its sole justifying motive, and did justice to it precisely as a union of love. Margaret Miles looks to ancient and medieval ecclesiastical iconography as well as written word and finds little if anything in the Church at all favorable to sexual love, even within marriage, or to the "bodily" equality of the woman with the man.[15]

James Brundage admits to pluralism in the early and medieval Church's sexology: medieval European society "encompassed diverse views about various kinds of sexual behavior.... Christian sexual ethics have been neither uniform nor static." He concedes that prior to the

THE CRAFT OF LOVE

Reformation there were some (unnamed, unmentioned through the whole of his book) who "emphasized sexual relations as a source of intimacy, as a symbol and expression of conjugal love." However, though there were such as these who "commended married love as a virtue," they were rare; and we are not to "fabricate from these scattered and fragmentary references a tradition of Christian tolerance toward sexual desires, much less a school of eroticism, either in the patristic period or in the Middle Ages." Brundage's judgment on Augustine and the medieval penitentials on the question of marriage, at least in its sexual dimension, may stand as his commentary on the whole of the medieval Church: "Sex, Augustine believed, was a shameful, sordid business." The penitentials by and large took a gloomy view of the sexual proclivities of both men and women."[16]

Peter Lamont Brown limits his study to the ancient Church. He is more reserved and tentative in his judgments than those mentioned above, perhaps because his explorations are deeper if not broader than theirs, and he brings to his subject the same compassion he asks of his readers: "the Church Fathers might strike us as unduely severe in the matter of love and marriage, but most of them did much to bring marital love along, to save its 'body' from being etherealized in the spiritualism of Manichaean Gnosticism or degraded by an unbridled sensualism." His happy phrase on Augustine tells much about the whole of the early Church, as Brown reads it: "The body was a problem to him precisely because it was to be loved and cherished."[17]

The value of modern criticisms

These criticisms of Christian marriage, and the fundamentally dualistic attitudes toward the human person, were addressed in a positive if indirect way by the teaching of John Paul II. The Pope gave a series of 129 lectures at his Wednesday audiences from 1979 to 1984. These were later published in a single work: *The Theology of the Body: Human Love in the Divine Plan*. In his teaching, the body is not as the Dualist would have, it a mere instrument of the mind; or as Manichæism would have it a source of evil. It is a sacramental sign—a symbol and an effective conduit of Divine grace. On this basis the Pope provides a rich pastoral analysis of masculine and feminine roles and the nature of love, sexual emotion, and sexual excitement within

PROLOGUE

Christian marriage. The Pope discusses Christian and pre-Christian ethics as part of his analysis but does not directly deal with the questions raised here in regard to the Churches position in earlier times.

While present-day historians and theologians have found ample evidence for criticisms and censures in the past two thousand years, what is needed is a critical examination of history to see if such views are valid and to see if Pope John Paul II's analysis is in the mainstream of traditional Christian ethics. Has the Church encouraged the ideal as given by what John Paul II describes as "from the beginning"—before sin entered the world? Has the Church been pastoral in the help it offered to fallen nature? It will surely be found that the critical views are not untrue so much as incomplete and untrue only when they are offered as the whole story.

We have noted that in the search for truth it is futile to sift through and select desirable authorities in the two thousand year Christian history. A better approach is to make a broad review of a period that can stand as emblematic of the mind of Christendom. I have chosen to center upon one locale and relatively brief period of time—the England of the fourteenth and early fifteenth centuries. If, as I propose, a certain convergence of both doctrine and praxis in this period is revealed in liturgy and in the writings of iconic theologians, poets, philosophers, and laymen it will show to what extent romantic love was revolutionary or new.

An era emblematic of Christian values

We must remember what the Oxford scholar, Richard Southern tells us, "for those who invented the term [Middle Ages].... it meant the age of barbarism, superstition, and ignorance, lying between the ages of civilization, ancient and modern."[18] Not surprisingly the depiction of Christian theory and practice as retrograde when compared to 'modern' romantic love often centers on the Medieval Church. For this reason our search for a fuller understanding of Christian theory and practice must also center on the Middle Ages.

Looking beyond the stereotype it will be found that a study of the medieval period is uniquely suited to our purpose. It suffered from the

THE CRAFT OF LOVE

ageless problem of human frailty. It suffered from the problems of the age such as the Church's conflict with the civil authorities and with Islamic aggression. But the medieval Church was large and its time-span long, as was also the body of theory and poetry, and both were various and complex. Then as now—and perhaps more then than now—not everyone thought or felt alike. There were divergent points of view within the Church and society as a whole, and theologians and poets were not shy about expressing them. However, a more attentive reading of the teaching Church and poetry of the Middle Ages will suggest, paradoxically, a wider range of thought and feeling of both Church and poet and a *closer agreement* between them in the matter of love than has hitherto been acknowledged.

It has been necessary to be selective and I acknowledge my bias in this regard. My prime concern has not been to tell the whole truth but to present evidence that may serve to challenge, correct, balance and complete testimony already submitted many times over. My aim is also to suggest and respect fullness of context in which alone any selected extract or instance has its proper meaning. And, finally, I intend that what I offer serve as an intimation that more of the same may be found if looked for.

Why center on fourteenth-century England? One reason, certainly, is my intimacy with it. I have long lived with its mystics - the author of *The Cloud of Unknowing*; Julian of Norwich, Richard Rolle, Walter Hilton—and have enjoyed and taught its poetry both secular and religious; and I am at home in the principal theologies alive there at that time in its great universities of Cambridge and Oxford.

The history of this period, having been popularized through books, is relatively accessible. I think of Barbara Tuchman and her rich and lively history, *A Distant Mirror*, intriguingly subtitled "The Calamitous 14th Century"; Umberto Eco and his *Name of the Rose*, long a best-selling novel (and film) of fourteenth-century monkery and mystery; Donald Howard and his scholarly and marvelously engaging biography, *Chaucer: His Life, His Works, His World*. These and many others assure us that perennial beauty and truth and goodness, together with their opposites, are to be found in abundance in this period.

PROLOGUE

But a further reason, more apposite to the purposes of our analysis, is that it is in this time and place that the laity begins to match the best of the clergy in knowledge and in ecclesiastical concerns. W. A. Pantin, who studied the influence of theology upon the English laity of the fourteenth and fifteenth centuries, and the laity's corresponding involvement in the thought and life of the Church assures us, "it was possible for a devout and literate layman, with the help of all the apparatus of religious instruction, sermons, and devotional literature, to take a more intelligent, educated, active, and, so to speak, professional part in the life of the Church."[19] Beryl Smalley shares his view. "It was the educated laity," she affirms, "who did much to force the friars and other clergy into better, more engaging and thoughtful preaching." They were "critical, eager for novelty, and hopeful of entertainment, wanting to be stimulated and amused."[20]

Furthermore, a review of romance and marriage at a later time would involve the views of Christian marriage when it had retreated toward an older pre-Christian view of marriage as only a civil contract. Certainly the Reformers of the sixteenth century saw the evils possible where the Church laid emphasis on the sacramental aspect of marriage. They accepted marriage as a human contract and insisted on parental consent as the grounds of marriage.

The human contract aspect of marriage was clear in Roman law. G. H. Joyce, discussing the marriage customs of the Germanic peoples Lombards, Franks, and Visigoths, says, "In most of these peoples marriage was normally accompanied by the transfer of authoritative guardianship (*mundium*) over the bride from her parents or natural guardians to the husband .... This transfer required the observance of certain prescribed formalities both at the betrothal and at the actual marriage."[21] Joyce adds that a sum of money was paid for the "*mundium*" and this was employed as the dowry of the woman and, after the manner of the Romans, the transaction was written up in a *libellus dotis* and was regarded as the distinctive sign of marriage, and a woman's proof that her marriage was a true one.

For the contractual aspects of marriage of North American Indians, Driver and Massey say, "... the parents and other elder relatives of a bride or groom normally had more to do with the selection of a marriage partner than did either of the principals. Marriage among most primitive peoples is regarded as a contract between two individuals. In general, a bride and groom had more voice in the matter among the economically less advanced tribes .... Those areas which were economically more advanced or possessed sib systems tended to give more weight to the opinions of elders."[22]

The poets are considered for two reasons. The first is to observe the teaching of the Church on love and marriage in action, albeit "poetic action" as it were—to see if and how that teaching affected the laity in their idealization of love. We must, of course, say "some" of the laity. Some were affected, but it is not possible here to plough so wide, and rough, a field as that of the *de facto* sociology of fourteenth-century England. Secondly the finer poets of our period were consciously and conscientiously a part of the Church, often critical of it, but aware that they were as much members of the Body of Christ, and *teachers within it*, as were cleric, priest, and bishop. By the fourteenth century the *auctores,* or classical poets, such as Ovid, Fulgentius, and Virgil, had begun to be classified as ethicists as well as poets and were used by preachers and theologians as such. The more serious of the contemporary poets entered into the same spirit: precisely as poets their job was to teach as well as please.[23] Accordingly, *both* Church and poet ought to be consulted if we would know what either was about.

Besides its historical worth an analysis of fourteenth-century and fifteenth-century England will have current moral value. Much of what the medieval Church and poets had to say about love and marriage is mere chaff and best forgotten. But there remains after the winnowing some fine and precious grain. A new look into the old wisdom may help heal, deepen, and broaden our present capacity for love. At least it may serve as salutary challenge to views in serious need of it.

CHAPTER 2

Priests and Poets

The relationship between Church and poet in the matter of love has engaged the attention of many medievalists. But this attention was mainly in reference to earlier times and other places. For instance, the twelfth century and thirteenth century in southern France of the troubadour commanded attention as well as northern France of the trouvere, of Andreas Capellanus, Chretien de Troyes, Guillaume de Lorris, and Jeun de Meun.

The literary critique of the troubadours

When the love celebrated in medieval poetry is taken literally as real human passionate love, scholars are generally agreed that Church and poet stood opposed. It might seem they could scarcely judge it to be otherwise. For on the one hand, there is the strong suspicion, resulting from the accumulations of a century of literary scholarship, that much of the poetry is adulterous in theme and idolatrous in tone; and on the other hand, it has long since been a common accepted tenet of literary critics and ecclesiastical historians alike that the medieval Church was generally intolerant of passionate love altogether, even when experienced within the marriage bond. To be sure, some Christian values together with undercurrents of fundamental orthodox belief have been recognized in the poetry, but only when the love themes of the poets are viewed as symbolic of a higher, unearthly love —the woman extolled and cherished seen as a figure of the Virgin or God himself—have there been some who have found the Church and poet to be in complete accord.

THE CRAFT OF LOVE

The critique of the English literary world

This opinion of the earlier situation has carried over into the scholarship concerned with the English literary world. With the poetry of Chaucer, Gower, and Lydgate before him as well as that of the earlier poets, C. S. Lewis set poet and theologian side by side and drew the conclusion that has done much to harden and propagate the belief in the opposition between Church and poet through the whole of the Middle Ages:

> The general impression left on the medieval mind by its official teachers was that all love—at least all such passionate and exalted devotion as a courtly poet thought worthy of the name—was more or less wicked. And this impression combining with the nature of feudal marriage ... produced in the poets a certain wilfulness, a readiness to emphasize rather than conceal the antagonism between their amatory and their religious ideals. Thus if the Church tells them that the ardent lover of his own wife is in mortal sin, they presently reply with the rule that true love is impossible in marriage. If the Church says that the sexual act can be "excused" only by the desire for offspring, then it becomes the mark of a true lover, like Chauntecleer, that he served Venus "more for delyt than world to multiplye."[1]

Some might hesitate before Lewis's surmise that the Church by her antagonism toward love within marriage was, in part, responsible for the poet's "truant" love outside marriage; but after Lewis and largely because of him few have ventured to deny that Church and poet, whether of twelfth-century France or fourteenth-century England, were at odds over love.

An expansive view of the literature

As with the earlier poetry, attempts to reconcile Church and poet can also be found. But once again it is on the basis of an interpretation of the poet's love theme as symbolic of, or as, inculcating something other than mere human love. The work of D. W. Robertson and his "school" remains the classic example in point.

PRIESTS AND POETS

Lewis, though assuredly aware of the medieval use of allegory, nevertheless, took the poet's love theme literally and seriously and found the theology when ranged beside it sadly and coldly wanting. Robertson, on the other hand, looks first to the theology, in its method of symbolic or allegoric interpretation of the Scriptures, and in its doctrine of charity. Then, insisting that such was the only method and doctrine allowable—indeed, available—in that medieval culture, he searches beneath the "letter" of the poetry and in the underlying *sententia* (meaning) finds no longer human passionate love, but the Church's universal law of charity. Robertson thus sees Church and poet in fullest harmony, but only because the poet, like the Church, would have nothing to do with love."[2] Robertsonian criticism, active in the area of medieval and renaissance literature as early as 1941, remains a major factor in any serious consideration of that literature.[3]

Where, however, the poets are taken literally as celebrating human love there are some who have been unable to accept the common verdict of disparity between priest and poet. D. S. Brewer, with an eye certainly to the morality (and so the Church) of Chaucer's own time, will not allow that the love celebrated by that poet was unlawful. He writes:

> The incompatibility of love with marriage in the poetry of Chaucer is a platitude so widely accepted that it is worth pointing out that it is quite untrue. Chaucer nowhere celebrates illicit love, though it is sometimes material for a joke, or satire. The only exception seems to be the Troilus, and it may be argued that this exception is more apparent than real.[4]

Jack A. W. Bennett has gone further. For him poetry and theology, though divided in the days of the troubadours, had by the fourteenth century converged, the one with a happier view of marriage, the other with a more sympathetic evaluation of love. He says:

> The doctrine of amour courtois had changed somewhat since the days of the troubadours: it had long since admitted that love was possible within marriage; but it still placed on love between men and women a supreme value which the Church could not allow .... None the less, the developments in philosophic and religious thought throughout the twelfth and thirteenth

centuries did conduce to a new evaluation of human love, which inevitably affected the poetry.[5]

Gervase Mathew and T. P. Dunning have also noted the nearness of the fourteenth-century love-poet to the doctrine of the Church and suggest the Church's positive influence upon the poetry.[6] Matthew is concerned with indicating parallels between the poet's and the scholastic's ideas of friendship, but he touches on marriage when he points out that the scholastic viewed it as a species of friendship. Such a view, he says "provided the framework for the new analyses of love. It did much to humanize the medieval conception of marriage."[7] In T. P. Dunning's essay, "Chaucer's Icarus-Complex," Chaucer is seen in the person of the Parson as justifying love in marriage and as finding ample precedent in the contemporary theology of Thomas Aquinas, Nicholas Oresme, Friar Lorens, and Peraidus for doing so.[8]

A more recent and detailed study of the subject is that of Henry Ansgar Kelly. He finds not only that the poets were all for marriage, but also that their chief source and mentor, Ovid, celebrated not just love but conjugal love. He also cites ecclesiastical canons and mystical literature that evince an appreciation of human love compatible with that which the poets were celebrating.[9]

Mine is one more voice added to the above. But in fairness to the critics just cited, who might not care to find themselves placed in unqualified alliance with the readings and results here offered, it should be noted that though it may be agreed that Church and poet were generally one in their treatment of love and marriage, opinions may differ as to the kind and degree of the love involved. If Chauntecleer married "more for delight than world to multiply," whose side was he on Chaucer's, the Church's, neither, both? The Knight of La Tour-Landry loved the wife of his youth, but with a love *peramours,* that is with romance and passion. Did the Church approve, did she applaud; or was she merely tolerant, grudgingly consenting to the inevitability of human weakness and the temporary lustiness of the young?

Thus, though Bennett holds for the mutual approximation of Church teaching and the doctrine of *amour courtois* by Chaucer's time, the latter, he says, "still placed on love between men and women a supreme value which the Church could not allow." Dorothy Bethurum also argues that *eros* and *caritas* are not so far apart in Chaucer or in the medieval world in general, and yet she hesitates before the marriage question. Love in that medieval world, she says, might follow marriage—and if so all "well and good"—but the social climate, at least among the aristocracy and nobility, would not allow marriages to be made from love. Thus the poets celebrate love and *not* marriage.[10] And T. P. Dunning, though convinced of late medieval theology's support of love within marriage, does not seem to be so sure concerning the specifically sexual aspects of that love. He sees the Parson's doctrine that there is venial sin in every marriage act as an instance of Chaucer, the layman, anxious "to be on the safe side when undertaking to discuss theological topics."

Was it then in point of fact "unsafe" in the theological climate of the time to hold a more liberal view than that which the Parson is believed to have held? If so, then we are back with C. S. Lewis *et al* in their claims against the late, as well as early, medieval Church's sexology.

Henry A. Kelly for all his harmonization of Church and poet on love and marriage is not sure about the theology on the sexual expressions of love within marriage. Love "spiritualized," yes; but the physical emotion of love, the *delectatio* of conjugal coitus, is quite another matter.[11]

A reasoned approach to the conflict of Church and poet

C. S. Lewis believed that the theologians were altogether ignorant of the kind of love the poets described. Was he right? And if they did know of such romantic, passionate love in and through the mystics in their celebration of divine love, were they prepared to approve of it when its object was all and only human? What of the Church's insistence on the superiority of virginity over marriage, her consideration of marriage and the marriage act more in terms of justice (the *debitum*) than love, her teaching that conjugal love-making must intend children if it would be entirely "excused" from sin and that, in any case, it must not be "too ardent" but rather "chaste" and "tempered" by reason?

How does all this square with the conception and practice of the free, spontaneous, often sensual and sexual springtime love that

THE CRAFT OF LOVE

brightens the poetry of Chaucer, Gower, Lydgate? These are critical questions which, to my knowledge are unanswered. I shall provide evidence and argument that may serve to resolve them.

In the study of the medieval theologians and poets one of the more vexing problems is that of selection. Of the various theologies and numerous theologians and different modes of ecclesiastical expression found in the late medieval Church, and of all the rich and diverse poetry produced in the England of that period, which of these should engage our more serious and detailed concentration?

There are several possibilities. One might select one theologian and one poet and compare their respective conceptions of and attitudes toward love. This would have the advantage of allowing the study to be exhaustive with respect to two individuals, but it would tell us little if anything about the Church at large and the poetry in general. Or one might attempt to survey all of the ecclesiastical expressions of doctrine and all of the poetry. The result here, however, would be superficial and a distortion and caricature of the truth; for theologies as well as poems must be lingered over, their treatment of particular subjects or motifs viewed in the context of their full doctrine and larger themes if we are to understand what was really thought and felt.

Accordingly, I have tried to steer a middle course. I have concentrated on a limited but respectfully wide area of the most prominent and influential poetry and ecclesiastical expression of the period. Further, from among the poets those have been chosen who, because they were learned and informed men as well as gifted artists, were likely to have been conversant with the Church's doctrine on love and marriage; this in the hope of discovering whether or not they felt their love themes and "doctrine" to be in conflict with their Church's ideals. The same reason has influenced my choice of one who was a reputable priest and monk as well as a popular poet of love, John Lydgate. Did he, or his ecclesiastical superiors, suspect conflict or feel any tension between his poetry and theology? Obviously the answers to these questions will be of some consequence in the final resolution.

On the ecclesiastical side we shall consider the theologies of several of the most noted representatives of the two great schools of speculative theology active in England and throughout Europe by the late fourteenth century. Also reviewed will be the nuptial rite with its marriage sermon. The liturgy as it appeared in fourteenth-century and fifteenth-century England will be reproduced and examined. In addition we will examine the ecclesiastical doctrine on love and marriage as it begins to find expression in the homelier, warmer, less abstract, less technical language of the vernacular, and thus as it achieves a direct and immediate hearing among less learned clergy and the common layperson. Here, too, authors and works notable and popular in their time have been selected.

As Eamon Duffy remarks in his revisionist exploration of Catholic worship on the eve of the Reformation, "Any study of late medieval religion must begin with the liturgy, for within that great seasonal cycle of fast and festival, of ritual observance and symbolic gesture, lay Christians found the paradigms and the stories which shaped their perception of the world and their place in it." [12]

I have judged it best to consider each expression of ecclesiastical teaching and the poems of each poet separately. The advantage gained by this procedure is that of clarity and completeness, and the freedom and ease it allows the reader to judge each case in and by itself, unprejudiced and unmodified by statements introduced from a foreign source. One night easily choose different points of doctrine from several theologians and mesh them into an overall teaching which, in its entirety, may actually have been held by none of them. But if each author and instance is treated singly, then in the end it should be clear if, and to what extent, a common doctrine was in historical fact shared by all. The disadvantage of the procedure is that of the perhaps tedious repetition of topics and ideas, and a long delay before expected comparisons begin to emerge. But it is one that must be suffered in fairness to those studied and in the interest of truth.

Poets as Christians

There is a further complication that must be resolved, or at least recognized, at the start. We have been speaking of Church and poet as though they were two separate entities functioning apart from each other. The Church, however, though distinct from and transcending each of its individual members, entered into the very lifeblood of the

THE CRAFT OF LOVE

medieval poet as into that of all Christians of that time. A reflective poet could not help being aware of this, for he heard the doctrine of the Mystical Body, the original name for the Church universal, read or preached from the pulpit frequently enough, with exhortations to live and fulfill one's duties as a responsible member of it; and the very structure of medieval society and the routine of each day (the liturgy and its extensions) were further reminders.[13]

It was another expression of the "great Chain of Love" which, as we shall see, was the overall context of the thinking as well as believing in the High Middle Ages. Each person had his or her place within the Body, the Church, the Chain, and all were to try to fulfill their responsibilities accordingly; and daily fast or feast were there to help toward this end. From the theologians and preachers to Chaucer's *Wife of Bath* and Gower's *Lover*, the doctrine was known and voiced, if not always lived.

Precisely as poet he knew that a good part of his responsibility was to share in the teaching ministry of the Church. He was certainly not identified with the Church; his teaching did not have the authority of pope, bishop, or theologian. He was, however, *of* the Church as was also to be his teaching. We must continue to speak of Church and poet, as also Church and bishop, Church and theologian, Church and priest, as distinct, for so they were; but we must realize that they were also one, feeding and being fed by each other; and the Church of the Middle Ages, as always, was all people together rather than any one individual or group of individuals apart.

We will begin with the theologians and other formal ecclesiastical teaching and practice. This seems appropriate because in that medieval world, not excluding the England of the fourteenth-century, ecclesiastical teaching and practice enjoyed priority over the poet's sentential. The poet, like the rest of the faithful was expected, in life and teaching, to measure up to the Church, not vice-versa. Such procedure seems fitting also, because in this matter of love and marriage it is the Church's teaching that has been most critiqued and criticized in our time, and therefore is the more inviting, or rather demanding, of attention.

PRIESTS AND POETS

Patristic influence on the Middle Ages

Before examining the later medieval theology a word must be said about the earlier theology of the Fathers of the Church. For, it is argued: that the Fathers were hostile to sexual love, that they were infected with Manichaeism, and that their emphasis on virginity disparaged marriage.

It is a common conclusion that together with the Bible the writings of the Fathers, in themselves, and as incorporated into the canonical legislation of the Church became the authority for subsequent thought. If, then, the Fathers were hostile toward passionate, sexual manifestations of love, as appears to be the case, it would seem the later medieval Church would have been similarly disposed?

It is also thought that the Fathers were contaminated by the same disease they sought to eradicate, that of Manichaeism, with its vilification of the corporeal and its condemnation of marriage especially in its procreative intention. Years ago H. C. Lea in his *History of Sacerdotal Celibacy* (revived and reissued in the 1960s) wrote:

> It would be easy to show from the hagiologies how soon the Church virtually assented to the Manichaean notion that the body was to be mortified and macerated as the only mode of triumphing in the perennial struggle with the evil principle .... It is sufficient for us here to indicate how narrowly in the process of time she escaped from adopting practically, if not theoretically, the Manichaean condemnation of marriage. This is clearly demonstrated by the writings of the orthodox Fathers, who in their extravagant praise of virginity could not escape from decrying wedlock. It was stigmatized as the means of transmitting and perpetuating original sin, an act which necessarily entailed sin on its participants, and one which at best could only look for mercy and pardon and be allowed only on sufferance.[14]

Present-day studies have done little to modify Lea's indictment. We need only open the books of Uta Ranke-Heinemann, James Brundage, Vern Bullough, Margaret Miles, to find the same patristic texts quoted or referred to and similar conclusions drawn.[15]

THE CRAFT OF LOVE

As Lea maintains in the above quotation, the Fathers' "extravagant praise of virginity" resulted in the disparagement of marriage. And since virginity continued to be extolled above marriage into the High Middle Ages the supposition is that the disparagement of marriage also continued.

For yet another reading of the Fathers different from that of Lea and company, this one directly concerned with marital love, see John R. Connery, S.J.[16] Marital love, which many find absent in the early theology on marriage, Connery uncovers in the sacramentum, the "sacramentality" of marriage: "In general it is under the heading of sacramentality that the Fathers deal with marital love. While the term does not have the technical meaning of a later date, it clearly refers to the symbolic meaning of marriage in reference to Christ and his Church. The basis for this meaning is the love of the spouses for each other. The Fathers clearly assume that this love is present. It is only because of this love that marriage has the symbolic meaning they attribute to it."[17] As we will see, the idea of the sacramentum, with explicit reference to a full love—both spiritual and physical—between spouses, looms large in later medieval theology. If, then, such was the attitude of the Fathers, the antecedent probability is that it was also that of the later theologians.

That the later medieval theology might enjoy a fairer, less prejudiced reading, let me suggest some of the limitations of the above arguments. It can be shown that the authority of the Fathers was not absolute in the Middle Ages. Of course, the Fathers can be shown to be combative with Manichaeism. Furthermore the relation of the charism of virginity to ideas about marriage is more complex than portrayed.

Though the Fathers of the Church were authoritative throughout the Middle Ages, their authority was far from being absolute. True, they set the stage and sometimes the tone of much of the later thinking. However, the great theologians of the High Middle Ages were independent thinkers in their own right. They might sometimes adjust their thinking to that of the Fathers but just as often the reverse was true: the patristic authority would be respectfully cited but then distinguished (a key word in the later theology) to fit the truth as now perceived. St. Thomas expresses the common belief and practice, with the authority of St. Augustine to back him up:

> sacred doctrine [theology] makes use of these authorities [the philosophers] as extrinsic and probable arguments. But it properly uses the authority of the canonical scriptures as a necessary argument, and the authority of the doctors [Fathers] of the Church as one that may properly be used, though only as probable. For our faith rests upon the revelation made to the apostles and prophets, who wrote the canonical books, and not on the revelations (if any such there are) made to other doctors. Hence Augustine says (Epistle to Jerome): "Only those books of Scripture which are called canonical have I learnt to hold in such honor as to believe their authors have not erred in any way in writing them. But other authors I so read as not to deem anything in their works to be true merely on account of their having thought and written it, whatever may have been their holiness and learning."[18]

To categorize the Fathers en bloc as Manichees in the matter of marriage or in anything else is, to say the least, intemperate. Certainly a number of them spent a good deal of time and energy combating the dark heresy, and with considerable success. That, as some propose, they ended up being infected by the disease they labored to cure seems much less likely than that they would have moved to the opposite extreme, meticulously careful to remain clean of anything Manichaean. Such at any rate is the implication of a contemporary historian who, although not particularly enamored of the teaching of the Fathers on marriage, admits that it was their unrelenting work that rescued marriage, in its function of procreation, from the negativity of the Manichees and, in its function of purification, from the sensuality of the pagans; and, our historian speculates, in the heat of the polemic and anxious to distance themselves from either camp, the Fathers exaggerated procreation, making of it the exclusive aim of marriage, and diminished the sensual, making of it a sin.[19]

But a deeper and broader view of the early Church might well reveal an appreciation of marriage not only as procreative but as a blessed way of life, both in body and in spirit, for the spouses themselves. Thus we have the younger Tertullian's encomium of marriage in which, it should be observed, only the spouses are considered with no mention of procreation:

> How shall we be able adequately to describe the happiness of that marriage which the Church arranges, the Sacrifice strengthens, upon which the blessing sets a seal, at which angels are present as witnesses, and to which the Father gives his consent?
>
> How beautiful, then, the marriage of two Christians, two who are one in hope, one in desire, one in the way of life they follow, one in the religion they practice. They are as brother and sister, both servants of the same Master. Nothing divides them, either in flesh or in spirit. They are, in very truth, two in one flesh; and where there is but one flesh there is also one spirit. They pray together, they worship together, they fast together; instructing one another, encouraging one another, strengthening one another. Side by side they visit God's church and partake of God's Banquet; side by side they face difficulties and persecution, share their consolations. They have no secrets from one another; they never shun each other's company; they never bring sorrow to each other's hearts .... Hearing and seeing this, Christ rejoices. To such as these He gives his peace. Where there are two together, there also He is present; and where He is, there evil is not.[20]

High praise for marriage precisely as a love bond, in flesh as well as spirit, and as a total way of life; and it comes from one of the earliest of the Fathers. True, as he grew older Tertullian suffered a radical change of mind, occasioned, supposedly, by the question of the legitimacy of "second marriages," i.e. when one's former spouse has died. One might surmise, from the above epithalamium, that his opposition to such marriage was due to his belief in the eternal fidelity required by the original marriage, but other, less romantic motivation reveals itself as he builds his argument.:

> But if spiritual insensibility, which results from the use of sex in even a single marriage, repels the Holy Spirit, how much more will this be the case if the practice continues in a second marriage! Here a man's reason for shame is doubled, since after a

second marriage he has two wives by his side, one in the flesh, the other in the spirit. Your affection for your first wife will become even more devoted, now that she is secure in the Lord. You certainly will not be able to hate her. You pray for her soul. You offer the annual Sacrifice for her. Do you wish, then, to stand before the Lord with as many wives as you remember in your prayers?

We admit but one marriage, just as we recognize but one God. The covenant of marriage is most honorable when it is associated with modesty. But the Sensualists, not receiving the Spirit, take no pleasure in such things that are of the Spirit. Therefore, since such things that are of the Spirit do not please them, they will find their joy in things of the flesh, as being contrary to the Spirit.[21]

The "Sensualists" mentioned here and in other of Tertullian's later heterodox writings were the orthodox "Catholics" who, apparently, not only favored second marriages but also looked kindly upon the physical delights, the "sensuality" of marital intimacy. Others note that "In his Montanist writings Tertullian habitually uses the epithet 'Sensualists' or 'Psychics' in speaking of Catholics."[22] The word psychics is derived from St. Paul's distinction of carnal or animal man as opposed to the spiritual.

When Tertullian praised marriage as a bond of flesh as well as spirit he was Catholic and accepted by the community as such. But when he raised his voice against marriage in its carnal dimension he found himself outside the fold.[23] This tells us, among other things, that there must have been a formidable corpus of ecclesiastical teaching and practice that continued Tertullian's early praise of marriage after he had abandoned it. The same phenomenon appears in another of the Fathers, St. Jerome, who, like the later Tertullian, was not altogether happy about second marriages or, seemingly, with the carnal love of first marriages. But unlike Tertullian, he was anxious to conform, though with little enthusiasm, to the prevailing orthodoxy and bowed before its pressures.

Let the royal road be this: so to desire virginity as not to condemn marriage. And who will be so unfair a judge of my little works as to say that I condemn first marriages, even after he has read what I have to say about second marriages? ... Let my calumniator blush with shame for saying that I condemn first marriages, whereas he reads: "I condemn neither the second marriage nor the third nor (if one can speak so) the eighth marriage." But it is one thing to allow for a weakness, another to praise a virtue ... Whatever, I say, they speak in praise of marriage, we gladly hear. And if we gladly hear the praises of marriage, do we then condemn marriage?[24]

The concluding lines of this same epistle (col. 509) are also worth noting if only as illustration that this Father distinguished the right and the wrong, the good and the better, not in terms of subjective state or disposition or private inspiration, but, apparently, according to an objective rule of Faith: "Therefore, with this final word I protest that I have never condemned, nor do I condemn marriage .... But virginity I praise to the sky, not because I have it, but because what I do not have I all the more admire (*magis mirer quod non habeo*)."

Who was this "calumniator," who were "they" who were of such power that they could bring the proud and irascible Jerome to his knees and force him to admit where orthodoxy lay? Those who maintain the early Church's negative stance on marriage inevitably quote St. Jerome in evidence. But what of the anonymous authority Jerome himself felt obliged to accede to? If we are in search of the early Church's teaching on marriage it would seem we should look to such authority rather than to individuals, however reputable for other reasons, who taught or tended to teach otherwise. My point is that in judging the patristic theology we are not simply to consider the "letter" of this or that theologian but are to reach to the underlying "spirit," not just of the theologian in question but of the Church whose mind he is laboring to express. For it is this, more than isolated or even group opinions and feelings of the Fathers, that exercised directive force in the shaping Of the later theology. Such "spirit" is not always easy to detect but, as in our present instances of two of the more prominent of the Fathers, and precisely on the matter of our present study, it is easily observed.

In view of the exalted authority attributed to St. Jerome by many students of the ancient Church, it is salutary to note recorded indications of Jerome's subordinate place within that Church. When Jerome's admirer and protector, Pope Damasus, died in 384, Jerome, because of his pronounced ascetic views, was summoned by a council of Roman clergy and told to leave the City. Later, from a distance, he again intervened in Roman affairs, chastising a certain Jovinian for expressing the view that marriage was of equal worth with virginity. His pamphlet, *Against Jovinian*, was, as Peter Brown reports, "a disaster." It attracted some, repelled others who, eventually, were responsible for Jerome's "apologies" quoted above in our text.[25] That the later English medieval world did not take Jerome too seriously in his views on sex is delightfully illustrated in Chaucer's parodying of them in and through his *Wife of Bath*.

But when we do consider individual sources, and texts culled from them, we should try to be as complete as we can, as the greater medieval theologians tried to be. The common tendency today has been to isolate passages from the Fathers that are depreciative of conjugal love, add them together and so come up with a sum negative in the extreme. But what of a Father like Lactantius, in good standing with the early Church, and praised by St. Jerome himself (though more, perhaps, for his rhetoric than for his doctrine)? William Fletcher, in a preface to his translation of Lactantius notes that "Lactantius has always held a very high place among the Christian Fathers, not only on account of the subject-matter of his writings, but also on account of the varied erudition, the sweetness of expression, and the grace and elegance of style, by which they are characterized." Critics find his theology superficial, but in his own time (third century and early fourth century) he was known and respected both as teacher of rhetoric and a defender of the Christian faith.[26] With his anti-Manichaean Aristotelian appreciation of the oneness of body and spirit he argued to the rightness of sexual passion in the conjugal embrace:

> for sensual desire (*libido*), if it does not wander from one's spouse (*legitimum torus*) although it be ardent (*vehemens*) yet is without fault. But if it desires an unlawful object (*alienum*), although it be moderate, yet it is a great vice.... The whole matter ought to turn on this, that since the force (*impetus*) of these things [i.e. emotions] cannot be restrained, nor is it right that it should be, because it is necessarily implanted for maintaining the

duties of life, it might rather be directed into the right way, where one may even run [emphasis mine] without stumbling or danger (*ubi etiam cursus Qaoffensione ac pericule careat*).²⁷

As Thomas Aquinas, also a student of Aristotle, would later say: if the object is right—and one's legitimate spouse is a right object—the more passion in loving the better.

Here is thinking in accord with the earlier Tertullian quoted above and, apparently, in conformity to the authority insisting that both the later Tertullian and truant Jerome shape up and think more kindly about marriage. It also harmonizes with the thought of the early Fathers behind some of the fourth-century formulations called the Apostolic Canons or Constitutions: "If any bishop or priest or deacon or, indeed, anyone from the body of clerics, abstains from marriage, meat and wine, not from the motive of mortification, but because of detestation for them, forgetful that all things are exceedingly good and that God made man male and female; but blaspheming, finds fault with creation, let him either be corrected, or deposed and cast out of the Church."²⁸

Peter Brown, at the end of his history of the early Church's sexology, which, he agrees, upheld celibacy at the expense of marriage, and spirit to the neglect of body, nevertheless cautions his readers to "remember that we have followed the destinies of a small and vociferous minority, in an ancient society that changed very slowly. Even the minority was divided in its opinions. The early Church was so creative largely because its most vocal members so frequently disagreed with each other."²⁹ This is good counsel for the reading of the early Church. It should also be kept in mind as we move into the Church of the later Middle Ages.

That the early and later Church's high regard for virginity worked to the detriment of marriage is debatable. One might plausibly argue to the contrary that the repeated comparison of the two eventually helped secure the honorable status of wedlock. Marriage in itself is nothing extraordinary: it is as natural and inevitable as eating and drinking. But, much as a hitherto unknown poet gains in prestige as critics begin to compare him or her favorably to an Eliot or a Yeats, so with marriage when matched with what in the early Church was regarded with special reverence. Rather than being diminished through its comparison with celibacy, marriage may thereby have gained in esteem. But we need not limit ourselves to speculation. There is satisfactory evidence that strong and authoritative voices in the early Church did all possible to forestall and/or correct any pejorative effects that might issue from the comparison. Thus the canons formulated by the Fathers of the fourth-century Council of Gangra:

> If anyone despises wedlock, abhorring and blaming the woman who sleeps with her husband, even if she is a believer and devout, as if she could not enter the kingdom of God, let him be anathema ... if anyone lives unmarried and in continence, avoiding marriage from contempt, and not because of the beauty and holiness of virginity, let him be anathema ... if anyone in pride exalts himself above those who are married, let him be anathema ... if a woman leaves her husband and separates herself, from abhorrence of the marriage state, let her be anathema.

And the Council concludes:

> We ... admire the virginity which is accompanied with humility, and approve continence when joined to dignity and virtue. We approve the renunciation of worldly affairs, if done with humility, and honor married intercourse as seemly, nor do we despise riches if united with righteousness and benevolence.[30]

Patristic texts regarding marriage and virginity have been cited to the contrary by Lea, Brundage, and others. Margaret Miles quotes passages from the Fathers that do indicate that marriage suffered as virginity was extolled.[31] She cites Gregory of Nyssa among others: "The more exactly we understand the riches of virginity, the more we must bewail the other life (marriage) ... how poor it is." However, she recognizes that "Patristic authors frequently had to defend themselves against charges that they harbored a Gnostic disdain for marriage" Again, as noted above with regard to St. Jerome and Tertullian, we must take into account this higher authority in the early Church whose appreciation of marriage was dominant and the norm to be followed by all. Here was the *Church* in its teaching rather than the individuals who taught otherwise, however orthodox and prestigious they were or came to be in other respects.

The fact that both the early and later medieval Church preached times of conjugal sexual abstinence has served as a further example of Manichaean infestation and consequent devaluation of marriage. There were, indeed, some churchmen who even commanded abstinence and multiplied the times of its observance to an intolerable degree, practically requiring of the married the same continence as was demanded of the virgin. In the twelfth century, to cite a later instance reflective of earlier teaching, Pierre le Chantre and his disciples class as "semi-heretics" those who prohibit conjugal intercourse to such an extent that it is allowed no more than twice a week.[32] Since such rigorists are censured by le Chantre as "semi-heretics," they must have had some reputation for orthodoxy and been regarded by some (many?) as theologians within the Church; though evidently there were others, like le Chantre and his school, whose opposing opinions on conjugal love-making were of equal if not greater force.

The counsel for sexual restraint in marriage

It is true, however, that the Church in general, both ancient and medieval, did in fact preach periodic restraint in marital intercourse, as it did with regard to food and drink and other matters however good in themselves. Individual churchmen may have had their private reasons for this, but one of the "official" reasons for the practice and preaching of sexual abstinence, especially during Lent and other penitential tines, was to keep the faithful from mistaking the creature for the Creator. Human love, marriage and sex were good, but they were not everything. Infinitely above and beyond them was the dear God toward whom they and all else were to aim; and it was the human spirit more than the body that was to inform marriage, make it *humane*, and give it thrust toward the divine.

Such an attitude may be difficult for the citizen of this twenty-first-century world to understand let alone appreciate. We live in good measure in a closed world, where matter, not spirit, is our business and pleasure. We extol, advertise, and demand immediate satisfaction of whatever appetite, especially, in recent years, the sexual, and we rebel

PRIESTS AND POETS

against any law or even suggestion to the contrary. But this may be our vice rather than virtue.

Alice Thomas Ellis takes those clergymen to task who, with the rest of our world, are now "starry-eyed" over sexuality and marriage. She refers to a letter to The Tablet by a priest who regrets the fact that "in the first 1,500 years of the Church not a single Western theologian is to be found praising redeemed man and woman walking equal, naked, and unashamed in the garden of God ...." "This," she writes, "shows their grasp of reality. We are not in the garden of God. We are in the world and most people look like hell with no clothes on. We have an adequate number of pornographers and romantic novelists to divert us with inflated and unrealistic ideas of the value and importance of sexuality without the priesthood adding its tuppence worth. Believe it or not, there are other, more important and even more interesting things in life—God, for one."[33]

In that medieval world, however, it was recognized, at least in theory, that "there is a time to embrace and a time to be far from embraces" (Eccl 3:5), in order to satisfy one's religious aspirations, but also to make for a better, happier marriage. Yet in sober moments we, too, can glimpse something of the worth of such renunciation. The poetry of Kahlil Gibran comes to mind. Accepted by a good segment of our secular as well as religious world as wisdom, it is often heard at weddings when love is still fresh and pure, or at least when we like to think it is:

Then Almitra spoke again and said, "And what of Marriage, Master?"

And he answered saying: "You were born together, and together you shall be forevermore. You shall be together when the white wings of death scatter your days. Aye, you shall be together even in the silent memory of God.

"But let there be spaces in your togetherness, and let the winds of the heavens dance between you .... Sing and dance together and be joyous, but let each one of you be alone.[34]

THE CRAFT OF LOVE

Scholastic scientific language

One final introductory word, this one directly related to the later medieval theology we are about to consider. There in the classical scholastic theologians we come as near to a non-rhetorical style of writing as is perhaps possible this side of pure science. There is little heart, little warmth manifested even where, as in the question of love, we would most expect to find it. This must not be taken as a sign of the theologian's cold indifference toward his subject, but is simply the inevitable consequence of his scientific technique. There is often emotion aplenty, but it flows from the ideas themselves *when seen in their totality*, and not from the author's "rhetoric."

Historians of medieval thought like Gilson, de Wulf, and Chenu, all pronounce similar warnings with respect to the study of 'the golden age of scholasticism.' Gilson says, "Even the theological style ... can be said to be classical in its own order. The technique of the 'question' has been perfectly mastered; the language of the theologians and philosophers has become precise and supple and no writers have ever said more with a stricter economy of words. Historians have created a different reputation for them, but among those who judge the language of the great scholastics, how many can understand its meaning?"[35]

CHAPTER 3

ARISTOTELIAN THOMISM

The importance of Thomas Aquinas as a philosopher and theologian for the twenty-first century as well for the thirteenth century must be acknowledged. He was born to a prosperous family near Aquino in the Liri Valley, Italy. He was a pious youth and his family sent him to nearby Monte Cassino for his early education. Later he was a student at the University of Naples, which had been recently founded in 1224 by Frederick II in the interests of service to the State. There he studied under Thomas of Ireland who introduced him to the wonders of Greek learning. In Naples to the great displeasure of his family he joined the Order of Preachers —the Dominicans.

In his early years due to his girth and gift for contemplation he was called "the dumb ox." His brilliance, though, was recognized by the Dominicans who sent him to study in Paris and later under that man of encyclopedic knowledge, Albert the Great. His life-long friendships with Albert and with the Hellenist William of Moerbeke were providential for his learned output.

In a 1500-year odyssey and through a circuitous route from the Lyceum through Christian Syria, Arabic Baghdad, Arabic Spain, and Flemish scholarship much of Aristotle's learning came to be absorbed by Thomas. In a short life of about fifty years and through his extraordinary power of synthesis and eristic skills he introduced Aristotelianism to the West. This was a revolution in thought and "Christian thought henceforth was never to lose the temper of science."[1] But revolutions do not happen without opposition, and there was antagonism from Platonists and those who associated the Thomistic synthesis with that of Averroes. The objections culminated in 1277, three years after his death, in propositions of censure directed against Thomas and Averroes by Etienne Tempier, the bishop of Paris.

THE CRAFT OF LOVE

Thomas's style of exposition treats the Fathers of the Church, as well as the Greeks, in an ahistorical fashion. He quoted them "as though they spoke directly to him," and agreed or disagreed with them as he saw fit.[2] However, his teaching in regard to marriage does not repudiate Patristic doctrines. W. Kasper describes it thus:

> Whereas Augustine was concerned principally with the grounds for marriage, Thomas was able to use these grounds to express the human dignity of marriage. Purely sensual love tended, he believed, to break away from humanity's total orientation in life, assume an independent value of its own and thus threaten the dignity of human beings. It was, however, integrated into the total meaning of human life by the three goods of marriage as given by St. Augustine: the good of progeny, the good of fidelity, and the good of the sacrament.[3]

The Aristotelian revolution and early Thomism

In 1277 Etienne Tempier condemned a long list of propositions, some related to the *de amore* of Andreas Capellanus, others traceable to the new philosophy of Thomas Aquinas. By that time Thomism was a force to be reckoned with in England as well as at Paris and throughout Europe.[4]

Etienne Gilson, speaking of the support given to the Paris condemnation by the then Archbishop of Canterbury, Robert Kilwardby, says that the Archbishop was probably exaggerating when he claimed that the "prohibition" (Kilwardby's benign interpretation of the condemnation) had met with the approval of all the masters of Oxford. "If one thinks," writes Gilson, "of the early pro-Thomist reactions on the part of certain Dominicans of Oxford ... who followed the prohibition but very little, one cannot help thinking that, as early as 1277, Thomistic theology found at Oxford some sympathy."[5]

Gilson is no doubt referring to such young innovators as William Hothum, Richard Knapwell, Robert Orford, Thomas Sutton, and William Macclesfield, all contemporary with the prohibition. All were prominent theologians in the Oxford of that time, and all loyal, though by no means slavish defenders of their brother and master, Thomas Aquinas. They formed only the modest beginnings of Thomism in

ARISTOTELIAN-THOMISM

England, and at the price of severe attack and often condemnation on the part of local authorities and older theologians. But in a relatively few years their numbers had grown to legion and all authoritative opposition had ceased.

In June of 1286 the Dominican General Chapter, meeting in Paris, obliged every Dominican "insofar as he was able and capable, to devote himself effectively to the study, promotion and defense of the doctrine of the venerable master, Friar Thomas Aquino, of celebrated memory."[6] In 1313 the chapter at Metz ordered that "No one may be sent to the Paris *studio*, unless he has diligently studied the doctrine of Brother Thomas for at least three years."[7] By 1317 Thomas was recognized at the University of Paris as *doctor communis* and on July 18, 1323 he was canonized by Pope John XXII on February 14, 1325.

"Stephen of Bouret, Bishop of Paris, proclaimed that the censure of 1277 promulgated by Bishop Tempier had no canonical value insofar as it concerned St. Thomas."[8] Thus by the end of the first quarter of the fourteenth-century Thomist teaching had achieved a prominence and respectability throughout whole of the western Church, and its eminent position both at Paris and at Oxford was secured.[9]

He was also depicted in art and in literature. Angelus Walz writes, "Christian art was not slow to occupy itself with the portrayal of the holy Doctor, and there are several well-known examples of the 'triumph' of St. Thomas in various conventual churches ...."[10] Walz is thinking of the painting at Florence by Bonaiuto and the "trionfo" in St. Catherine's at Pisa of the mid-fourteenth-century Florentine school. Other examples of fourteenth-century and fifteenth-century iconography devoted to the Saint's life and teaching are given by M. D. Chenu in his beautifully illustrated book.[11] In a fourteenth-century painting in Pisa by Simone Martini, St. Thomas with book in hand, open and shining as the sun, stands directly beside St. Augustine also holding a book which is significantly closed.

We should also recall Dante's early immortalizing of Thomas in Cantos X and XI of the *Paradiso*, finished in 1321. In light of such an abundance of contemporary testimony, it is difficult to accept D. W. Robertson's view that even as late as the late-fourteenth century traditional Augustinianism still held almost exclusive sway in matters theological and exegetical.¹² Both in exegesis and in theology the "new" scholastic and "literal"-minded Aristotelianism represented especially by St. Thomas but also as modifying the theologies of those of an Augustinian bent and loyalty, was already old by mid-fourteenth century and was widely taught and respected throughout the Western Church.¹³

Extensive teaching on marriage

St. Thomas's reflections on love and marriage are found scattered here and there through his vast *opera*, but his teaching appears in full and concentrated form in his *Commentary on the Sentences of Peter Lombard*.¹⁴ This early teaching of St. Thomas was, in the middle of the fourteenth century, incorporated into a *Supplement* to the *Summa Theologiae* by an unknown Dominican friar in an attempt to complete the Saint's master work.

Accordingly, it is these two loci, the *Commentary* and the *Supplement*, that serve as the principal sources for this present examination of Thomas's fourteenth-century theology of human sexual love. But the *Summa Theologiae* itself together with that other master work of Thomas's maturity, the *Summa Contra Gentiles*, will also be called in evidence, for in these Thomas's doctrine on marriage is rounded out, deepened, and detailed. Questions left unanswered or undeveloped in the earlier, ex *professo* treatment of marriage are resolved when in later tracts—charity, passion, love (*amor*), justice all integral to the question of marriage—are each dealt with singly and in fullness of detail. And it is within the *weltanschauung* of his *summae* that Thomas would have us view what he has to say about marriage as about every other subject he considers.¹⁵

It is, indeed, in the broad metaphysical and theological context of God and the universe that St. Thomas treats of human love in general and as it is realized in marriage. The pattern is similar in the *summae* and *commentaria* of other medieval scholastics. There is an infinite God and a finite world. Within God there is a Trinity of Persons and "beyond" God—but created, loved, supported, and directed by Him— there is a universe of things, people, events, actions, institutions; and all is hierarchically ordered, though the order is often veiled in mystery. As part of this whole, as an instinct implanted by God and reflective of what is deepest within Him, created love or desire of whatever sort is fundamentally good, and human love in particular is very good.

The comprehensive, encyclopedic view of the late scholastics—their attempt to see all the facets of life and learning as a systematic and ordered whole beginning and ending with God—derives especially from Hugh of St. Victor's twelfth-century *De Sacramentis christianae fidei*. To quote D. Knowles, this is "the first attempt on the grand scale ... to give a really comprehensive view of theology in all its branches .... The *De Sacramentis* is important for its influence on theological teaching; joined to the different approach of Abelard, it became the grandmother of all the *summae* of the following hundred years."[16]

James Brundage seems strangely unaware of this overall perspective of medieval theological thought.[17] For him, it was not the theologians but the poets who harmonized the world and saw sex as a manifestation of nature. As illustration of the poet's unique vision, he offers the early-fourteenth-century *Breviari d'amor* by the Franciscan poet, Matfre Ermengau. Here, Brundage summarizes, we have God above all and the source of all; beneath him is Nature who rules all created beings. Nature in turn is the source of natural law, of the *ius gentium*. Sexual love descends from natural law, of which it is a product. In Matfre's cosmology, sexual attraction was an intrinsic element in God's design for the world, and, concludes Brundage, "he clearly rejected that sex resulted from sinful defiance of the Creator's will." Brundage adds that "A few theologians [unnamed] took positions akin to those of the love poets, but conventional theologians and canonists distanced themselves from such fancies."

And among these "conventional theologians" he places Thomas Aquinas and Bonaventure. But in light of what we have just seen of Thomas in our text and what we shall further see as we continue to expose his thought, the same vision Brundage notes in the *Breviari* he might also discover—and with greater depth and breadth—in the "conventional" theology of St. Thomas.

THE CRAFT OF LOVE

The goods of marriage comes from the goodness of God

Thus St. Thomas argues that there is love (*amor*) in God from, of course, St. John's "God is love," but also by an argument that notes love to be the very first movement of the will, the "prime root" of every other stirring of appetite.[18] Echoing an ancient and common theological tradition he affirms that there is a "vestige" of the Trinity in everything created, but especially in the rational creature in whom, as in the godhead, there is an intellectual awareness (*verbum conceptum*) imaging the divine Son, and a consequent love (*amor procedens*) that reflects the Holy Spirit.[19] He asks if our every desire is toward our ultimate end? The reply is affirmative, for whatever else one may consciously desire is but a beginning (*inchoatio*) of the total perfection to be found in the final good, which in fact is God.[20]

Simply on the natural plane, St. Thomas, as all the scholastics, found his logic wanting when he came to distinguish created good and so created love, from the uncreated. "Each thing," he says, "is called good because of the likeness of the divine goodness inhering in it (*sibi inhaerente*) which is formally (*formaliter*) its own goodness .... And thus *there is one goodness for all*; and yet there are many goodnesses"[21]

The problem was only intensified when grace had to be considered. For through grace an added, a special mode of union with the divine was effected, especially when the grace in question was the most excellent grace of charity (*caritas*). Some theologians, including the great Peter Lombard, hazarded explanations that terminated in a kind of supernatural pantheism: they *identified* charity with the Holy Spirit. Thomas Aquinas avoided the heresy by, it would seem, transcending logic and intuitively holding that graced human love when looked at from above, from God's side as it were, was uncreated, was God's own love, the Holy Spirit; but when looked at from below, from our side, it was created. For Thomas, therefore, charity is not identical with divine love, but is "a kind of (*quaedam*) participation" in it.[22] However vague and abstruse and unsatisfying his explanation may be (and must be, since we are in the darkness of divine mystery) Thomas's *belief* is clear and definite: through grace, particularly that of charity, our one love, whether directly or consciously for God, or indirectly or unconsciously for Him in and through another, is both human and divine—fully God's love but fully ours as well.

There is thus no possibility of confounding Thomistic doctrine on love with either pantheism or Manichaean dualism. "The teaching of Aquinas concerning the moral and spiritual order stands in sharp contrast to all views, ancient and modern, which cannot do justice to the difference between the divine and the creaturely without appearing to regard them as essentially antagonistic as well as discontinuous. For Aquinas, no such opposition obtains between God and the world which he has made."[23]

Since human love shares in divine love it is good and can be holy; but because it is not identical with divine love it is limited and can fail. And the fact is it has failed: sin has entered the world and in consequence a tension has resulted between the divine and the human. Thus St. Thomas, along with the whole of the Christian medieval world, was very much aware of the possibility and fact of sin, especially in the ways of love: *corruptio optimi pessima*. He treats, therefore, no virtue without due consideration of its opposite vices.[24] But ethical failure is never strong enough to sever fundamental metaphysical bonds. Human love, no matter how marred and twisted, is still basically good by reason of the divine goodness creative of and inhering in it. And because of the superabundance of grace flowing from the Incarnation, love after sin can be even more divine, and more perfectly human, than it was before sin. Of this, the *Beata nox* and *felix culpa*, of the ancient Easter liturgy was an ever-present and unqualified assurance for the medieval Christian.

Natural Love is perfected by grace in marriage

Such was the broad and universal context in which St. Thomas treated love, including that of marriage. But as much as some, and more than most, of his contemporaries he also viewed conjugal love in the less general, more immediate context of *natura*. The very first question he asks in his long treatise on marriage is: "Whether marriage is natural?"[25] The fact that it is the first question, affirmatively answered, illustrates Thomas's all-pervading respect for the natural, and would have served to alert his medieval readers to the paramount importance of giving nature its due in any consideration of conjugal living, much as Lactantius had done for his readership in the earlier Church.

In his response Thomas first invokes the authority of Aristotle: man, says the Philosopher is, "more naturally conjugal than political." The argument proper explains and elaborates. First, since nature "inclines" not just to the generation of the human species but also to the preservation, education, and, advancement of the child to full maturity, man and woman are meant to live together in a permanent union, which, accordingly, is likewise of nature. Secondly, man and woman are by nature complementary: they owe to each other a mutual service and obedience (*motuum obsequium*), since neither alone is capable of coping with the large and varied business of living in which "some matters are in the competence of men and others of women." And, it is emphasized, it is this determinate union of the sexes, their communal life together, "that makes for marriage."

Note how simply Thomas conceives of valid marriage: marriage is "the association of a man with a woman," it is "the binding (*obligatio*) of a man to a definite woman." In the Middle Ages there were other requirements for a *licit* marriage (a formal contract, solemnization, and so on) but for a *valid* marriage the requirements were extremely simple. This should be born in mind when considering some of the medieval love poetry. The formalities of marriage and even the word "marriage" may not be mentioned, but the *reality* of marriage may well be implied. The binding of a man (in intended lasting fidelity) to a woman is, says Thomas, "*quae matrimonium facit*." The definition needs expansion, and Thomas, as he moves into his subject, will expand it, but not by much.[26]

The marriage community

In Thomistic doctrine the root relationship in the body politic is the "community" (*obligatio, associatio*) of husband and wife in "mutual service." Out of this relationship grows the complex relationships that constitute society at large. This is the order required by nature. It is also the order of grace, which, for Thomas generally, "does not destroy but perfects nature."[27]

ARISTOTELIAN-THOMISM

Speaking specifically of Christian marriage he asks the question whether *sacramentum*—the indissoluble union itself between husband and wife as reflective of the union of Christ and the Church's—principal among the three marriage goods, his answer is that though in the order of finality progeny and fidelity are of prime importance (They are what marriage "intends"), the *sacramentum* is more noble (*dignius*) than either of the other two and, with respect to marriage as such (*secundum se*), it is more essential (*essentialius*). The first of the marriage goods (offspring), he says, "belongs to marriage insofar as man is animal, the second (fidelity or mutual service) insofar as man is human, and the third (the sacramental union of husband and wife) insofar as he is Christian."[28] This is the common teaching among the great scholastics and, as we shall see later, is reflected in the contemporary nuptial ritual. It is a salient point overlooked by practically all of the critics of the medieval theology on marriage who, consequently, view that theology as justifying marriage only in its procreative intention.

Since the early twelfth-century scholastic theology, and with it St. Thomas, distinguished between the *sacramentum tantum*, which is the transient sensible sign of the particular invisible grace of the sacrament being received, the *res sacramenti*, which is the hidden grace itself, and the *res et sacramentum*, which is the lasting effect of the sacrament. So in the sacrament of marriage, the *sacramentum tantum* is the words and/or other sensible expressions by which the man and woman vow themselves to each other until death separates them. It is what we may designate as the wedding ceremony. The *res sacramenti* is the sanctifying and other graces the couple receives when they "plight their troth" and as they try to live their married life as God wills them to. This, however, may be lost along the way, though it may be regained through penitence. The *res et sacramentum* is the indissoluble bond of marriage, which in addition to being a grace itself and a claim upon grace also points, "signs" or "signifies," beyond itself to Christ's lasting love for the Church, to God's eternal love for each individual person. It is the res *et sacramentum* that Thomas and other scholastics most have in mind when they speak of marriage as *sacramentum*.[29]

Certainly there is heavy stress placed by St. Thomas, as by other medieval theologians, on the *bonum prolis*, and it ever remains for him the chief (though not the only) end of marriage. But such stress does not preclude his further and heavier emphasis upon the bond between the spouses themselves. Husband and wife are first and fundamentally for one another, though in and through their union they must also be for their children and society at large. The better they are for and with one another—such is the implication—the better they will be for others. St. Thomas stresses the *bonum prolis* and the *mutuum obsequium* as the ends (*fines*) of marriage, and of these the former is called principal (*principalem*) and the latter secondary (*secundarium*).[30]

Two observations are in order. First, in Thomas's thinking "secondary" does not connote, as it does to us, unimportance or even relative unimportance. Indeed, for Thomas the *mutuum obsequium* is indispensable if only to secure the *bonum prolis* (conception, birth, and education of the child), though in the present context it is viewed as a good in and for itself. Secondly, Thomas is saying here that there is something even more fundamental than either of these two *ends* or goals, and that is the union itself, which is the marriage. It is in and through this union, which in the Christian is the *bonum sacramenti,* that the ends of marriage are realized. Thus it is the union of husband and wife, in love and in justice, as we shall see that is foremost in Thomas's mind when treating of marriage. This is what is most essential and most honorable in the state of matrimony, ranking even above the *bonum prolis*, which now in its turn becomes secondary, though again in no depreciative sense. For Thomas all is important, and generally everything is more important than everything else *in some sense or other*.

This community or *sacramentum* between husband and wife is a matter of both justice and love, says Thomas. Here again present-day critics of the medieval marriage theology often mis-read and mis-interpret. F. Schlosser, for instance, claims that for the medieval theologians generally, the conjugal union was merely a matter of justice. One might think, he says, that the *bonum sacramenti* left room for mutual love between spouses. Not so, for according to St. Augustine, who had originated the idea of the marriage goods, husband and wife were to love each other, not as spouses, but as creatures of God; and Schlösser cites the relevant text. Then he suggests that perhaps the *bonum fidei* (fidelity) might have served in the interest of love. Again, not so; and this time he recalls that for so late a theologian as St.

ARISTOTELIAN-THOMISM

Thomas *fides* as referring to the faithful union of husband and wife belonged, not to the virtue of charity or love, but to that of justice.[31]

But this is to presume that the medieval theologian's thinking was dichotomous, whereas in fact it was extraordinarily synthetic—the kind of thinking that could produce the great summations and encyclopedias of learning and experience that proliferated through the late medieval world and create such massive, encyclopedic poems as *Le Roman de la Rose* and *Les Echecs Amoureux*. As noted above the twelfth and thirteenth centuries were the age of the *Sententiae* (opinions, i.e. of the Fathers) and the, *Summae* (summations of thought)—the gathering together of past and present thought into a schematic whole. There were then great analytic minds, but more characteristic of those centuries was the desire and ability to synthesize. It is this characteristic that Kenelm Foster attributes *in its perfection* to St. Thomas in a beautiful chapter on the Saint's "tact." "It is this power of active discrimination, of measuring one thing against another, of reserving its limited place for each limited thing, of balancing part and part, of distinguishing the lesser and the greater and relating the one to the other, it is all this that I call tact; and if I were asked to name the distinctive characteristic of St. Thomas's genius I should point to this."[32]

Thus if St. Thomas says that fidelity belongs to the virtue of justice he is not thereby excluding the presence of charity or love. On the contrary, for him, just as the natural and supernatural, though radically distinct and worlds apart, are nevertheless inseparable in the *de facto* history of each of us, so also, though there is a multiplicity of different virtues, in concrete human activity every virtue presupposes and requires every other; and this, notes Thomas, is not his own private opinion, but is held by almost everyone (*ut fere ab omnibus ponitur.*)[33] For Thomas, then, as for his contemporaries, if there is to be in marriage the supernatural or grace, there must also be, and be left intact, the natural; and if there is to be true justice in the union between husband and wife there must also be love.

Why St. Thomas sometimes prefers to think of conjugal fidelity specifically in terms of justice rather than of love is understandable, for marriage yesterday and today, Christian and non-Christian, has always been regarded distinctively as a *contract* involving the exchange of

THE CRAFT OF LOVE

bodies and material goods, an exchange which for the good of society and the security of the spouses must be rooted in objective justice over and above subjective love. But it is also understandable in terms of love itself. Before marriage a man and a woman might simply love each other for a day, a month, or a year. But if their love reaches a certain depth it itself will want to continue to their life's end (and beyond), and will seek assurance that it might. This is the moment of marriage, in which quite freely, quite willingly, the two lovers *swear* (an act of justice) to be faithful to each other till death.

That St. Thomas quite explicitly taught the need and worth of love in marriage is amply evidenced. Consider this passage from the *Contra Gentiles* where the question concerns the indissolubility of marriage:

> The greater friendship is, the stronger and more lasting it is. But between a man and a woman there seems to be the greatest friendship; for they are united not only in the act of intercourse, which even among the animals produces a certain sweet society, but also throughout the whole of domestic living. In sign of this it is said, in Genesis ii, that "for the sake of his wife a man leaves father and mother." Thus it is fitting that marriage be altogether indissoluble.[34]

Here, not just friendship, or love—for in the Middle Ages *amicitia* was definitely a matter of love, and often passionate, emotional love. Note that for St. Thomas, as for medieval theology and literature generally, "*amicitia*" is a wider, fuller affair than that denoted by our "friendship", embracing heterosexual "romantic" love as well as other forms.[35] But "the greatest friendship" is postulated between husband and wife. It is quite definitely considered to involve the love act and all the 'sweetness' thereof. It is on the basis of this friendship, and not of justice that St. Thomas concludes that marriage must be indissoluble. Fidelity unto death is seen as a product of a great *love*.

In this same question of the *Contra Gentiles* another argument is presented linking love and fidelity. It is, to be sure, the same argument, only in reverse. If love of itself tends toward indissolubility, indissolubility quickens and confirms love: "For so the love (*amor* is the word now, not *amicitia*) of the one for the other will be the more faithful, since they know they are indivisibly united." Lovers, Thomas believes, want to be bound (in justice) to each other precisely because they feel such a bond will preserve and deepen their love.

Spousal equality

In question 124, which follows that outlining the arguments for monogamous marriage, the theme of conjugal love is pursued and enlarged as the note of spousal equality is introduced. "The love of friendship comprises a certain equality." But, observes Thomas, where one man has several wives "the love between husband and wife is not free but, as it were, slavish." In such marriages "wives are treated as though they were servants."

Further, "intense love cannot be exercised toward many." Thus, the man who has several wives while they have only one husband cannot love them as much as they love him. Consequently, the love between husband and wife "will not be the friendship of equals ... but a kind of servility." The presuppositions here are obvious and significant: there is to be an "intense love" (*amicitia intense*) between husband and wife; it should be a love that is free and equal (*liberalis, equalis*); and accordingly the wife is not to be treated as a servant (*ancillariter*).

The spiritual aspects of physical love

Thomas again argues for love, and a great love, in the conjugal union when, like other theologians of the time, and some poets, he inquires concerning the appropriateness of the derivation of the first woman from the first man. One of the reasons given for the suitability of that particular mode of production is "that man might love his wife the more, and cling the more inseparably to her, realizing that she has been derived from him." And this, it is added, "was especially necessary in the human species in which male and female live together through the whole of life, which does not happen among other animals."[36]

But what precisely is the nature of this love that should, according to Thomistic teaching, inform the union between husband and wife? C. S. Lewis claimed—and he was thinking specifically of St. Thomas—that the medieval theologians knew nothing of the kind of love that featured in the poetry of the time: a love of fine, human passion, transformative and perfective of the lover.[37] From what we have already seen of Thomas's respect for the natural, and from what we may learn from Thomistic specialists who tell of his unrelenting, though remarkably easy efforts to preserve the natural throughout the whole of the Christian dispensation,[38] we must suspect Lewis's judgment here as elsewhere relative to our subject.

Our suspicions are fully verified when we turn to Thomas's long and detailed treatise on human passion in the *Summa Theologiae* on the love-passion alone.[39] Love, says Thomas, is manifestly a passion since it affects the physical, concupiscible appetite, though it is also, *extenso nomine*, said to be lodged in the spiritual faculty of will. It is the first and most basic passion, and is the underlying motive of all that a person does, even when one's action quite visibly emanates from another, even opposing passion, for "every action that proceeds from any passion proceeds also from love, as from a first cause." The lover is in the one loved who is likewise in the lover. One who loves is not satisfied with a mere superficial knowledge of the beloved but "strives to search within for a knowledge of everything about the beloved and so enters into the depths of the beloved." Ecstasy is a product of love: intense meditation upon the beloved distracts the lover, "draws him away from other things," and to the extent that it is the love of friendship, that is, other-directed, the ecstasy is even more complete, for then the lover is entirely (*simpliciter*) outside himself, being entirely within the beloved.

Jealousy (*zelus*) is also *an effect* of love, for "intense love seeks to exclude all that is hostile to it," and the love of friendship sets one "against everything that is inimical to the good of one's friend." Finally, the love-passion, when its objective is right, far from being harmful to the lover, is perfective of him: "Nothing ... which is adapted to that which suits it is harmed thereby; rather, if it is possible, it is bettered and perfected."

All of this is in the context of a purely natural love which, as we have seen, has Thomas's blessing. It cannot be argued, as has been maintained with regard to mystics like Bernard of Clairvaux and Gerard de Liege, that Thomas is here using the fervent language of love because he is really thinking of God.[40] As a matter of fact, whereas the mystics borrow the notions of natural love and apply them to divine love, Thomas, especially in his response concerning the perfective power of love where he expressly uses the language of the *Song of Songs*, does just the opposite:[41] Like many a troubadour and courtly poet of his own time, he adapts the language of the mystics to natural love. When he describes love as a *liquefactio*, i.e. a melting or softening of the heart in preparation for the entrance of the lover; when he speaks of enjoyment or pleasure (*delectatio, fruitio*) experienced in the presence and possession of the beloved; when he refers to the languishment (*languor*) caused by the absence of the beloved and the intense desire (*fervor*) to have and to hold him—he is thinking of human love pure and simple. In other words, the conversion is not from earth to heaven, but from heaven to earth, as with the poets of secular love. The context of the question Thomas proposes and the tenor as well as content of his reply will allow for no other judgment. The appreciation is for human love precisely as such.

Further, when Thomas speaks of the love-passion as perfective of the lover he has in mind moral as well as aesthetic and psychological perfection. This is clear from his response to a question concerning human passion in general.[42] He asks: "Whether passion increases or diminishes the goodness or malice of an act?" He replies: "As ... it is better when one both wills good and by act accomplishes it so it is of the perfection of moral goodness for one to be moved to good not only in will but also in sensitive appetite, as Psalm 84 has it: 'my heart and my flesh sing for joy to the living God,' where heart stands for intellective appetite or will, and flesh for the sensitive."

In answer to the objection that passion must be harmful since it impedes the judgment of reason, Thomas grants that, if passion "precedes" reason then it "diminishes" (not necessarily destroys) the moral goodness of the act. But if passion follows reason (*se babet consequenter*), then it is both sign and cause of deeper moral worth. As we shall presently see, St. Thomas in reply to another question concerning human passion will exonerate the most ardent passion and pleasure in the very love act of husband and wife. But here the implication is clear: it is better to love one's spouse with flesh as well as spirit since by *reason* of lawful marriage they are "antecedently" right and good for one another.

THE CRAFT OF LOVE

In light of his golden rule that grace does not destroy but perfects nature, Thomas maintains the naturalness and human quality of conjugal love as he considers the effects and demands of the specifically Christian *caritas*.[43] In reply to a question asking if we should love those nearer to us (because of some natural bond) with greater charity, he argues that those who are not naturally united to us we are the friends of "simply" by the friendship of charity; but for those who are naturally one with us we have other kinds of love, and these natural loves, if they be "honest", charity draws to itself, not by absorbing them, much less by cancelling them out, but by "imperating" or commanding them, by summoning them and taking them into its service. They are left very much intact. Precisely by remaining what they are they become the loves of charity. Only now they have an added, supernatural objective, but one which by no means eliminates the original natural one; otherwise they would not be the same original loves, and charity would have nothing to "imperate."

In this same context St. Thomas singles out the love of husband and wife as perhaps the greatest of these "imperated" loves.[44] One's parents, he says, are to receive the greater reverential and appreciative love, but the "more intense" love is to be reserved for one's wife (*intensius diligitur uxor*); and this because the relationship is most intimate, husband and wife being but "one flesh" as Scripture has it. Of all the love relationships under God that Thomas treats in this question *de ordine caritatis*—love between fellow-citizens, rulers and subjects, simple friends, children for parents, etc.—at the pinnacle stands conjugal love. There is only one other relationship, not mentioned by Thomas here, that might possibly be conceived of as superior: the love of parent for child. Is it, or should it be, greater than one's love for one's spouse? It is strange that St. Thomas does not ask this question. But whatever the reason for the lacuna, it is clear that for Thomas conjugal love is, or should be, among the greatest of loves, both in the order of nature and of grace.

The error of Manichean thought

The physical sexual expression of conjugal love is treated by St. Thomas in considerable detail. His first concern is to justify the marriage act in face of the Manichaean denial.[45] In reply to the question: "Whether the act of marriage is always a sin?" he offers three texts from St. Paul which he regards as evident justification of marital intercourse: "A virgin if she should marry does not sin ... I wish young people to marry, to beget children .... Let the husband surrender to his wife that which is due her." As he elaborates his argument he is exceptionally definite in his affirmation and severe with the opposition. Twice he says that it is "impossible" that the sexual act be unrestrictedly sinful. Only those who follow the madness (*insaniam*) of the "worst of heresies" (*pessima haeresis*) claim that it is. Thomas would (and did, as we shall see) readily admit that the sexual act can, even within marriage, be sinful, but here he declares, what he is soon to prove, that in the act a "mean of virtue" can be found.

In this same question Thomas lists and disposes of all the relevant objections. It is argued that because the conjugal act interrupts one's union with God it is sinful. Thomas replies that though the act may interfere with one's immediate "contemplative" union with God it need not sever one's habitual union with Him "by grace." Thus it is no different for the conjugal act than for any other legitimate and required activity—eating, drinking, preaching, healing, tending to one's child. We cannot, nor should we always be in a state of actual contemplation.

Another objection claims that since the act is evidently shameful (*turpis*, i.e. causing one embarrassment or shame) it must be sinful. The reply is that the shame experienced in the act is not due to any "moral" defect therein but to a disorder resulting from original sin. One may fault Thomas here and insist that there is nothing at all disordered about sex whether in its activity or orientation; if shame is experienced it is, or should be, only when the privacy of sex is violated, and this is not a matter of disorder but simply the nature of sex. Thomas would agree that sex is by nature a private affair and therefore shame attaches to the violation of its privacy. This, after all, is simply one of the demands of marital fidelity, and one of its beauties: sexual intimacy is not for public viewing but is exclusively and secretly between one woman and one man.

But were he living today, Thomas would continue to hold his ground. He would have little trouble pointing to the disorders, often tragic, of sexual relationships even when guardedly private. He would not like us to translate his *turpis* as "shameful," for the word now connotes moral fault or sin (Thomas's *alum culpae*), but he would insist that in matters sexual, as in those of other appetites, there is a fundamental disorientation (original sin) beyond personal responsibility that often makes of sex a burden and a suffering (his *malum poenae*) rather than the joy it was originally meant to be.[46]

It is further argued in the objections to this question that since the act has to be "excused" by the marriage goods—as theologians generally held—there must be something sinful about it. Thomas answers that not only do we speak of inordinate or illicit acts as requiring excuse but also those acts that "appear" totally disordered, and such is the conjugal act. However, in itself it is "entirely (*ex toto*) excused by reason of the goodness of marriage, so that it is not a sin." For Thomas, sexual intercourse really needs no excuse since it is inbuilt into marriage itself and so shares in the goodness of marriage. It is only when sex is severed from marriage that it becomes wrong and only when considered apart from marriage that we must think of it as requiring excuse.

Passionate sexual fulfillment

Finally, it is urged that since an excess of passion corrupts virtue, the marriage act, in which passion and pleasure are always in excess, must be sinful. Thomas replies as we would expect from what we have seen of his doctrine on human passion in general:

> ...the excess of passion that corrupts virtue not only interferes with the act of reason but takes away the order of reason, which the intensity of pleasure in the marriage act does not do, because even if within the act one is not ordered according to reason, he has been pre-ordered to it by reason.

Elsewhere a still clearer and more forceful response is given to a similar objection:

> Only when the limits of reason are exceeded is passion considered to be immoderate. But the delight experienced in the marriage act although it be most intense quantitatively speaking,

does not exceed the limits prefixed by reason prior to its inception ..."[47]

By *reason* of marriage the conjugal act is antecedently rectified. Therefore let passion and pleasure therein be "most intense" (*intensissima*) and the "act" of reason suspended, still the "order" and "limits" of reason are observed, and the act emerges as good and virtuous.

Conjugal sex is meritorious

With the Manichees settled, the way lies open for a more positive approach to conjugal sexuality; and so the very next question asked is: "Whether the marriage act is meritorious?"[48] Thomas's full answer to this question is spread over a number of articles, and our understanding of it depends on just consideration of the whole of his doctrine on love.

His response in the present article is a qualified affirmation. First, the conjugal act is meritorious providing one is in grace and charity; that is, according to Thomas's general teaching, one must be united with God (grace) and must be disposed in love toward God and others (charity), and, under God, must love one's spouse above all others with both natural and supernatural love (the "order" of charity). Here the Thomistic doctrine on the relevance of love to sexuality is apparent: not only marriage but the marriage act itself is ultimately a matter of love and is of real and lasting value only insofar as it is rooted in and inspired by love.

Thomas's second qualification is that the act must have one or other of two purposes: the begetting of children or rendering to the other due love. Note that one or other of these purposes or motives satisfies the requirement for merit: "*vel ... ut debitum reddat, vel ... ut proles ... procreetur.*" Both may be present, but need not be. Just as marriage in general is not only for the begetting of children, but is also for the personal good of the spouses themselves, so too the act of marriage is for generation but is also for the love and well-being of husband and wife. That the *redditio debiti* here spoken of is a matter of love as well as justice should be evident from what has been noted above concerning the interrelationship of the virtues in the theology of St. Thomas and his contemporaries. It is also confirmed by the placement of *caritas* the source and prime condition of a meritorious act.

Because of our dichotomous dissociation of justice from love we do wrong to translate *redditio debiti* as "paying one's marital debt." A real *translation* rather than transliteration is called for, and "rendering due love" comes nearer St. Thomas's meaning, providing we understand the responsible, obligatory nature of the love he has in mind: it is *amor amicitiae*, the love of friendship, which looks to the needs and desires of the *other*, to what belongs to him or her more than to oneself. This other-centeredness of love is key to much of what Thomas is saying here and elsewhere when considering the marriage act as well as other facets of Christian living. Specifically Christian love, *caritas*, looks to the other not so much for one's own profit or pleasure (though this also will be involved) but for the sake of the other. Thus Thomas, along with other theologians of his day, distinguished between the *redditio debiti* and the *petitio debiti*. The latter, which is an "asking" for the sake of one's own private satisfaction, Thomas considers to be venially sinful, whereas the former, which is a "surrender" (in love) to the desires and needs of the other, is of virtue.

Libido —the marriage act for selfish reasons

Thus St. Thomas says that the marriage act is not meritorious but sinful when *libido* is its motive. "Libido" here obviously does not mean simply passion, pleasure, desire. We have already seen that St. Thomas recognizes the place and value of even the most intense passion and pleasure within the act. Nor is he ruling out all self-directed love (*amor concupiscentiae*), but only that self-love which is exclusive and makes of pleasure its only motivating force:

> If pleasure is sought beyond the honesty of marriage, as when someone considers his wife not as his wife but merely as a woman, and is prepared to do the same with her even were she not his wife, he sins mortally. Such a one is said to be "too ardent a lover of his wife" (*ardentior amator propriae uxoris*), because his ardor overleaps the good of marriage. If, however, pleasure is sought in none but one's wife, the sin is venial.[49]

ARISTOTELIAN-THOMISM

This is in reply to the question: "Whether one sins mortally *when* he knows his wife without intending any of the marriage goods but desires pleasure alone?" Herein is the marriage act vitiated: when one's concern is neither for spouse or progeny, when pleasure "alone" (*solam delectationem*) is "sought" (*quaeratur*). Here is the *ardentior amator* of his own wife, loving not her but his own solitary pleasure, seeing in her not his wife but a woman, any woman, who happened to be there for his personal gratification. He is not interested in society at large for he has no desire to procreate. He is not concerned for his partner for he does not consider her personal needs. This is brute, and perhaps brutal sexuality. Such behavior Thomas tolerates as venially sinful in the man who still has enough consideration for his spouse as to want to restrict his love-making to her alone. But for the one who has lost all love and concern for his wife and is prepared in his heart to seek his satisfaction elsewhere the judgment must be severe.

C. S. Lewis speaks of Peter Lombard as quoting "with approval from a supposedly Pythagorean source a sentence which is all-important for the historian of courtly love—*omnis ardentior amator propriae uxoris adulter est*, passionate love of a man's own wife is adultery."[50] Lewis mistranslates the phrase to fit his thesis. Peter is not here concerned with the "passionate lover" of his own wife (*ardens amator*) but, as in Lewis's quotation of the Lombard's Latin and the quotation from St. Thomas in our text, the concern is with the *"too passionate lover"* (*ardentior amator*) of one's own wife.

Similarly, Thomas offers the "avoidance of infidelity" (*vitatio fornicationis*) as a meritorious motive for the conjugal act only when one is anxious not to occasion the other's infidelity.[51] Then it is not only a meritorious motive but, like the *redditio debiti*, a morally and seriously compelling one, even, Thomas adds, when the sexual desires of one's spouse are, perhaps through modesty or shame, unexpressed: the husband must feel out, "interpret" the desires of his wife and fulfill them.[52] But when one uses the act simply to guard (as he *thinks*) his own chastity then it is vitiated, though only slightly so if his desire does not over-reach his wife.

According to Thomas, the wife need not "interpret" the desires of her husband, since it is supposed the male is naturally forward in his sexual drives. However, the wife is expected also to be "in tune with" her husband's health and general well-being. As he, then, is not to force himself upon his wife when she for some good reason is indisposed, neither is she to force herself upon him at inopportune times.[53] For St. Albert, Thomas's early mentor and teacher, it seems the wife must also "interpret" the desires of her husband and satisfy them. He may not express them at the moment, but they are inbuilt into the original marriage contract and as such are always being expressed unless withdrawn for some reason.[54]

In all the casuistry that marks, and perhaps for the modern mentality mars much of St. Thomas's sexology, his fundamental intention may be grasped, and appreciated: to keep husband and wife looking to each other in genuine concern and courtesy, and beyond to society at large and to God's kingdom here and hereafter. The "mutual service," the "sweet society," the "love of friendship" that Thomas would have in marriage generally must likewise be realized within the marriage act.

Nor need we regard Thomas as "puritanically medieval" in his morality and naive in his psychology for failing, as some would have it, to make the "modern breakthrough" in which pleasure becomes an exclusively justifying motive for conjugal intercourse. I. A. Richards, relying on the authority of Théodule Ribot's *Problems de psychologie affective* and, of course, his own sensitivity in art and literature, speaks of "the exclusive quest of pleasure for itself" as "a morbid form of activity and self-destructive:"

> Instructed by experience, man and animal alike place themselves in circumstances which will arouse desire and so through satisfaction lead to pleasure. The gourmet, the libertine, the aesthete, the mystic do alike. But when the pleasure which is the result of satisfying the tendency becomes the end pursued rather than the satisfying of the tendency itself, then an inversion of the psychological mechanism comes about. In the one case the activity is propagated from below upwards, in the other from above downwards, from the brain to the organic functions. The result is often an exhaustion of the tendency, 'disillusionment' and the blasé, world-wearied attitude .... Every

ARISTOTELIAN-THOMISM

activity has its own specific goal. Pleasure very probably ensues in most cases when the goal is reached, but that is a different matter .... The orientation is wrong if we put pleasure in the forefront.[55]

"The surest way to get pleasure is to forget about it," remarks Charles Bruehi, and he too admonishes against being actuated "directly by the desire for pleasure," for "pleasure seeking, when erected into an end, defeats itself, and is of all pursuits the most disappointing in which a man can engage."[56] I do not think St. Thomas is saying anything much different from this. This is why he could speak of pleasure as being a force implanted by God in sexual activity precisely to induce us to give ourselves to it and yet deny its validity as the reason for making love and warn against pleasure seeking not pleasure experiencing, in love.[57] Love must continually open out into the other; to the extent that it becomes closed off and ingrown, using the other solely for self-gratification, it ceases to be love and takes on the viciousness of lust.

Free choice essential for marriage

The question of the medieval Church's teaching and practice relative to liberty in love—the freedom of a man and woman to marry or not to marry, to choose this person or that—is of interest to the historical theologian; and it has, as we shall see, relevance to the literature of the time. But we need not linger over it here since, whatever the secular practice and ecclesiastical abuse of the time, the Church's formal teaching of the subject as manifest in St. Thomas and many other *loci*, is quite clear. What makes a marriage is the consent of both the woman and the man to be married: this is necessary and it alone suffices for a valid marriage. As St. Thomas succinctly puts it: "Through mutual consent ... matrimonial union is made." Even parental consent, though desired, is not deemed necessary:

> It must be said that a girl (*puella*) is not in the power of her father as a servant (*ancilla*), such that she does not have power over her own body .... Therefore she is free and so can give herself into the power of another without her father's consent. Just as someone, be it a young man or woman (*aiquis vel aliqua*)

THE CRAFT OF LOVE

can enter a religious order without parental consent, since that person is free.[58]

For an historical study of the Church's insistence on the free consent of the marrying couple as necessary, and sufficient, for a valid marriage, see Joyce, "The Church had throughout maintained the principle that before God all men are free to choose their state of life; that those who are called to be children of God are not chattels. But with the development of sacramental theology in the twelfth century a new reason was urged, viz., that the consent of the parents is not an essential element in the sacrament of marriage, that as soon as the consent is given by the parties concerned, the sacrament is realized and the marriage an accomplished fact."[59]

For a much less favorable view of the Church for having eliminated the need for parental consent see G. E. Howard:

> While she [the Church] very naturally strove to gain control of the nuptial celebration, to give more and more a religious form to the institution already declared by her to be a sacrament, she doubtless foresaw something of the evils which would ensue from clandestine or private unions, now that the consent of the parent or natural guardian was no longer necessary, as in the early days, for a valid marriage, and therefore began to legislate in the interest of publicity.[60]

Joyce too recognizes that one result of the Church's "innovation" was the evil of the clandestine marriage, but he believes that the Church was forced to its position by the very nature of marriage and the sacrament and maintains that the good accomplished by its demand for freedom in so vital an area far outweighed the corresponding evil. As we shall see, the idea of the desirability and need for freedom in contracting marriage, precisely because of the evils attaching to the forced, arranged marriage of the time, was not foreign to the best of the late medieval love poets.

Further, this mutual consent on the part of the marrying couple must be free of all compulsion, both physical and moral. Persuasion may be used, but if it should reach the point of force or violence the marriage, should it take place, is *ipso facto* invalidated.[61]

ARISTOTELIAN-THOMISM

The consequences of such teaching were not all happy. Since the consent of the couple alone sufficed, marriages could take place in secret; and though to marry clandestinely was regarded as gravely sinful, such marriages were nevertheless held to be valid. Thus the terrible and common blight of concubinage which eventually led Martin Luther to rage against the Church's doctrine and insist that parental consent was absolutely necessary for a valid marriage.[62] Without public ceremony or witness who could say who was married to whom? And a woman (or man) married in secret could easily be put aside in favor of another to be married in public (or in secret again). The medieval Church in general, as each theologian in particular, realized the evil, but hands were tied. The very nature of the sacrament, it was thought, demanded the complete liberty of choice of the couple involved, and nothing could be allowed that might interfere with it.

Pre-marriage engagement

For St. Thomas, as for the whole of the medieval ecclesiastical discipline, consummated sexual love was reserved for marriage. But such love was to have its beginnings prior to marriage. There were the *sponsalia*—the betrothal or engagement period, and this was sanctioned and blessed by a special liturgical rite; and the bond contracted thereby was regarded as a serious one. The *sponsalia* were early recognized and hallowed by the Church. Peter Lombard reviews some of the early opinions and legislation and, while he is careful to note the distinction between marriage and engagement, he emphasizes their similarity. In his eyes—and in the eyes of his many commentators—engagement is indeed a serious matter. He quotes St. Gregory: "He who takes in marriage a woman engaged to his neighbor, let him be anathema ...."[63] An early description of the rite of the *sponsalia* as performed in the Roman Church is found in a letter of Pope Nicholas I written in 866: it consisted of the mutual promise of intended marriage by the parties concerned; the *subarrhatio*, or giving of the ring (*annulum pronubum*) to the woman by her betrothed; agreement upon the dowry and a legal act (*tabulae nuptiales*) sanctioning it.[64]

Cohabitation was forbidden, of course, since the relationship was not yet marriage, but there is nothing to suggest that the engaged couple were not to love each other with a special and exclusive love and demonstrate their love by saying and doing the things that would preserve and deepen it. On the contrary, the betrothal ceremony itself might involve an exchange of visible tokens of love and fidelity: betrothal gifts and pledges (*datis arddzsponsaliis*), an engagement ring (*anuli subarrhatione*), etc:"[65] And each was required to keep chaste in mind and body for the sake of the other, such that an act of fornication by one was regarded as sufficient cause for the other to break the engagement.[66]

Even prior to the *sponsalia*, an "honest" love seems to have had the Church's approval and encouragement. This is the implication of the Church's demand that betrothal, as marriage, be grounded on the free choice and mutual consent of the contracting parties. Betrothal by parental arrangement was allowed at an early age, but it could be dissolved, with no adverse effects, by either party, when the age of puberty was reached.[67]

It is true a couple may not know each other before betrothal or marriage; the marriage may be arranged and their love begin with the wedding ceremony. But the emphasis placed by the Church on liberty of choice, the need for the couple themselves to decide on uniting in the intimacy of marriage until death, suggests a preference for *prior* knowledge and love. As to the ways in which premarital love might express itself, certainly nothing is allowed that is proper to marriage alone, and there should be nothing libidinous. St. Thomas, when speaking of extra-marital kissing, embracing, and touching (*osculum, amplexus vel tactus*) condemns as grievously sinful any act that proceeds from "corrupt intention." But he also affirms that these acts in themselves (*secundum speciem suam*) are not wrong and therefore may be free of lust either "by reason of native custom, or because of necessity, or for some other reasonable cause."[68] These conditions, it would seem, leave ample room for an honest and relatively intimate and tender show of love between those who are not yet married.

The purpose of celibacy

St. Thomas is one with the long-standing ecclesiastical tradition that ranked the state of virginity (celibacy) above that of marriage. But, like the Fathers of the fourth-century Council of Gangra and others, he insists that virginity is a worthier state not because of what is surrendered thereby but because of what virginity aims at.

In reply to the question as to whether or not virginity is illicit, Thomas says that if it is undertaken "contrary to right reason, as in the case of one who loathes pleasure (*quasi delectationes secundum se abhorens*)," then it is wrong; it becomes the mark of the "insensitive boor" (*insensibilis, quasi agrestis*). But true, that is devoted, loving virginity (*pia virginitas*) abstains from venereal delight in order that it might "be freer for the service of God (*ut liberius divinae contemplationi vacet, ad vacand rebus divinis*)."[69]

The same positive motivation is found to underlie the ecclesiastical, counsel, after St. Paul (1 Cor. 7:6), of periodic sexual abstinence within marriage. The one who abstains from sexual intercourse with his wife because he abhors sex (*detestatur mulierum usum*) sins. Such sin, Thomas says, has no proper name, but falls into the general category of "insensibility."[70]

But it is required, and is virtuous, for husband and wife to separate for a time for the sake of prayer: "on days that are set aside as being particularly for worship it is not for intercourse (*petere debitum*);" though one must always fulfill the desires of the other "whatever the day or the hour."[71] Thomas stresses that there is no *mortal* sin involved in seeking the sexual act at holy times (and no sin at all in rendering it), but there does seem to be venial sin, since during these times one should be preoccupied with the strictly spiritual demands of feast or fast. Still, Thomas seems loathe to use the word "sin" at all in the present context; he simply says that such an act at such time is "incongruous." Thus in answer to an objection which cites the authority of the Old Testament against intercourse in a sacred time, Thomas says: "from that authority it cannot be proved that it is a mortal sin, but that it is incongruous (*incongruum*). For many things pertaining to the cleanness of flesh are exacted by precept in the old law, which was given to the 'carnal,' these are not exacted in the new law, the law of spirit.[72]

Though virginity is preferred to marriage, the latter's worth and prestige is not, in the language of Thomas, diminished thereby. In his

THE CRAFT OF LOVE

long and positive treatment of marriage, Thomas rarely mentions virginity, and then only the more clearly and forcefully to secure the dignity of marriage. Thus in reply to an objection that the marriage act cannot be meritorious because by it virginity, which is "praiseworthy", is lost; he argues that there is "merit in both greater and in lesser goods so that when one leaves aside a lesser good that he might do the greater he is to be praised for having abstained from the less meritorious act."[73] Marriage might not be the best there is, still it has its worth and merit.

As noted earlier, Thomas shares the world-view of his contemporaries in which everything, great and small, has a proper and necessary place in the "fair chain of love." Nothing good is to be despised; all is rather to be appreciated and promoted for the benefit of each and of the whole. So to another objection, this one against the "sterility" of virginity, Thomas replies:

> The multitude of mankind will be secured if some give themselves to the work of generation; but others, abstaining from this, are thus free for the contemplation of divine things unto the beauty and welfare of the whole of mankind, as in an army there are those who guard the camp, those who carry the banners, those who fight with the sword. All is an obligation for the whole, but no one person can do everything (*omnia debita sunt multitudini, sed per unum impleri non possunt*).[74]

It is the kind of thinking manifested by St. Thomas here that led J. Huizinga to write in his chapter on "The hierarchic Conception of Society at the close of the Middle Ages:"

> Medieval political speculation is imbued to the marrow with the idea of a structure of society based upon distinct orders... The functions or groupings, which the Middle Ages designated by the words 'estate' and 'order', are of very diverse natures. There are, first of all, the estates of the realm, but there are also the trades, the state of matrimony and that of virginity, the state of sin ... That which, in medieval thought, establishes unity in the very dissimilar meanings of the word, is the conviction that every one of the groupings represents a divine institution, an element of the organism of Creation emanating from the will of God,

ARISTOTELIAN-THOMISM

constituting an actual entity, and being, at bottom, as venerable as the angelic hierarchy.[75]

Finally, to the argument that since the marriage act (unlike virginity) is granted by way of "indulgence" (1 Cor. 7:6) it is a gift (*beneficium*) and therefore cannot be a means of merit, Thomas replies: "It is not incongruous that he who uses a 'concession' should merit; because the good use of God's gifts is meritorious"[76] Marriage and the marriage act are gifts of God. Those, then, who use them rightly do well and merit thereby God's grace and the Kingdom of Heaven.

CHAPTER 4

FRANCISCAN AUGUSTINIANISM

Aristotelian Thomism was not, certainly, the only school of theology effective in the late medieval Church. Side by side with it and probably of broader influence, was the Augustinianism that entered into the teaching and preaching of the thirteenth-century and fourteenth-century Franciscans and many others. It is to this tradition in its doctrine on conjugal love that we now turn.

We will consider the writings of three Franciscan theologians, eminently authoritative in their own time and beyond: Alexander of Hales, St. Bonaventure, and John Duns Scotus. Alexander, an Englishman by birth and rearing, was a renowned master of theology at the University of Paris in the first half of the thirteenth century and may be said to have originated the Franciscan school of theology. St. Bonaventure, a contemporary of St. Thomas and as eminent a theologian in his time as, the Angelic Doctor, was Minister General of his Order, and so had political as well as theological influence over Franciscans everywhere. Duns Scotus was born and reared in Scotland and was a revered theologian first at Oxford. Later he was an enormously popular lecturer both at Paris and Cologne at the beginning of the fourteenth century.

ALEXANDER OF HALES

The teaching of Alexander of Hales is embodied in a monumental work, a *Summa Theologiae*.[1] Roger Bacon claimed the Franciscans attributed this work to Alexander, "although it was not done by him but by others."[2] Etienne Gilson thinks that Bacon was largely right. But for the very reason that it cannot be called exclusively Alexander's work the *Summa* has the greater historical value for our purpose, showing its widespread influence. As Gilson expresses it, "Despite its composite character, it has a unity of its own due to the fact that its component fragments are all borrowed from Franciscan theologians belonging to the same doctrinal school. Owing to this unity of inspiration, it remarkably illustrates what may be called 'the spirit of the thirteenth-century Franciscan school of theology at the University of Paris.'"[3]

We may justly conclude, then, that the hundreds, and perhaps thousands, of Franciscans, both English and continental, who walked the fields of Europe and the streets of its cities in the thirteenth and fourteenth centuries, who taught in its universities and preached from its pulpits and counseled in its confessionals, who were simple priests and lordly bishops, had their thinking shaped in large measure by what they read and studied in their representative book of theology, *The Summa Theologica* of Brother Alexander.

Love is natural

Though lacking the architectural harmony and detail of St. Thomas's *Summae*, the same grand sweep of vision permeates that of Alexander, and, as with Bonaventure and Scotus after him, love is always seen within the context that God is the beginning and end of the universe. The individual, the personal, the private concerns are there, and are respected—but never in isolation. Every item of the universe is a part of the whole, intimately interlinked with it and with every other part.

It is, then, in this broad context that Alexander views sexual love. It first appears in his treatment of creation. The question is asked: "Whether it was fitting that the whole of humankind derive from a single man for the sake of mutual love?"[4] The answer is affirmative: it was indeed proper that we should all derive from a person so that, aware of our common origin, we might be impelled to love each other all the more. In opposition it is argued that carnal love (*amor carnalis*) is an impediment to spiritual love and therefore, since a common origin would only serve to intensify carnal love, it is not proper that we should have derived from a single ancestor. In his reply to this objection Alexander manifests the same respect for the natural and its harmonious interworking with grace that we have observed in the teaching of St. Thomas. He distinguishes three kinds of love: carnal, natural, and spiritual. Natural love is carnal love but as purged of all lust (*amor modo libidinosus*). It is no obstacle to spiritual love; on the contrary it is through it that spiritual love is born (*induceretur*) and it is through spiritual love that natural or carnal love is to be perfected (*perficiendus*).

However, the approval of natural or carnal love is a qualified one. First, it must not be lustful—though as we are warned here against sins of the flesh we are likewise reminded of the perhaps more serious sins of the spirit: not every *amor Spiritus*, Alexander tells us is 'spiritual.' Secondly, Alexander concedes that perhaps (*fortasse*) carnal love may hinder the advance toward perfection, and he offers the example of Christ before and after his resurrection.

By no means did Christ's physical presence constitute an impediment to grace. However, the fullness of grace (*abundantia gratiae*) came only with the Spirit *after* Christ's physical presence was removed. Perhaps, then, suggests Alexander, even a good carnal love must be surrendered if the perfection or fullness of grace is to be had. However, the care and hesitancy in which the author expresses himself on this point suggests that he is not one who would hastily recommend the sacrifice of carnal love. Just as Christ's physical presence before his Ascension was absolutely (*simpliciter*) necessary for the faith and love of his disciples, so a given carnal love may be needed both for present proficiency in the life of grace and for future perfection.

Sexual love

In this question of our common origin the love treated is not specifically sexual love, but rather the more generalized natural love of each for all—although Alexander's reference here to lust (*pullo modo libidinosus*) indicates that sexual love may also be involved.

Sexual love, however, receives direct and explicit treatment in a following question concerning the origin of humankind: "Whether the woman should have been formed as a helpmate for the man?"[5] The affirmative answer lists four substantiating reasons according to the fourfold meaning of the Scriptures:

THE CRAFT OF LOVE

1. The *literal* value of a female helpmate is the consequent avoidance of the "confusion of the sexes" which, as evidenced in the hermaphrodite, nature abhors;

2. The *moral* value is that "man (*homo* that is man and woman) might be instructed thereby in the exercise of humility and charity, for seeing himself in need of the other he learns to humble himself, while seeing the other in need of him he strives to be charitable and generous;

3. The *allegorical* value lies in the supernatural symbolism thus made possible: "in the distinction of the sexes and their consequent meeting in carnal union (*in carnis unitatem*) there is signified "the union of Christ and the Church;"

4. The *anagogical*, value, "that in the loving embrace (*amicabili coniunctione*] of a man and a woman there might be symbolized the union of the soul with God both as to the intensity of that union (*magnitudo adhaerentiae*), and its fecund fruitfulness (*fructus foecunditas*)."

In all of this exposition not a single negative note is struck. Alexander seems to be all for love, the fullness of love between a man and a woman: a love that is intimate and intense; that involves both spirit and flesh; a need-love fostering humility as well as a gift-love promoting charity; a love, moreover, that is based on the equality of man and woman, for there is *mutual* need and help.

We should, of course, be aware that Latin is less exclusive in gender than English. Thus when our theologians want to refer to both male and female they use the word *homo*, while they refer to the male as *vir* and the female as *mulier*. Our English translation of *homo* as "man," is therefore, currently misleading. Our theologians may be prejudiced in favor of the male but not as much as it appears from our translations of them.

Equality of men and women

The subject of love and of equality in love is pursued as the question is asked: "Whether the rib, or some other member, should have been the principal material [in the formation] of Eve?"[6] Alexander, of course, is for the rib, and he gives his reasons. One is that thereby "the equality

FRANCISCAN-AUGUSTINIANISM

between man and woman in the begetting and rearing of children" might be made manifest. Another reason is that there might also be symbolized the "union of love" between husband and wife. The full significance of his response Alexander reveals in his answer to one of the objections to it. The objector counters that if it was love that was meant to be symbolized, a better organ (of greater dignity?) than the rib might have been chosen. Alexander replies that the woman "was not formed from man's side only to express a union of love," and he elaborates both then (and thereafter) frequently quoted words of Hugh of St. Victor:

> Woman was made from the side of man that it might be shown that she was created to share in a life of love. For if she had been made from his head it might seem that she was to be preferred to him and was to dominate him; or if from his feet it might seem that she was to be subjected to him in servitude. But because the man was to be provided with neither a ruler (*domina*) nor a servant (*ancilla*) but a companion (*socia*) she was produced neither from the head nor the feet but from his side that he might realize that she who had been formed from him was to be placed beside him (*iuxta se ponendam*) .

The union of husband and wife was to be not just of love but of equality in love, and this, add our two theologians, must endure through the whole of "their life of love together" (*in consortium ... dilectionis*).

The woman's equality with her husband is underscored in a response given to an objection raised in a subsequent question.[7] In the body of the article it is agreed that the woman is 'naturally' (physically?) weaker than the man; but in reply to the objection her equality is defended where for the Christian it most matters. In the faith of Christ, Alexander recalls, there is neither male nor female, the one is not more worthy than the other, and "each is the other's equal in virtue, in struggle, and in reward," as the Gloss on Gal. 3:28 explains: "Let not the woman say she is weak," says St. Basil as quoted by Alexander, "for weakness is of the flesh, power, however, is of the spirit."

THE CRAFT OF LOVE

The equality that Alexander here argues for the woman may not satisfy a growing number of present-day theologians, especially of the feminist school. From our perspective it may seem a mere sop for the socially suppressed woman. The woman may be said to be man's equal in spirit, but what does this amount to if she is inferior to him in body? For, first of all, in this world it is the body—the corporal, the tangible, the visible interrelationships of bodily human beings—that, for the most part, is identified with life itself. The world is body (celestial bodies), society is body (the body politic), even the Church is said to be body (the mystical body). How, then, is the woman the equal of the man if she is his inferior in this bodily world?

And secondly, even though in that medieval society the spirit had its place and even pride of place, it was dependent upon the body—upon visible and tangible books of devotion written by men, sermons preached by men, laws made and enforced by men, liturgy shaped and directed by men, religious rules and constitutions determined, often dictated by men, stained glass windows, statues, paintings created by men. The very prayers that spontaneously arose in the intimacy of her own heart were, in all probability, fashioned after the manner of male praying. It would seem then, that here too, in the realm of spirit, the woman, rather than being the equal of the man, was subject to him.

It is further argued that even within herself, at the center of her own soul, she was the subject of the male. The man had his own self-image, his "subjectivity"; he determined who he was in himself and in his relation to the rest of the world. But the woman had only the image of herself given to her by the man who, again, did the theologizing and writing and preaching about her, who sculpted and painted her body, who told her why she was in the world and what she should do within it. What then of Alexander's and other theologians' protestations that she was the equal of man and was to be regarded and treated as such? All down the line, in just about everything, she was the creature of man.

In regard to the equality of women we are indebted to Margaret Miles in her two books as well the whole current of thought prominent in our time.[8] Following the lead of Simone de Beauvoir and others, Miles defines "subjectivity" as "an inner life, a construction and cultivation of a 'self.'"⁹ Her claim is that, unlike her male counterpart, ancient and medieval woman received her identity as woman from outside, from the male, rather than developing it from within. She was not a subject of her own making but merely an object of man's dreams and desires, which were mainly sexual and thus we have the carnal exploitation of women by men in the ancient, medieval, and modern world.

It is true that viewed from our point in time, in light of contemporary achievements of and future hopes for male and female equality, the medieval theologians must be found wanting. In medieval Christianity, however, the Church's teaching of sexual equality, limited though it may have been, was an advance over what women had to contend with prior to and outside of Christianity, and so, we may surmise, preparation for further advances in the future.

Miles begins her *Carnal Knowing* not with women in Christianity but with those who appear long before in Babylonian and Greek epics as mere "foils for the hero's developing awareness of what is entailed in being human" (p. 3). So it was before Christianity, and so it is outside of Christianity in much of the world today.

At the Aug. 16-20, 1993 conference at Leuven, Belgium, of the Society for European Women Theologians, it is reported that perhaps the most moving of the lectures was from the "Muslim Perspective" by Fatima Ahmed Ibrahim, a Sudanese theologian exiled in Britain. She "came from a society where women are the leftovers after the men had finished; where girls were circumcised when young; where female illiteracy is over ninty-eight percent; where women seen in the company of a man not their husband are now convicted of adultery and given eighty lashes, a fine and a year's imprisonment; where women (in western Sudan) do all the agricultural work while their husbands sit and drink; and, not surprisingly, where a growing number of wives are murdering their husbands." Ibrahim does not accuse the Koran for such conduct against women. She finds from the speeches of Mohammed and from the Qur'an that Islam "does not oppose equal rights for women or does it teach male superiority."The opposition comes from those who use the Qura'an as a cover-up for their own ambitions and agendas.¹⁰ We must, then, be wary of accusing Christianity or the

THE CRAFT OF LOVE

Church of suppressing women. There is something more primitive, more chronic at work, which the Christian Church perhaps has done more than many other religions to check and correct.

In times when men were physically stronger than women and most occupations (including war and other ways of maintaining government) required physical strength, and when education was for *men* (some of them) and rarely for women, and when, consequently, men had the roles of secular and ecclesiastical leadership, it was nigh revolutionary to declare woman the equal of man in *anything*. But the Church, after her founder and in the express words of his apostle (Gal. 3:28), did declare the woman the equal of man, and in areas that at the time were regarded, at least in theory, as the most critical, namely those of the spirit.

This last we must not take lightly! The spirit was everywhere to be found in the Christian Middle Ages, and if the body was also there, it was mainly to promote and manifest the spirit. This was the belief, and however little it may have worked out in practice in individual lives, it was a respected and sought after ideal. If women, then, were declared by Christ and his Church to be the equal of man in the spirit, then they had a dignity equal to man where dignity ought mainly or only, to be sought.

Self Image

It is likewise true that medieval women found images of themselves in and through the theology, art and literature created by the male. Such images, however, simply because produced by the male need not have been distortions of the truly feminine. Divine revelation and a perceptive theology based upon it, and some good thinking and feeling by poets and artists in touch with the feminine within them as well as appreciative of it in women themselves, might well have had true things to say about the woman, who she was and was to become, thus aiding rather than hindering her self-realization. At any rate, supposing the worst, it would not have been much different for the average medieval male. Then as now, it was not "man in general" who created and so expressed for all men what maleness truly is, but particular writers and artists who may have been much different in

FRANCISCAN-AUGUSTINIANISM

their persons and ideals than most other men. Accordingly, the images of manhood they projected may have been quite foreign to the common man. If then, we say that women were deprived of their true identity, their 'subjectivity,' by men, should we not likewise say that so were most men by far? I am thinking of the macho image imposed upon the male through the ages: the image of man the aggressor, the lover, the "jock," the athlete, the knight, the soldier, the avenger, the "boss," the money-maker, the senator, the president, the bishop, the pope ... and "the failure" when none of this is realized in his life. Man "in general" is not responsible for the image, but particular men—those especially who happen to be involved in the media of one sort or another—and women who happen to like the image as complementary of their own image given them in and through that same media.

I should think the judgment here would be the same as it might be in our own day. Some there are, whether male or female, who have no self-created self-image. All they know of themselves is what they find in and through the media or, more directly, in the expectations of what family and friends have of them. Their formation is externally imposed. But there are others who take what they see and hear externally, use it to build something new within them, and leap beyond what is within and without to what they, as individuals, are striving to become. Most of us fluctuate in the process. Sometimes we, women and men alike, are merely pawns manipulated from without, at other times we are moved and shaped from within; but hopefully as we grow in years more and more of the latter is realized in our lives. Why should we suppose it to have been different in the Middle Ages?

There were women (and men) who knew of themselves only according to what they passively saw and heard of themselves through the art and theology of their time. But there were others who became more and more *themselves* as they searched within and beyond the words and images given to them. All through the Middle Ages we find creativity in art and literature, almost exclusively exercised by the male. But it would be a mistake to limit creativity to *ex-professo* artists, poets, musicians. As today many more people are creative in quiet non-professional ways, both outside themselves and within, than those reputedly creative, so it must have been in the Middle Ages. And the Middle Ages themselves matured as they grew older in that, as we have already noted, more and more people began to read, think for themselves, and challenge their traditional teachers. People continued to be formed from outside, as are all in whatever age, but many, both men and women, were at the same time doing their own personal formation as well.

Discrepancy has also been found between the Church's supposed belief in the equality and dignity of women and the particular self-image it was trying to inflict upon them. Two pictures were placed before them as symbolic of who they were and were to be. One was that of Eve, "fallen" Eve. Here was woman the seductress, the temptress, the cause of the fall of man the male. She was at once sexually desirable and hateful. The other picture was that of Mary, the Virgin, who was all and only good. Both pictures, it is claimed, insinuate a rejection of the sexual. If sex is, it is bad or soon becomes bad—thus Eve. The only sure way sex can be good is not to be at all, to be virginal—thus Mary. In either case the full stature of womanhood, in itself and vis-à-vis the male, was diminished.

It would be difficult to gauge the frequency of "fallen Eve" in the theologizing and preaching of the medieval Church. In the reputedly great theology examined here, there is very little mention of Eve and none of it is derogatory of women as such. And if it is Eve who tempted Adam to sin, the sin itself, with all its dire consequences, is attributed to Adam. He, more than Eve, is held responsible for the Fall. So says the theology.

As for the preaching, there are more references to Eve than in the theology proper, and some of it must have been offensive to women while pleasing the men, as delightfully fictionalized by Chaucer in his *Wife of Bath* and her fifth and final husband (to date!).[11] But this is only one type of preaching, what G. R. Owst calls the preaching of "satire and complaint." Most other sermons were silent about Eve and had nothing but good to say about women.

But with Mary it is another matter. In her *Image as Insight*, Margaret Miles devotes several pages to the listing of later medieval Marian iconographic material alone (cathedrals, sculptures, paintings, frescoes, etc.), and she just begins to scratch the surface.[12] If we add to this all the Marian devotions and pilgrimages, the liturgies, the preaching, the

FRANCISCAN-AUGUSTINIANISM

theologizing about Mary, all the poetry and hymns sung to her praise, we can be sure that one of the dominant figures in the life of the medieval woman and man, if not *the* dominant figure, was that of Mary. If to the medieval mind it was a woman who caused the man to sin, much more in mind and heart was the realization that it was only through the woman that we have the Redeemer and redemption. Not to the old but the new Eve did medieval man and woman look. Satirical and comical literature may have held onto fallen Eve and so continued to bait and batter women, but the Church in its theology and preaching, its art and architecture, its liturgy and song could only praise this particular woman, and so through her all womankind.

That Mary, being a virgin, was therefore regarded as counter-sexual cannot be proved. Certainly none of the classical theologians or poets reviewed in the present instance may be called in witness of it. The counter-sexual image is speculation growing out of the particular interests and prejudices of our age. We may find Mary's virginity restrictive and stifling; it must be proved that medieval men and women found it so. It might be more plausibly argued to the contrary. Mary may have been virgin, but she was also mother, and as such received the prayers of countless numbers of women who at that time wanted, *needed*, to be pregnant, and wanted their children to live and live well and happily in this world. And unlike Mary, they could become pregnant in only one way.

Mary, then, rather promoted sexual intercourse than discouraged it. Even as a virgin, Mary would have done no harm to the medieval women's lives and loves, but rather would have broadened and deepened them. In her they found a woman who lived a full and rich life, a life honored by all the world, not because she was the satisfying object of man's sexual desires, or simply because she was a mother and home-maker, but because, precisely as virgin, she remained at liberty to live a higher, creative life, unrestricted by the desires and demands of male aggression. Margaret Miles who recently has written, negatively, of the early and medieval Church's sexology and its suppression and sexual exploitation of medieval woman,[13] in an earlier book seems, at least in places, of a wider, more tolerant understanding. She describes and illustrates the medieval fondness for juxtaposing the image of the Virgin Mary, who lived without sex, and Mary Magdalene,

THE CRAFT OF LOVE

who rejected it. She then sounds a warning and alerts us to a truth our present prejudices are likely to hide from us:

> If we try to inspect these images [of Mary] without prior assumptions from twentieth-century experience, the plays, paintings, and popular devotions that deal with the life of the Virgin reveal a woman who was able to experience the events of girlhood, young womanhood, motherhood, old age, and death without being overwhelmed by their physical aspects. Through all biological changes she pursued a life of spiritual intensity and personal power. That this spiritual autonomy was even possible, medieval women would have known from no other source. The Virgin's biology was ancillary to her life cycle, a spiritual process that must have reversed—and compensated—the experience of actual medieval women.[14]

But Miles goes on to qualify: "If this hypothesis seems fruitful for making us aware of other messages than the 'message given' by fourteenth-century paintings, it does not negate this message; it does not ignore in the message a page from the history of the oppression of women. But it also honors the creativity and ingenuity with which visual images can be and were used by women."

It is, then, more likely than not that when men and women read or heard the theologians and preachers on the matter of women's spiritual equality with men, they found not fiction but something real and determinative. Woman had a dignity equal to that of the man, and, though it might be violated and probably often was, it was the God-given law to respect and cultivate it. And in and through it the woman could find her own self-image, develop her own 'subjectivity,' beyond the dictates of her body or the body of the world. That such development was not uncommon, is instanced in many women in those late medieval centuries, women widely respected and admired and sometimes followed by their male contemporaries—a Hilda of Whitby, a Hedwig of Bavaria, a Hildegard of Bingen, a Catherine of Siena, a Bridget of Sweden, a Julian of Norwich, abbesses, nuns of incredible energy and originality, women from high social places and low, mainly religious but also some who were married or had been married. These, though they had their art and liturgy, their books of devotion, their preaching and the laws that governed their lives, all from men, knew how to use what they received toward their own ends, break out of whatever restrictions were placed upon them, and shape their lives beyond men's and their own imaginings.

When, therefore, we reflect upon the Middle Ages, especially their later centuries, we think of their great women along with their great men. And how many unknown women, quietly great, were also there exerting their influence upon the men of the time and directly upon society, we will never know. But the opportunity and incentive were there, as illustrated in the above texts from Alexander's theology, voicing a common and ancient Christian belief. We may justly suppose that more than a few took advantage of it.

Marriage and sexual expression

When, in the context of the other sacraments, Alexander comes to treat marriage as a subject in itself, he, like St. Thomas, poses the question as to whether or not marriage is "of the natural law."[15] But less 'naturalistic' than Thomas he hastens to locate the natural component of marriage in its full and specifically Christian context. St. Thomas dwells on the natural aspect of things, firmly securing the worth of the natural before moving on to the order of grace, thereby providing us with a detailed exposition of the indispensable function of nature within the Christian life. Alexander, and the Franciscan theologians generally, recognizes and respects the natural, but does not linger over it; he leaves us to infer the particular details of its functioning.

Thus in reply to the present question he argues that the union of the spouses is of nature, but without any elaboration of the point immediately goes on to say that the *significatio*, that is the symbolism of the union, is of divine institution, while the *sanctificatio* is "through the passion of Christ, which sanctifies all the sacraments, and through which all the sacraments have the power to sanctify." But it is clear that for Alexander nature is of prime importance: it is responsible for the union itself. It is left fully intact and is only strengthened in and through all the graces and blessings added to it.

THE CRAFT OF LOVE

This same respect for what is of nature is manifest in Alexander's argument for conjugal inseparability and exclusiveness. Here, too, it is asked whether inseparability is "of natural law."[16] The purely natural instincts of the spouses provide the answer:

> No one wants his wife to share (*dividat*) herself with others. Likewise, [natural law] dictates that one do to others what he wills to be done to himself, and thus it demands inseparability; for as a man wills that his wife's affection cleave to him inseparably, so must he will his own affection to be inseparably hers.

When the question is posed: "Whether intercourse with one's spouse is a sin?"[17] the *solutio* is prefaced by three brief arguments affirming its sinlessness and, indeed, its holiness. A more positive attitude toward the worth of conjugal love-making is scarcely conceivable than that expressed here. Marital intercourse is held to be not only sinless but meritorious, and this in the express context of fallen nature.

Alexander's argument runs as follows. First, it is granted that in the *de facto* state of things, that is the state of fallen humanity, the law of the flesh is opposed to that of the spirit. However, our present condition is also one of grace, and since it is grace, the principle of merit, which has restored order to marriage by means of the marriage goods, the marriage act is now not just sinless but meritorious. Secondly, according to St. Augustine, while punishment comes from sin, merit (because of Christ) comes from punishment. Therefore again, the marriage act, though once involved in punishment (because of sin), because of grace is now of merit. And, it is added, since it is meritorious it is even without venial sin. Finally, it is argued that since Christ is not just a good but a very good and most able physician, the healing He effects is complete; therefore, the conjugal act though once vitiated by sin has been entirely restored so as now to be in no way (*nullatenus*) sinful.

However, Alexander continues, conjugal intercourse may become sinful. His teaching here is identical to that which we found in St. Thomas. When a man makes love with his wife *simply* for the pleasure of it—"*si propter se quaereretur delectatio*"—he sins. The sin is located not in the experiencing of pleasure but in *exclusive*, pleasure-seeking. When one seeks his pleasure contrary to love of spouse, treating her like a common whore (*per meretritias blanditias... adulteram*) with the sole purpose of fulfilling his lust (*ad satiandum libidinem*) his sin is mortal. Such intercourse is, accordingly, "prohibited." But "permitted" is "that intercourse which results from fragility or weakness of the flesh, such that sexual pleasure is sought, but so subject to God (*sub Deo*) that the love of God is preferred to it. Such intercourse is venially sinful."

There is, however, a liberality in Alexander's teaching which seems broader than that of St. Thomas. The latter speaks of procreation and fidelity as the two marriage goods which render the conjugal act meritorious. A third good or end of marriage—the *remedium concupiscentiae* (the healing of libido) or *vitatio fornicationis* (avoidance of infidelity)—fully justifies the act only when it is the *other's* sexual needs that are in question. When one's own needs are in the balance then other remedies, such as prayer and fasting, should be applied.[18] Thomas is loathe to allow the love act, as love in general, to become self-centered; self-interested, yes, but always it must be centered on the other. But Alexander seems to regard the *remedium concupiscentiae* as fully justifying even when it is a question of satisfying one's own needs exclusively. Thus in reply to the query as to whether by the sixth commandment all conjugal intercourse is forbidden,[19] he specifies that "from the words of Scripture it is manifest that the conjugal act when it is for procreation, or for rendering due love or for avoiding unchastity (*vitandi incontinentiam*) is not prohibited." One (*vel ... vel*) of the *three* goods of marriage, therefore, would seem to justify the marriage act. How they secure the justice of the act is described in the reply to the fifth objection of this same question: "The first motive (procreation) orders conjugal intercourse to God that is the begetting of children for the Kingdom of God), the second (fidelity) to one's neighbor (spouses looking to the good of each other); the third (the *remedium* or *vitatio*) orders the act to oneself (each spouse looking to his or her own good)." It would seem, then, that the *remedium* or *vitatio* precisely as referring to oneself, takes its place as a completely legitimate and meritorious motive for the conjugal act.

Alexander, even under the close scrutiny of theological casuistry, finds room aplenty for a full and intimately loving life for the married.

THE CRAFT OF LOVE

That life in all its public and private detail is blessed by both God and Church and, if persevered in to the end, merits the Kingdom of Heaven.

Virginity

For Alexander, then, marriage with all its intimacies is fully justified. But is its value diminished when compared with the state of virginity? In Alexander's treatment of marriage there is scarcely any mention of virginity. When it is mentioned it is in reply to objections raised against marriage.[20] The opposition quotes 1 Con 7, 1, which, apparently, argues for continence: "It is good for a man not to touch a woman." Alexander replies that this refers to the unmarried. There is a legitimate touching and one that is illegitimate. Touching that is in marriage is legitimate; as St. Paul declares when he commands men to render due love to their wives. He then quotes, with approval, the words of St. Augustine in *De bono coniugali* (ch. 9): "Certain goods have been given us by God which are desirable in themselves, such as wisdom, health, friendship; while other things are necessary because they serve some other end, such as food and marriage.

Whoever uses those goods, such as food and marriage, for reasons other than those for which they were instituted, sins. But those who use them according to their institution do well, while the one who abstains does better. Alexander also quotes St. Ambrose who refers to St. Paul not as commanding virginity but only as recommending it: "It is," says Ambrose, "of counsel, not precept." It is much the same with St. Thomas and other renowned theologians of the time—virginity as an ideal is to be preferred to marriage; but mention of it occupies only a small corner of their long and detailed considerations of marriage; and then only the better to secure the justification and worth of the totality of conjugal life and love.

BONAVENTURE

An account of Bonaventure's life, work, and contemporary influence may be found in the work of Etienne Gilson.[21] Gilson notes that Bonaventure had been nominated to the archbishopric of York, but, at his earnest petitioning, was allowed to continue on as Minister General of his Order.

FRANCISCAN-AUGUSTINIANISM

In his *Commentary on the Sentences* St. Bonaventure asks (again, in the broad setting of God and the world as a whole) the customary question as to the propriety of Eve's having been formed from a rib of Adam's side.[22] His response shows some originality and fresh imagination, and clearly reveals his basic positive attitude toward human sexual love. The one sex, says Bonaventure, is taken from the other in order to show the strength and exclusiveness of the bond that must exist between them (*forti vincula et singulari*). The "operation" is performed while Adam sleeps in symbol of the peace and joy (*quietatio*) the man is meant to experience in union (*coniunctio*) with the woman, and the woman is derived from the man's "bone" in symbol of the strength and support (*fortitudinem et sustentationem*) she is meant to draw from him. Finally, the woman is taken from her husband's side in proof of the equality that must be in their life together (*equalitas mutuae societatis*). No considerations external to the couple themselves intrude. In this first moment of the formation of woman, only the mutual relationship of the man and woman is envisioned. The woman is not viewed as having been produced for the sake of procreation or of society at large or even for the Kingdom of God; rather she is seen as being for her man, as he for her. As for St. Thomas, so for Bonaventure, the prime social relationship, the very first and best love under God is that between husband and wife.

Natural love

Elsewhere, Bonaventure uses this same theology, with some expansion, as background for a sermon on the magnitude of the Blessed Mother's love.[23] "The greatest natural love (*amor naturalis*)," he observes, "is that of a mother for her child (*filium*)... The greatest acquired love (*amor acquisita*) is that of wife for her husband (*sponsae ad sponsum*) ... and the greatest gift love (*amor gratuita*) is the love of God (*caritas*)." Mary has all three loves to perfection: her supreme love for her child, Jesus; her supreme acquired love for Jesus the Christ; her supreme love for Jesus as God. We may speculate as to why Bonaventure speaks here only of the wife's love for her husband (*sponsae ad sponsum*) rather than, as in the exegesis just cited, their mutual love. Is it because he had Mary in mind and so in this context was concerned only with the feminine, just as he used the masculine for child, since in the present case the child of Mary is masculine! Or did he think that within this greatest "acquired love" that of the woman outweighed that of the man? In any case, here, in a sermon for the people at large, as in his theologizing for the specialists, it is evident that spousal love held Bonaventure's respect and reverence.

This sermon is referred to by Robert P. Prentice, O.F.M.[24] At the beginning of his study of human love in Bonaventure's works Prentice notes that though the Saint's treatment of charity is vast, his consideration of strictly human love is minimal (p. 7). This does not mean that Bonaventure had little regard for human love. It is simply that for Bonaventure human love must also be of charity. St. Thomas, though he was willing to abstract human love, as all of nature, from its intended divine context and consider it in itself, would and did agree with Bonaventure. In real life, human love to be true to itself must be grounded in and imbued with caritas.

Marriage created by God in Paradise

Bonaventure visualizes the first historical moment of love when he asks the question: "By whom was the sacrament of marriage instituted?"[25] He replies with just about every theologian of his day that it was instituted by God himself in Paradise, but qualifies with an original and gracious nuance: God instituted marriage, not directly, but by enlightening Adam interiorly to accept Eve as his bride: "He did not command Adam to take Eve as his wife but enlightened him within that she was to be given to him as his wife, so that in this way through free consent wives would be united to all his descendents."

Here in Bonaventure is another illustration of the Church's traditional insistence that marriage based on freedom of choice, which is the ground of love. As we have seen in our study of St. Thomas, a marriage contracted through compulsion or fear, a marriage forced by parents or relatives, was not only unlawful but also invalid. True, Bonaventure concedes marriage once was of precept—there at the beginning when the world had to be populated—but it was not man's precept but God's, which works *interiorly* through an inspired acceptance. It is freely obeyed in an act of love. So in answer to an objection claiming that since marriage was originally of precept (and

FRANCISCAN-AUGUSTINIANISM

therefore of justice) it is not meant to be free, Bonaventure replies: "as that precept did not take away the movement of charity, which is supremely (*maxime*) gratuitous and free; so it does not remove nor diminish freedom of consent."[26] Neither for Bonaventure nor for Thomas are justice and love opposed. For there always is liberty to accept or reject the precept, and there is the "enlightenment from within" to consent out of love (*motum caritatis*).

Bonaventure, like Aquinas and Alexander of Hales, respects the natural instincts of love even when it is "supernaturalized" by charity, as evidenced in the following passage.

> In marriage there is a certain exclusivity of love in which an outsider (alienus) does not share. Thus one is naturally jealous of his wife that she should love no one as she loves him in the conjugal act (*in actu illo*); and every wife is similarly jealous of her husband.... Likewise, with the influx of charity, which makes all things to be in common, it never does so with respect to one's wife, because of the private nature of that love (*privatum amorem*) which must be in marriage. For marriage is the symbol (*sacramentum*) of that love by which God is jealous of the individual soul that it love no one as much as Him, and the soul in no way wants to be deserted by God for another.[27]

Charity does not interfere with the natural, intense, and exclusive love between husband and wife but rather demands and, in its own order, illustrates it. St. Thomas's teachings on the harmony of nature and grace and of the "imperation" of charity (charity taking to itself and using toward its own ends what is of nature) are not here formally proposed, but they are clearly implied. Bonaventure assuredly knew of both principles and employed them in his theologizing. So in a question concerning the "order of charity," he denies that to love one's parents more than one's own children is a violation of the principle "grace must conform to nature," even though by "natural love" parents must love their children more than their own parents.[28] It is, he says, as also in the sermon referred to above, by another kind of love, a love of gratitude that they are to love their own parents more.

The other principle, that of imperation, he employs when he distinguishes the virtue of charity from the other virtues.[29] Charity is a distinct habit within the soul and has a distinct object, God himself, and so it is a distinct virtue. But it is one with the other virtues in that it moves them beyond their own proper objects into God. The former is *caritas eliciens*, the latter *caritas imperans*. Bonaventure does not make as extensive use of these principles as does Thomas, but they are operative as he forms his theology, as in his theology of marriage as of all else. The Franciscan and the Dominican are one in their respect and reverence for nature as they are for what is above and beyond it.

For the medieval theologian generally, marriage reached its ultimate perfection *(finis primarius)* in and through the child *(bonum prolis)*. But, at least for the greater theologians, it did only by reason of having reached a prior and more important reflection simply by being what it is: a lasting union of love between a man and a woman (the *sacramentum*). And the marriage act had much to do with that union: it expressed it, confirmed and deepened it, helped preserve it, and gave it transcendental or supernatural significance. St. Bonaventure shared in this teaching. We have already sampled his appreciation of the union between husband and wife as basic to and preeminent within marriage. His conception of the marriage act relative to this union is revealed in his answer to the question as to whether carnal intercourse is of the "integrity" of marriage.[30] He replies that it is not of integrity "*quod esse necessitatis*, that is a valid marriage may be had without it; but it is of integrity "*quod esse completionis*,", that is the marriage act completes and fulfills the conjugal union. Again, the significance of the marriage act relative to the conjugal union is illustrated in Bonaventure's discussion of "constrained consent" (*consensus coactus*).[31] A marriage, he says, is invalid if the consent of either party has been forced; but it can be validated without more ado by a subsequent act of intercourse freely consented to. In other words, the conjugal act has the power *practically* to make the marriage. Finally, the full import of the marriage act is outlined in an article which, we may note, makes no mention of the *bonum prolis*. The question is asked: "What in marriage is the sign, and what is signified?"[32] Bonaventure begins his answer by categorizing marriage as a sacrament that proceeds "from natural instinct," and he defines it simply as the union (*coniunctio*) of a man and a woman. He then says that the word or gesture (of bride and groom) expresses the interior union by way of "signification," that is as *conventional* sign. But the sex act expresses that union "naturally" (*naturaliter*). In other words, the conjugal act is the *natural* sign or expression of conjugal love. And that this particular expression of love is both good and holy, Saint Bonaventure clearly affirms when he adds that the marriage act further signifies "the union of Christ with the Church or of God with the individual soul."

How sin enters the conjugal act

In Bonaventure we find the same requirements for legitimate love-making as are to be found in Alexander and Thomas. Like them he sees the marriage act as licit and meritorious when *either* procreation or fidelity is its motive.[33] And like them he judges the one who knows his wife simply for pleasure (*ut delectetur*) and not as spouse (*matrimonialiter*) as sinning, venially if he limits himself in act and desire to his wife, mortally if he is prepared to violate God's law for the sake of his pleasure.[34]

However, as Thomas seems less tolerant of self-interested love than Alexander, Bonaventure may appear to be less tolerant than Thomas. This is suggested by his reply to the question: "Whether to have intercourse with one's wife in order to satisfy one's sensual appetite (*ration concupiscentiae satiandae*) is always a mortal sin?"[35] Thomas had asked a similar question. Both theologians begin with a summary of the opinion of those who hold that "to seek pleasure is a mortal sin, to accept it when offered is a venial sin, while simply to tolerate it is of perfection." Both theologians reject the opinion, but while Thomas's rejection is immediate and absolute, Bonaventure's is qualified and hesitant. The opinion, he says, is "too strict" (*nimis dura*), but he concedes it may have "probable" value, which means that it might be followed as a safe norm of conscience. He goes on to say that one may fondle and take pleasure (*iocari*) in his wife, though with venial sin; and what pleasure he does experience he ought to refer to God, otherwise, again, there is venial sin. Compared to Alexander's and Thomas's teachings on the matter, his view, like the one he rejects, is *nimis dura* (too much, hard.) Thomas says nothing about the love-play between husband and wife (supposing, we might surmise, its legitimate place in the total legitimate act). He makes no stipulation about any need to refer one's pleasure to God. And he will have nothing at all to do with the opinion in question. Of it he simply says: "This cannot be" (*sed hoc non potest esse*).

But whatever the indecision we may find in Bonaventure with regard to the finer details of the marital act, it is manifest that he is much more for it than against. As we have seen, he recognizes its high symbolism and its native power to confirm and express the conjugal bond, and what sin he unearths in pleasure-motivated sex he regards generally only as venial. But he is careful, perhaps over-careful, not to allow the physical in love to become isolated. He sees it as one element in a large love, and he does not regard it as the most important element. More important than the union of bodies is the union of hearts, and the grace of Christian marriage is meant to bring the former into harmony with the latter.

Thus he argues that as there is a threefold disorientation in the sexual appetite—the propensity to be promiscuous, to act solely for pleasure, and to be unfaithful—so there is a threefold conjugal grace giving rise to the three *bona matrimonii*: the grace of fidelity that holds a man to one woman in the intimacies of conjugal love (*copula singulari*); another grace that keeps husband and wife mindful that their love-making reaches beyond their private joy and pleasure into society and the kingdom of God by reason of its procreative power (*copula utili*); and a third grace, that of the *Sacrament*, that insures that they remain together in a lasting union (*copula insepargbili*).[36]

JOHN DUNS SCOTUS

Relatively little of John Duns Scotus's work—and none of it that concerns marriage—has been critically edited, and much has not been edited at all.[37] There are, however, Wadding's edition containing the Paris lectures and a redaction of Scotus's teaching the form of a *Summa Theologica*, and both contain doctrine on marriage. The former, Gilson declares, "represents the actual teaching of Duns Scotus," and the Franciscans who in the early eighteenth century issued the *Summa* testified that it contained nothing other than the doctrine of Scotus himself."[38] Accordingly we can with fair security rely on these sources for Scotus's teaching on love and marriage; though we must be aware that arguments drawn from them are seriously qualified by the still uncertain state of the texts that will be considered.

Marriage is a work of nature and grace

Scotus is in agreement with the other theologians of our study in viewing marriage within the context of the total Christian revelation and as a work of nature as well as of grace.[39] The goodness and holiness of marriage and the need for an intimate love (*unionem mutuae delectionis*) between husband and wife, are clearly enunciated. But he is no wide-eyed romantic. He is very much aware of the hardship involved in marriage, which is one reason why he postulates within marriage, an "honorable" state, the need for special grace:

> It is fitting that the conferring of grace be attached to the aforesaid contract [that of marriage], because it is a difficult contract, the difficulty of which is conjoined to the honorable (bonestati) ... But upon what is both honorable and difficult it is right that grace be conferred.[40]

This same realism coupled with respect for the marriage bond as it is sanctioned by God appears as Scotus argues the need of a divine precept to enforce indissolubility:

> Unless some law had commanded that it be done, with great difficulty could people be persuaded to undertake such a heavy task (onus) with such a condition attached to it [that is indissolubility]. Indeed, for the most part they would deny that they had entered into the conjugal contract under a condition of indissolubility.[41]

Some in the Middle Ages may have found it difficult to reconcile marital grace and merit with the comparative ease and pleasure of married life vis-à-vis the "sacrificial" life of virginity or celibacy. Others shunned and despised marriage precisely because it was onerous. Scotus was a party to neither attitude. For him, marriage was both honorable and difficult; *therefore* it contains the grace that makes it holy.

Scotus makes Peter Lombard's definition of marriage his own: "the marital union of a man and woman legitimately qualified (*legitimas personas*) and holding to a single way of life."⁴² What is essential, what marriage *is* is the union between husband and wife (*coniunctio maritalis ... vinculum coniugale*). In virtue of this union husband and wife are always and only for one another, cannot renounce the marriage act even for the purposes of prayer unless by mutual consent, and must live together as equals, each showing to the other the same consideration expected for oneself (*alter alteri exhibeat quod quisque sibi*).⁴³

Like St. Thomas, Scotus is able to sum up nicely in a single paragraph the fullness of what marriage is; and like Thomas, Alexander and Bonaventure he regards the *sacramentum*—the transcendentally significant indissoluble union between husband and wife—as the first and principal perfection of marriage. There are, he says, three perfections in marriage. The prime and intrinsic perfection, the essence (*forma*) of marriage, is the indissoluble union of the spouses as symbolic of the union between Christ and the Church. The second perfection is "extrinsic" and is the proximate goal toward which the essential union is "ordered": the conjugal act, which is to be rendered each to each when requested. The third perfection is also "extrinsic": the procreation and education of children, which is the principal end of marriage.⁴⁴

Note that this last is called the "principal end" (*finis principalis*) and not the "principal perfection" of marriage. Scotus's terminology is precise. In the passage under consideration, it is evident that he recognizes that the order of essence and the order of finality are on two different levels, each having its own importance and each in some respect more important than the other. True, it was axiomatic in scholastic philosophy that the final cause is the most noble of all the causes, and thus the end or goal of a thing or action is more noble even than its constituent elements, its "formal" cause. But it was also recognized by the scholastics that this was an abstraction which in a concrete event or situation could be enormously complicated. So, in the question at hand, carnal union and procreation are ends or final causes of marriage, and so they have their importance.

However, the *sacramentum* itself also has a good deal of finality simply as such. It is symbolic of the union between Christ and the

Church—by the *res et sacramentum* it actually finalizes that union within the marriage—and of itself it bespeaks the "intended" personal relations, carnal and spiritual, between the spouses. This is why St. Thomas, who certainly believed in the relative nobility of the final cause, could yet speak of the *bonum sacramenti*, and not the *bonum prolis*, as the most worthy of the marriage goods. And this is why Scotus could do the same—in the present passage by strong implication, and quite explicitly in his reply to a question specifically concerned with the relative importance of the several marriage goods:

> Marriage by reason of its perpetual bond is the sacrament [symbol] signifying Christ's indissoluble union with the Church. Therefore, the sacrament, as a good of marriage, is intrinsic to marriage itself, and its first and formal perfection. But what is the proper formal perfection of each thing has the greater primacy within it (princinalius in ipso). Therefore the sacrament is chief (praecipuum) among the goods of marriage.[45]

Loving sexual activity is meritorious

There is no mistaking where Scotus's emphasis lies: marriage is assuredly for children as it is also for the conjugal act, but only because it is first and foremost for the love itself between husband and wife. That Scotus regarded marriage as having worth independent of and beyond its procreative purpose is further evidenced in this question concerning the primacy of the *sacramentum*. The good of procreation, Scotus argues, does not mean that every conjugal act must eventuate in a child or even that it be "intended" to do so. It simply demands:

1. That if a child results (*si eveniat*) it be received gratefully and be reared religiously, and

2. That nothing be done positively to exclude the possibility of conception (*non impedire illud bonum studiose*).

And even where there is the sure impossibility (*certa impossibilitas*) of conception, marriage, including its proper act, is still justified. Here theologians are cited who explain how this is so by having recourse to the possibility of a miracle healing the sterility. But Scotus himself believes that even where such a miracle is unlikely (*sec ... probabile*) and, indeed, even unwanted by those making love (*nec intentu m ab istis utentibus tali actu*), still the act of love is justified, and this simply by reason of the presence of the other two marriage goods, fidelity and the sacrament. In this event, he concludes, though the marriage would not be *in officium*, that is for children, it would remain, as the other sacraments, in *remedium*, that is a source of healing grace."[46]

Like other commentators on the *Sentences*, Scotus uses Peter Lombard's term *excusantia* as applied to the marriage goods: the goods of marriage, said Peter, "excuse" the marriage act. But Scotus finds the term inept. The marriage goods, he argues, are "specificative," both intrinsically and extrinsically, of marriage and its proper act, rendering them, accordingly, good and virtuous in themselves (*sui ratione*). In other words the marriage act like marriage itself needs no excuse. St. Thomas, as we have seen, had held substantially the same opinion, but he accepted the Lombard's terminology. Scotus wants to abandon it. And if still, under the pressure of tradition he continues to use it, he does so having first radically qualified and altered its meaning. With him (as for Thomas too) the term *excusantia* has more of the meaning of "justifying" and, really, none of the sense of "excusing": the marriage goods are justifying factors which *constitute* marriage in its essence and function; they *are* what marriage is. Thus by eliminating what in his time had apparently become an ambiguity tainting the worth of marriage, Scotus thereby underlined his perfectly positive attitude toward marriage and the act of marriage.[47]

Of this teaching as it appears in Scotus's Paris Report[48] G. Le Bras says: "Duns Scotus ... does not at all want to speak of 'excuse,' since marriage, by its object and its end, is a virtuous act (*acte homnnete*); and because the goods of marriage already existed in the state of innocence, there can be no question of 'excuse.'" And Peter Auriol [a disciple of Scotus] ... declares [regards the marriage act]: "no act of virtue is in need of excuse."[49]

Like our other theologians, Scotus holds for the indubitable merit of the other-directed conjugal act. He also shares, in his own way, in Alexander of Hales's 'permissiveness,' or allowance for human frailty, however one might in those days have viewed it. As for all theologians in good standing, Scotus believed that the prime condition for merit in the conjugal act is the presence of charity: basically the act must be one of Christian love. If at root the act is of charity and the motive is either (*vel*) the desire for children or fidelity (which seems to combine both the *redditio* and *remedium*), then the act is meritorious, providing, of course, it is consummated in a way apt for generation. In his reply to the objection that those engaged in the act become immersed in and thence motivated by the sheer pleasure of it (*ad ipsam delectationem actus per se respicientes*) and thereby commit venial sin, Scotus argues that still this would not prevent the act from being meritorious, for venial sin, he notes, does not impede the flow of grace and so the possibility of merit. Thus even if (*etsi*—Scotus is not at all sure there would be even the least sin in this case) there should be venial sin in the love-making between husband and wife, more deeply there is goodness in it. It still may be virtuous (*honestus*), praiseworthy (*laudabilis*), and holy (*meritorius*).[50]

CHAPTER 5

THE MIND OF CHRISTENDOM

Having examined the doctrines of love and sex of the two leading schools of speculative theology in the late Middle Ages as expressed by the recognized leaders of those schools, we should have a fair understanding of what the "official" Church of the time, in England as elsewhere, was teaching concerning love and marriage. "Official" is here used loosely. It is meant simply to suggest that the teaching of these great theologians enjoyed considerable authority, sanction, and influence within the western Church at large, though not necessarily voicing its definitive doctrine. We will discuss the various expressions and channels of ecclesiastical teaching in the Middle Ages later.

What these theologians say about the pleasure of conjugal love-making and the sin that may or may not be in it perhaps needs further clarification for the contemporary reader, who may have little if any belief in sin but a firm belief in pleasure. Furthermore, the contemporary reader might find the scholastic relationship between reason and pleasure unexpected.

As already explained, what was considered at fault was not the experiencing of pleasure. The sin is in pleasure-seeking to the exclusion of the conjugal union, the love commitment of the partners.

Secondly, the sin that is mentioned is for the most part considered venial, mortal sin being reserved for the obviously brutal and completely self-centered act, what today we might call marital rape and condemn as such. But venial sin is infinitely distant from mortal, being only slightly aberrant from the ideal, weakening our union in love with God but by no means severing it. As St. Thomas, quoting St. Augustine, says relative to the sin in conjugal sex when *only pleasure is sought*: such sin is categorized among those "daily sins" for which we ask forgiveness in the *Our Father*.[1] We all fail in little ways, the married in their way, the celibate in theirs. But this says nothing at all against one's state of life or the actions and joys proper to that state or against those therein involved. And most people then, in the Middle Ages, as now, would not have scrupled over venial sin; though it was for the theologian to keep the Christian *ideal* alive and pure, and then, because of inevitable failures to live up to it, to proclaim the fundamental gospel message of forgiveness.

The third point that may need clarification is that of the theologians' demand that the pleasure of the conjugal act be kept within the bounds of and be subject to reason. "Reason" for us may suggest a coldness and calculation that should have nothing to do with love: heart not head should be the organ of love. But this was not the medieval theologians' meaning. Saint Albert here expresses succinctly the extraordinarily cohesive view of that time:

> It must be said that then [in Paradise] conception would have been without ardor, and delivery without pain. But by "ardor" is meant delight which stifles the act of reason. And well do I concede that then there would have been greater and more genuine delight in the conjugal act, but under the imperium of reason; for then reason would have been strengthened by the grace of innocence, so that nothing below it, no matter how powerful, could have withdrawn it from the vision of the first immutable good.[2]

For the theologians of the Middle Ages reason was not the isolated Cartesian faculty of abstract thought but something much fuller, much richer. Perhaps a better translation for *ratio*, at least in our present context, would be "spirit," that which, in the Holy Spirit (Love itself, *ipso Caritas*), is meant to pervade, humanize, and divinize that which might otherwise remain purely (or impurely) physical.

Thus for Scotus, as also for St. Albert the Great and St. Thomas, the conjugal act before the Fall, that is in the state of innocence when all was subject to reason and reason to God, would have been charged not with less passion, pleasure, and delight than now but with more, precisely because it would have been free of all the subtle (and not so subtle) psychological and physiological deformities that now often make of the act and the life surrounding it a torment and a bore.

Of the scholastic view of sex in Paradise, C. S. Lewis says: "... the scholastic picture of unfallen sexuality—a picture of physical pleasure at the maximum and emotional disturbance at the minimum—may suggest to us something much less like the purity of Adam in Paradise than the cold sensuality of Tiberius in Capri." It must be stated at once that this is entirely unjust to the scholastics.[3]

In his *Life of Tiberius* Suetonius, the prominent Roman historian and biographer, offers a description of the sexual excesses of a man who is powerful enough to go 'beyond good and evil.' The descriptions of the debauchery, and cruelty still has power to shock. John Crowe Ransom might seem to have such unrepented sins in mind when he penned these lines:

> Great lovers lie in Hell, the stubborn ones
> Infatuate of the flesh upon the bones;
> Stuprate, they rend each other when they kiss,
> The pieces kiss each other, no end to this.[4]

So much for sex in Hell, here or hereafter!

Indeed Lewis's suggestion is perverse, as hopefully, our discussion of St. Thomas and Franciscans in the preceding chapters has suggested. But Lewis is here like the lawyer who has made his point before the jury even though he has been forced to withdraw it. We must, however, insist with Lewis's fairer self, that this was definitely not the case. Pure love, as conceived by Alexander, Albert, Thomas, Scotus was emotional as well as passionate, but it was a fine as well as strong emotion and passion and a perfect pleasure, precisely because *both* spirit (*ratio, caritas*) and body shared in the love-making. Tiberius's interest (supposing the stories to be true) was merely genital and perversely so, and thus his pleasure was only genital. Adam and Eve's interest, according to the scholastics (and, we might add, according to Lewis in his *Perelandra*), was *total* love, and so their joy in it was complete.

THE CRAFT OF LOVE

Collective teachings of the great theologians

Here, then, is the teaching on love and marriage of four great theologians well-known, widely studied, and profoundly respected in England, as elsewhere in Europe, in the closing centuries of the Middle Ages, and together they represent the two main theologies of the period: the traditional Platonic Augustinianism and the new, though firmly established, Aristotelian Thomism. Whatever radical, metaphysical differences may have divided the two schools, it appears that when it came to the very practical matter of love, and sexual union in marriage there was little enough difference and an abundance of positive agreement.

To summarize: All of our theologians come to the matter of love and marriage out of a sweeping vision of God and his world. Sex, love, and marriage have their unique importance, but they are not isolated elements, and must not be viewed as such. They are to be seen in context, and the context is enormous. One has only to page through a table of contents or the indices of our theologians to be all but confounded by the near infinite number of matters treated, often in minute detail, and yet to see how all is interrelated. In my treatment of their theology of marriage, I have simply suggested this larger vision and the need to consider our topic within it. The difference is critical when one isolates sex and love and thinks of them as the only things in life and when they are seen as parts of an immense and infinitely variegated whole.

Within this global context natural, human, passionate love as fulfilled in the sacrament of marriage was held by all our theologians to be good and holy. Marriage must be entered into freely and must be grounded in love, natural love imbued and elevated by the still greater love of charity. Since freedom and love are the ground of marriage, an honest love prior to marriage in preparation for it is in order, but the sexual activity proper to marriage itself is forbidden outside of marriage. Husband and wife were recognized as equals, and if the woman was to be subject to her husband in what is of the body (external social relationships), she had a dignity in spirit that made her her own person; and since the bond was one of love, especially the love of charity, the husband's headship over his wife was not to be tyrannical but, like Christ's for his Church, a headship in service. All were agreed that marriage proposes *carnal* union and the begetting of children for the Kingdom of God, but all likewise believed that more worthy than either of these two "goals" of marriage was the value intrinsic and essential to marriage—the *sacramentum*: the lasting love-bond between husband and wife which is the visible sign of God's intimate love for each individual, Christ's undying love for his Church.

Natural love

The authorities given also were appreciative of sexual love as given and received in marriage, seeing it as the graced and meritorious confirmation and expression of the marital bond, a source of love and pleasure for the married couple, and of children for society and the Church at large. Spouses may sin in their love-making, but only to the extent that they become introverted, seeking only themselves rather than the good, the joy of the other as well. One might look to the Aristotelian Thomistic doctrine for a fuller exposition and appreciation of natural love, of human passion and emotion, of the profound harmony at every vital turn between what is of grace and what of nature in marriage. One might find in Scotus and Alexander's *Summa* a greater tolerance of the fallen human condition in the act of love, and in Thomas and Bonaventure less.

But though our theologians are all for love as leading to marriage and consummated within it, they are realists, aware of the corrosive, destructive nature of sin and of their responsibilities as theologians to present the full Christian ideal in the light of which all—not just the married—must continually perfect their love, purge it of every egotistic and narcissistic tendency, and strive to center it upon "the other." Along this way, it was believed, lies not the loss or diminution of love but its preservation and joyous fulfillment.

CHAPTER 6

PRAYING AND BELIEVING

With Church's liturgy we move from complex analytical ideas of the philosophers and theologians to their implications in the general society. The marriage liturgy and the sermons preached therein have been almost entirely ignored by past studies of love and sex in Christian marriage; yet they are of major importance since they were the point at which the teaching Church most nearly, most intimately touched the laity in the matter of love and marriage, and where the Church's theology itself became a kind of poetry of love.

The liturgy of York outside the church door

In "the renowned Church of York" of the fourteenth and fifteenth centuries,[1] the marriage rite began before the church door with the following exhortation spoken by the priest in both Latin and English (*lingua moderna*), as the directive reads:

> Lo, brethren, we are comen here before God and his angels and all his halowes, in the face and presence of our moder holy Chyrche, for to couple and to knyt these two bodyes togyder, that is to saye, of this man and of this woman, that they be from this tyme forthe but one body and two soules in the fayth and lawe of God and holy Chyrche, for to deserue everlastynge lyfe, what someuer that they done here be fore.
>
> I charge you on Goddes behalfe and holy Chirche, that yf there be any of you that can say anythynge why these two may not lawfully be wedded togyder at this tyme, say it nowe outher pryuely or appertly in helpynge of your soules and theirs bothe.
>
> Also I charge you both and eyther be your selfe, as ye wyll answer before God at the day of dome, that yf there be any thynge done pryuely or openly betwene yourselfe, or that ye

knowe any lawfull lettyng [hindrance] why that ye may nat be wedded togyder at thys tyme, say it nowe or we do any more to this mater.

If there are no objections to the marriage the priest immediately puts to the bride and groom the following questions, again in Latin and English. It may be noted that the Latin words *honorare* and *diligere* appear for both parties in all the manuscripts, but only the Cambridge manuscript gives the vernacular of the two words in both questions:[2]

N., Wylt thou haue this woman to thy wyfe and loue her [and wirschipe hir—*Cambridge ms.*] and keep her, in syknes and in helthe, and in all other degrese be to her as a husbande sholde be to his wyfe, and all other forsake for her, and holde the only to her to thy lyues ende.

N., Wylt thou haue this man to thy husbande, and be buxum [obedient] to hym, [luf hym, obeye to him, and wirchipe hym—*Cambridge ms.*] serue hym and kepe hym in sykenes and in helthe: and in all other degrees be unto him as a wyfe shulde be to hir husbande, and all other to forsake for hym, and holde the only to hym to thy lyues ende.

Then each pronounces, this time only in the vernacular, the "form" which expresses his and her consent to the marriage and which, accordingly, makes the marriage:

Here I take thee N. to my wedded wyfe [husbande], to haue and to holde, at bedde and at borde, for fayrer for fouler, for better for warse, in sekeness and in hele, tyl dethe us departe, and thereto I plyght thee me trouthe.

The ring ceremony follows, coupled with that of the giving of gold and silver, symbol of the woman's dowry (*dos mulieris*). First the priest blesses the ring (in Latin):

Bless, Lord, this ring, which in your name we bless, that she who will wear it stand in your peace and remain in your will, and may she live and grow old in your love and be multiplied unto length of days.

PRAYING AND BELIEVING

> Creator and preserver of human kind, giver of spiritual grace and bestower of eternal salvation, you, Lord, grant that your blessing come upon this your servant and this your handmaid, that armed with the strength of heavenly protection they may advance to eternal salvation ...

The groom then takes the blessed ring, touches it to the first three fingers of the bride's hand, saying "In the name of the Father, etc.," and places it on the fourth finger because, as the rubric states, in that finger "is a certain vein going to the heart." As he places the ring he repeats after the priest *(docente sacerdote):* "With this rynge I wedde thee, and with this golde and siluer I honoure thee, and with this gyft I dowe thee." If the woman's dowry is land, she is then to kneel before her husband. Otherwise she remains standing while the priest recites some verses from the psalms. He asks the congregation to pray for the couple and, in Latin, he himself prays for God's blessing once again upon "these young ones" *(istos adolescentes),* "that they might remain in your security, live and grow old in your love and be multiplied unto length of days."

The liturgy of York in the sanctuary

All now enter the church. The bride and groom prostrate themselves before the altarstep *(ante gradum altaris).* The priest says some versicles and again (in Latin) prays God's blessing upon the young couple that they might be joined in true love:

> All-powerful and eternal God, who by his power created Adam and Eve, sanctified them by his blessing, and joined them in community of love *(societate amoris copulavit);* may He sanctify and bless your hearts and bodies and join them in love that is true. [*amorem verae dilectionis*].

Bride and groom rise and take their place in the south side of the sanctuary, the bride standing to the right of her husband, and the solemn Mass of the Trinity is begun. There is an added oration, secret, and postcommunion prayer for the spouses (the secret prayer speaks of the *sacra connubili lege*—the sacred law of marriage),[3] and the epistle and gospel are special: the epistle (1 Cor. 6:15-20) reminding the couple that their bodies are members of Christ, that they are two in one flesh, and therefore they are to avoid sin, especially that of fornication. They are to "glorify and carry God" in their bodies. The gospel (John 3:27-29) speaks of John the Baptist as the "friend of the groom" who rejoices when he hears the groom's voice. The gospel ends: "This joy of mine has been fulfilled in order that your joy be complete."

At the breaking of the sacred bread, the spouses kneel before the altar and the *gallium* is held above them by two clerics. The priest turns and speaks over them three prayers, the middle prayer, the "sacramental blessing", being omitted in the case of a second marriage. Here there is a long rubric explaining why second marriages are not to receive this blessing. It states that though a second (or third, etc.) marriage is a perfect sacrament (*perfectum sacramentum*), something is missing of the sacramental signification, namely that of a single union between Christ and the Church. Besides, continues the rubric, one of the spouses will have received the blessing in a previous marriage, and so the other by becoming one flesh with the already blessed spouse will thereby share in it (*per carnem alias benedictam caro non benedicta, cum gua iungitur. benedicitur*). An exception is made for a second marriage in which the male is the widow and the bride a virgin. Here, it is argued, the full signification of the sacrament is preserved since the male represents Christ or the bishop who in a single union is wedded to many souls. In any case, the omission of the brief sacramental blessing is the sole noticeable difference in the whole wedding ceremony between first and second marriages.

Another slight difference is that if the woman is a widow she is to have her hand gloved; otherwise it is to be bare. Second marriages in the western Church were in marked contrast to those in the Eastern Church. In the West, as here indicated, there was little if any noticeable difference in the liturgy between first and second marriages. But in the liturgy of the Eastern Church the unfavorable attitude of that Church to second marriages is manifest where there are several long prayers apologizing for the "bigamist's" weakness of flesh and begging God's pardon for the spouses marrying for the second time.[4]

G. H. Joyce, remarks: "The Greek Church throughout took a harsher view of remarriages than was prevalent in the West."[5] Speaking generally, second marriages were regarded as a serious imperfection.

PRAYING AND BELIEVING

Third and fourth marriages were forbidden. I would disagree with Joyce in his implication here that the Western Church, at least in her liturgy, was at all "harsh" with regard to the remarriage of widows. There is no evidence of this.

The prayers said at this point (all in Latin) concentrate mainly upon the bride. We're reminded of the intimate and inseparable union established between man and woman from the beginning of creation, a union not abrogated either by original sin or the Flood. Then God is asked to look kindly upon the bride, to keep her pure, chaste, innocent, wise, faithful, fruitful, and of long life ... "and may she see her children's children unto the third and fourth generation."

At the conclusion of these prayers the husband mounts the altar steps and receives the kiss of peace from the priest. He returns to his place and kisses his bride alone and she him alone, "and no one else" (*et neminem alium, nec ipse nec ipsa*). Immediately preceding the kiss of peace the priest recites the simple formula: "Hold to the bond of peace and charity, that you may be worthy of the holy mysteries of God"—apparently indicating thereby that the bride and groom are about to receive Holy Communion. There is no specific directive as to whether or not the bride and groom are to communicate, nor is there such a directive in any of the rituals that I have consulted. However, Louis Duchesne referring to Pope Nicholas I's description of the rites of marriage in the Latin Church, claims the bride and groom did communicate. This certainly seems likely, judging from the solemnity of the occasion and the other privileges the bride and groom received in the nuptial Mass.[6]

The Mass continues, concluding with the special nuptial postcommunion prayer: "We beseech you, almighty God, to accompany that which has been instituted by your providence for the sake of love (*pro amore*), that you may keep in lasting peace those whom you join in lawful communion (*legitima societate*). Finally, "because of the solemnity of the sacrament" the priest is directed to give the last blessing with the chalice itself, saying:

> Lord, Holy Father, almighty and eternal God, we humbly beseech you, that you kindly deign to nourish with your blessing the union of your servants. We ask you, almighty God, that the

THE CRAFT OF LOVE

deceits of the enemy be thwarted, and that they, who by your providence have merited to be united, might imitate the holiness of the union itself.

The liturgy of York in the bridal chamber

That night *(nocte vero sequenti)* when the bride and groom have come into the bridal chamber, the priest enters and blesses the bed, saying: "Bless, Lord, this bridal chamber and all who dwell herein, that they may endure in your peace, and remain in your will; and that they may live in your love and grow old and multiply unto the length of days." A further brief prayer is prayed asking the protection of God's holy angel upon the couple. The bride and groom are then blessed with the simple Trinitarian formula and the chamber and bed are incensed. This ends the ecclesiastical ceremonies.

The nuptial liturgy at Salisbury

The Sarum, or Salisbury, nuptial liturgy was almost identical with that of York.[7] The differences between them are to be found not so much in the printed editions of the Sarum rite as in the early fifteenth-century manuscript of that rite preserved in the library of St. John's College, Oxford.[8] Here the directive reads that the woman be given in the first place to the Church. She is likewise to kneel and kiss the groom's right foot, whether there is land in the dowry or not. Also, while in the manuscript there is the rubric that the final blessing be given with the chalice, as at York, there is no mention of this in the printed editions. Other differences between the two rites are:

1. In the Sarum ritual there is the directive for the priest to speak the introductory words, admonition, and the initial questions *"in lingua materna,"* but whereas in the York manual the English is given, here we find only the Latin. However, the introduction, etc. are the same in content as those in the York manual.

2. The marriage "form", given in the vernacular, is slightly different for the man and woman, whereas in the York rite it is the same for both. In the Sarum rite the woman adds: "to be *bonere* and buxum in bedde and atte borde." And both the man and the woman add the words "if holy Churche it woll ordeyne" after "tyl dethe us departe."

PRAYING AND BELIEVING

3. The formula for giving the ring, the gold and the silver, is somewhat more elaborate in the Sarum rite: "With this rynge I thee wed, and this gold and siluer I thee geue, and with my bodi I thee worshipe, and with all my worldely catel I thee endowe." The ceremony of the placing of the ring is the same as at York, but with an addition in the rubrical commentary. After the words "in the fourth finger is a certain vein proceding to the heart," there is added an explanation of the symbolism of the gold and silver: "in the sonorous sound of silver is symbolized the internal love which must always be new *(recens)* between them." It is at this point that the Sarum *manuscript* (not the printed edition) directs the bride to kneel before her husband and kiss his right foot.

4. The epistle is the same as at York, but the gospel is different—Matt. 19:2-6, in which Jesus upholds the inseparability of the marriage bond, since "they are no longer two, but one flesh."

5. In the Sarum rite, immediately after the Mass bread and wine are blessed with a prayer that recalls the miracles of the multiplication of the five loaves and the changing of water into wine. Of this bread and wine the newly-weds taste *in nomine domini.*

6. The blessing of the bridal-chamber and bed is different from that of York, most noticeably in that here the last blessing is given while the couple are "in bed" or "on the bed" *(in lecto)* After the brief blessing the final directive for the priest is: "These things done, let him asperse them with blessed water, and so depart and leave them in peace *(dimittat eos in pace).*

The same practice of blessing the newly-weds while sitting upon or lying in the marriage bed is to be found in the fourteenth-century marriage rite of the Church of Paris. Here the priest is directed to incense the bridal-chamber, and then the bride and groom "sitting or lying in their bed .... "[9]. There are several others present, and a woman holds the pail for holy water. See below for Chaucer's use of the custom in *The Merchant's Tale*: apparently January and May are under the covers "whan the bed was with the preest blessed."

THE CRAFT OF LOVE

The nuptial liturgy at Hereford

Still another prominent English liturgy of the fourteenth and fifteenth centuries was that of the diocese of Hereford. Here the marriage rite, as it appears in the medieval Hereford missal, is similar to and often identical with the rites of York and Sarum. Some of its noteworthy and distinguishing features are as follows:

1. After the priest has inquired about the existence of any impediments, he is directed to announce to the bride and groom "the law of marriage ... namely, that they shall be two in one flesh, and each obedient to the other *(uterque alteri obnoxius sit)* unto the keeping of each other in sickness or in health, and for no cause can they be separated." This is from the manuscript Hereford missal;[10] it does not appear in the printed version.

It should be observed that in the manuscript the whole of the service till the end of the exchange of vows is quite markedly abridged. For example, the questions put to the couple are simply: "Man, do you wish to have this woman united to you? ... Woman, do you wish to have this man united to you?" This may suggest that a certain spontaneity or originality of expression on both the part of the priest and the marrying couple was tolerated or even encouraged as long as the essential content of the various formulas was respected, much as occurs in present-day marriage ritual.

2. In the printed version of the missal, after the priest has inquired as to the freedom of the couple to marry, he asks the groom (the question is printed in Latin, but surely it was asked in English): "N., Do you wish to have this woman and receive her as your legitimate wife, and, in God's fidelity and yours, keep her as a Christian man ought to keep his wife, in sickness and in health?" A like question is asked of the bride. Then holding the bride's right hand in his the groom repeats after the priest "in the mother tongue": I, N., underfynge þe N., for my wedded wyf, for betere for vvorse, for richer for porer, in sekenes & in helþe, tyl deþ us de-parte, as holy churche haþ ordeyned, & þerto y

plyzth þe my trovvþe." The bride says the same, adding the phrase "to be buxum to þe."¹

3. In the giving of the ring, the gold and silver, the man is directed to say either in Latin or the mother tongue: "with this ring I thee wed, and with this gold and silver I thee endow; and with my body I thee honour." The ring is placed as at York and Sarum. The rubric here contains a slightly varied explanation of the ceremony and gives the authoritative source for the explanation: "I ask why the ring is placed on the fourth finger counting the thumb, rather than on the second or third." Isidore says "it is because a certain vein extends from that finger to the heart, and this gives us to understand the unity and perfection of love; (quaest. v. cap.) *Feminae in fine.*" This last is the reference to the particular work of St. Isidore in question.[11]

4. As at York and Sarum, there is the Mass of the Trinity, with the couple in the sanctuary throughout. The epistle and gospel are as at Sarum, and all else in the mass is as in the Sarum or York rituals. There is the blessing of the bread and wine "or some other potable good" after the final blessing has been imparted with the chalice, and husband and wife share them. In the evening the bridal bed and chamber are blessed with the same simple blessings as at York and Sarum. And again the final rubric is that the priest departs and leaves husband and wife "in peace."

Nuptial prayers at Hanley

Finally, mention may be made of two prayers from the thirteenth-century missal of Hanley Castle, Worcestershire, which do not appear in the nuptial rites of York, Sarum, or Hereford, though the Hanley rite seems to be like the others in all other respects.[12] The first of these prayers occurs immediately after the ring ceremony while all are still standing before the church door. It recalls God's institution and sanctification of marriage in the Old Testament, his being born of it and his blessing upon it in the New Testament; it asks God to bless and

---

¹ þ –Thorn is a letter in some dialects of Middle English, it was later replaced with the digraph *th*.

sanctify the present nuptials, to join the couple in true love *(verae dilectionis societate)*, to give to the couple "peaceful corporal health, joy of mind and body, and the procreation of sons and daughters *(filiorum et filiarum)*; and after the labor of your life is ended may He lead you into the community of holy angels and archangels in Heaven." The second prayer is spoken over the bride and groom as they lay prostrate before the altar, just before the Mass of the Trinity is begun. It asks that God bless the couple "that they might be joined in conjugal union with equal effect, like mind, and mutual charity *(effectu compari, mente consimili, caritate mutua)* ... and that each may prefer the other to oneself *(invicem se praeferant sibi)* ...."

The liturgies express free self-giving love

Here, then, are four marriage rites practiced in different provinces of England in the fourteenth and fifteenth centuries. In all of them without exception marriage is regarded as a noble and holy state of life. The broad fact of the nature of the ceremony itself is ample evidence of this: it begins before the church door and is continued within the church in the sanctuary itself; the Mass is the most exalted there is, that of the Blessed Trinity, and bride and groom are explicitly drawn into it at different times for blessings and special prayers; in the end the final blessing is sometimes given with the Mass chalice; and all through there are prayers reminiscent of the theology which, as we have seen, maintains that marriage is not only good but holy and, as was sometimes preached, an order of perfection similar to and in some respects surpassing in dignity the great religious orders in the Church.

Nothing depreciative of marriage is in any way said or implied. There is no mention or suggestion that it may be a concession to human weakness or that it is a state of life inferior to some other. No apologies for marriage seem to be needed, nor are any given. And all of this is true for "second marriages" as for first. The very lavishness of the ceremony would have led bride and groom (and all who were witnessing the ceremony) to think that they stood before God as before the Church with every bit as much dignity and holiness as monk, priest, nun, or bishop.

PRAYING AND BELIEVING

And, again reminiscent of the theology, marriage is considered to be holy precisely as *sacramentum:* the inseparable love-union between a man and a woman involving both body and spirit. The ceremony begins with such words as: "Lo, brethren, we come here before God and his angels ... to couple and knit these two bodies together ... that they might be from this time forth but one body and two souls ..."; or with some statement of the "law of marriage," which is that husband and wife "be two in one flesh, subject to each other, and inseparable." It is the marrying couple who are center stage throughout the entire ceremony, standing or kneeling side by side, close to the altar and apart from all others. In the marriage promises there is the vow "to love and worship" each other till death.

In the giving and receiving of the ring, the gold and the silver, there is the reminder that this is a ceremony betokening a love that is rooted in the heart, an "interior love" that must remain always new *(recens),* a love that must be one and perfect *(unitatem et perfectionem amoris).* The Church prays that the woman be loving *(amabilis)* toward her man, and that God join them both "in a society of true love." Just before communion the man, after receiving the kiss of peace from the priest, kisses his bride "alone" and she him "alone." And in the evening, after all the festivities are over, the bridal bed is blessed—according to one of the rites, with the newly-weds apparently within (or upon) it. Of the traditional ends or purposes of marriage, the liturgy mentions the *remedium* or *redditio* not at all, and procreation only in passing. What is dwelt upon and emphasized is the union, the love-union in flesh as well as spirit, of the "young ones" there present and their projected mutual fidelity until death.

These declarations and enactments of the union between husband and wife are not dehumanized because of their holy or supernatural character, nor are they enfeebled by any negative qualifications relative to the conjugal act. Once again, the theology and liturgy are in agreement, this time on the principle of nature being perfected, not destroyed, by grace. The love that is to be between the spouses is spoken of as holy and chaste, but it is equally emphasized that the couple are to be "one in flesh," it is prayed that they be "multiplied," and at the end of all the marriage bed is blessed. True, there is no detailed exposition of the specifically sexual aspects of conjugal love.

THE CRAFT OF LOVE

But this is as we would expect in a public rite of this kind, the various rites manifesting a delicacy and modesty and respect for the privacy of love. Their statements on love are general and positive; the blessing of bridal chamber and bed simple, brief, tactful; there is not a rubric suggesting what ought not to be. Only the epistle of the Mass may seem to strike a negative note with its warning against fornication; but this imposes no limitation upon the lovemaking between husband and wife. They are to avoid sexual love with others since they are to have such love only for one another. It is simply a veiled expression of the *vitatio fornicationis* which, as we have seen, the theology, after St. Paul, offered as a just motive for marriage. Even here, then, as in the rest of the service, the natural bond between husband and wife is commended and indelicacy avoided. It is as though that final rubric after the blessing of the couple in the bridal chamber were meant to express the purpose of the whole of the Church's nuptial liturgy: "These things done, let him bless them with holy water, and so depart and leave them *in peace.*"

The several rites make it clear that the wife is to be obedient to her husband: she is to be "buxum in bedde and at borde," and at one point she kneels before her husband and kisses his foot, in feudal token, no doubt, of his lordship. The husband, however, is not to lord it over his wife but is to "love and worship" her as she him. They appear as equals as they stand and kneel side by side through the whole of the ceremony, and, indeed, if in the ceremony either might appear superior to the other, it is the bride, who, as in the liturgies of our own day, seems to receive the greater attention, consideration, and honor. In one rite (Hereford) it is said that husband and wife are to be "subject to one another," and in another (Worcestershire) it is prayed that "each prefer the other to oneself" and that they be united in the marriage partnership *(consortium)* "with equal effect, like mind, and mutual charity." And both marry because they freely choose to do so, which is evidenced by the nature of the admonitions and questions that the priest initially puts to the people at large and to the couple themselves. They must be free to marry and must choose each other in freedom. And freedom, as love, suggests equality.

The late medieval English marriage liturgy appears to have been a joyous affair. For in these thirteenth-century, fourteenth-century, and fifteenth-century rituals not a single note of gloom is struck; there is

PRAYING AND BELIEVING

nothing of cynicism or of mockery, whether against the woman or marriage. On the contrary, both marriage and woman are, as we have just noted, steeped in honor and in reverence; and there is much lightness, beauty, and joy—from the rhythmic, meaningful poetry of the marriage promises and the love symbolism of the ring ceremony to the joyful sung mass of the Trinity with its white or gold vestments, its *gloria,* its special prayers for mutual love and fidelity and fecundity, with its exclusive kiss of peace for bride and groom, and with the chalice raised above them in privileged blessing; and all the while the favored *adolescentes,* handsomely clothed we would suppose, standing and kneeling together in the sanctuary itself for all to see and admire. From what the rituals tell us we must conclude that if marriage in the late medieval world was in fact a happy occasion, it was not in spite of priest or Church, but largely because of them.

Léon Gautier gives a full, moment by moment description of a twelfth-century French marriage in which the grandeur and joy of the Church's ceremonies are underscored. As his exemplum of medieval marriage rites Gautier used that which appears in the Pontifical of the monastery Lyrensis in the twelfth century, as given in Martene, *De antiquis,* ordo iii.[13]

Mark Searle remarks in his concluding chapter, "Between the preoccupations of the families and the negativity of theologians, pastors, it seems, still found positive vision of marriage to present to believers on the occasion of their betrothal and their wedding ..."[14] We are in agreement as to the positive character of the liturgy, but as to the "negativity" of the theologians we are at odds. Searle's remark is gratuitous since he offers no theological presentation to support it; he is simply adopting and repeating the present-day common view. It should be evident by now in our study that the nuptial liturgy and a large and prestigious representation of the theology are very much in agreement as to the positive nature of marriage and the love within it.

Wedding sermons

The wedding sermon was evidently one of the 'popular' sources of medieval church doctrine. The following representative selections of wedding sermons is intended to complete our study of the major

THE CRAFT OF LOVE

current of ecclesiastical teaching on conjugal love in late medieval England. Of the marriage rites, those of the Sarum and York liturgies are certainly of prime importance. Of the marriage sermons which seem actually to have been preached, two will be highlighted. These have not until now appeared in print, though they have been judged, by one well schooled in the medieval English pulpit, typical of their kind.

Perhaps it was in the sermon preached at the marriage ceremony that a discordant note was sounded? Indeed, if in this instance the pulpit was as harsh as it is said to have been at other times when women and love were in question, then whatever the ritual may have promoted by way of joy the priest in his sermon must soon have dissipated! Speaking of the harsh, negative attitude of the fourteenth-century English preachers in general, G. R. Owst at one point exclaims: "Where alas is our merry England!"[15] Elsewhere he indicts that same negative, ranting pulpit for its generous share in the English Reformation, claiming that "as its smarting children reared mainly through repression, through taunts and threats of future punishment, grew to an independent manhood and a wisdom of their own, they turned to mock, to threaten, and then to eject their own short-sighted parents."[16] And when Owst treats specifically of the pulpit as related to women and marriage, he seems to be drawing from an inexhaustible well of medieval invective and vituperation.

But it may be suggested that the medieval pulpit was much more kindly toward women and marriage than Owst's chapter on "the sermon of satire and complaint" might lead us to believe. The sermons of Robert de Sorbon and others cited above, together with the manuals meant to aid the preaching, are testimony as to the esteem in which both the woman and mariage were held. And with regard to the Middle English sermons he has edited, W. O. Ross observes that "In none of these sermons are women contemned; in fact it is pointed out at least three times that though Eve brought sin into the world, Mary brought salvation ... "No man," says one of the sermons, "shuld haue voman in dispite, for it is no wisdom to dispise þat God loveþ."[17]

Owst himself is ambiguous. Perhaps it is because he tried to see the preaching as a whole, that we find in his histories almost as much

PRAYING AND BELIEVING

contradiction as we find in the preaching itself. Thus after describing the gloom of the medieval English pulpit, he goes on to tell of the "rollicking humor" and laughter of that same pulpit. He speaks of "our homilist now turned play-writer," and finds the clerical accent most clearly manifest in those very passages of medieval drama "which have been supposed hitherto to exhibit the birth of a native dramatic sense, struggling free of the old clerical traditions, uproarious with a people's mirth, fresh, realistic, and redolent of the soil."[18] As for the pulpit's treatment of woman and marriage, he carefully notes that the examples he cites are confined to one specific type of sermon, the satirical, and concedes that a "kindlier, fairer attitude is expressed ... in the typical marriage sermon of the day."[19]

Two such "typical" marriage sermons appear in ms. Gg. vi, 16 of the Cambridge University Library. It seems likely that they were sermons actually preached sometime during the fifteenth century, and the several glosses on one of them *(in solemnizatione matrimonii)* suggest that it likewise served as a pattern or model sermon. Each of the sermons should be read in its entirety so that not just the "matter" but the tone of our preacher(s) might be known and savored.

In Nupciis Sollacio[20]

Worschypull Soffereyns, here we assemylde [be] affore god, hys awngells and all hys seynts, by vertu off the blyssyd sacrament off matrimonye off too persawnes to make one, that is to been off one concente and off one wyll, the qwyche oned [unity] betwyx man and woman to be had was expressed by the sentence off god in hys ffyrst formacion, qwher as he seyd: *Erunt, inquit, duo in carne una*—here shall be, seythe allmyzty god, ii [two] dyfferent and diuerse persawnes in bodye and in sawle the qwyche shall be made one fflesche and blode thorw the blyssyd sacrament off matrimonye.

Thys seyd most blyssyd sacrament of matrimonye allmyzty god hymselff institute and ordenyd in the blyssyd and joyffull place off paradyse affore anye syn qwyche was thoght or doo, originall, veniall, or actuall; and so was ncow [initial, beginning?] off all the todyrvi [i.e. sacraments]; and so it was ordeynyd in

THE CRAFT OF LOVE

remedye anense [against] syn and to the conffyrmation and nobyll encresce off morall vertues to be possessyd in manys sawle in hys pilgrimage goynge honorablye to the ryall cyte off Jerusalem clepyd heven.

Allmyzty god seying by the merror off hys godhede that adam so beynge sole mankynde myght neuer abeen meliorate ne encresyd qwherffore blysfully he seyde: *Non est bonum hominem esse solum: faciamus ei adjutorium simile sibi*—it is not good, seyd allmyzty god, man to be alone; late us make to hym a creature to be to hym releve, socour and helpe lyke unto hym in fflesche and blode in qwhom he shall execute and excerscyse the inwarde beemys off hys luff and ther hys herte to sett above all odyr creatures next allmyzty god. And than þis glorious lorde *tulit unum de costis adam dormientis*—he toke one off the rybbys off adam leyng in slepe þorze þe disposycion off allmyzty god. And þan ffurmyd owre fyrst moder Eva þat she sholde be vnyd and knytt to owre fforne ffadyr adam with hym to be one in bodye, in fflesche and in blode, and one in sawle by þerre stedffast luff in mynd thorw þis blyssyd sacrament off matrimonye.

Qwyche sacrament was fullffyllyd and made perffyte qwhan adam, inspired with the spiret off gode knawlage, seyd theys wordes: *Hoc os de ossibus meis et caro de carne mea*—0 goode Lorde, seyd adam, this woman fformyd be thy myzty power, ordenyd to be my ffelawe, I vnderstande be þi blysfull inspirynge þat þlise materiall bonys off thys woman cummyth off my bonys and thys fflesche sensibyll cummyth off my fflesche, I and sche to be one body, one fflesche and one blode, and to [be] one in mynde by stedffaste luff by the mene off thys blyssyd sacrament now in thys glorius fformacion of the good lorde institute and ordeynyd, and so in man and woman to be continued to avoyed and aschewe all fornication and awowtrye vnto the ende off the worlde.

Here is to be had in remembrance þat allmyzty god fformyd woman not off the hyest party off man, þat is ffor to seye off the hede, not off the lawest party off, þet is, the ffoot, bot off a rybbe off the syde not ffer ffrom manys hert in token þat woman shulde not usurpe to have domination nor preemynence above man, nor man shulde not sett woman in hys conseyte in vile subjection or evill dignite off worschep and re[v]erence benethe hym; but woman to be egall and ffelawe unto man as a true ffere and mate in þerre stedffast luff.

Adam and Eve thus creatyd and formyd off allmyzty god, he blyssyd them and gaff to them thys comawndement: Crescite et multiplicamini et replete terrain et subjicite eam et dominamini piscibus maris et volatilibus coeli et universis animantibus quae moventur super terram encresethe and multiplieth and fulfyllthe the erthe with your ffrute, seythe allmyzty god, man to be lorde and prince, woman to be ladye and princess off ffyches and fowles and off all thynges that is induyed with lyffe sensative that arne mevyd vpon erthes; and I wyll that ye and yowre ffruite that cummythe by naturall cowrse and propagation be inhereditors off the blys off heven, and to þat johye [joy] to atteyne by perffytt luff and humill condicion off mekenes; ther to restore the casure [fall] & ydus ffall of awngell qwyche ffell thorw desyre off inordinate worschep, laborynge to usurpe the dignite off the hyest soffereyne allmyzty god, the originall maker and fformar off all creatours.

Qwherffore ye soffereyns, at þis tyme beynge present disposyd in mynd and will be one consente thor the meyns off perffyte luff, grwnde and begynnar off all vertues, to reseve this blyssyd sacrament of matrimonye, I shall saye to yowe at þis tyme as Christe seyd to hys discipulls: *Estote perffecti sicut pater wester celestis perffectus est*—be ze perffyte in body and in sawle as your fadyr off heven, allmyghzty god, is perffyte. The fader of heven is so perffyte that no straungenes off mankynde wyll cawse hym to withdrawe the sun beemys ffrom the herte; and he makethe the sun to doo hys offyce and to shyne bothe vpon them þat arne goode and vpon them þat arne oderweys disposyd. So in lyke wyse ye to soffereyns at this tyme, Stabyll yourselff so stedffastlye in luff þat nether worde, nor langwage, cowntenawnce, ne dede make yowe to withdrawe the beemys of perffyte luff as longe as ye lyff togeder, for luff is the begynnar and grounde off this blyssyd sacrament of matrimonye. As the

THE CRAFT OF LOVE

fadyr off heven is so perffyte that the fadyr and the son and the holy goost arne iii persawnys and one god, so that in thise iii persawnys restythe vnyte and onyd [oneness] in all theyr werkys, lyke wyse ye soffereyns at þis tyme by the mene off this blyssyd sacrament be ye perffite as longe as ye shall naturally lyff to gedyr. As ye shall be one in body, fflesche, and in blode, lyke wyse to be sted ffast and perffite with oned [unity] in luff in your sawles withowte discontinuawnce, the glorious apostyll giffynge to yowe holsom cownseyll þat nedyr poverte ne adversite, ryches or plentee, sekenes or defformite make yow, thorw anye blast off temptacion, to disowd or loos thys solemne knott of matrimonye þet I purpos to knytt affore god, his awngells and all hys sents in heven—*quod ergo deus conjunxit homo non separet.*

In Solemnizatione Matrimonii [21]

Goode cristen people.

Most worschipull ffrendys, we be cum hedyr at þis time in the name off the fader, son & holy gost, in þe honerabyll presens of our moder gostly, holy chyrche, to conjoynyn, knytt, and combyne thyse ii [two] persawnes by the holy sacrament off matrimonye, grauntyd to the holy dignite & ordyr of presthode. Qwyche sacrament off matrimonye is off this vertu and strengthe þat þise ii persawnes qwyche be nowe too bodyes and ii sawles, durynge theyr lyvys togeder schall be butt one fflesche and too sawles. Acordynge to thys, the holy Euaungeliste in the gospell (matt. 19) saythe: *Propter hoc dimittet homo patrem et matrem et adherebit uxori sue et erupt duo in carne una*—for thys, seythe the holy euaungeliste, a man shall leve ffader and modyr and drawe to hys wyffe, for thei shall be too souls in one fflesche.

This is wele figyred genesi primo qwhan allmyzty god had formyd [and made] owre fforne fader and moder in *agro damasceno* to the resemblauns, similitude and ymage off the blyssyd trinyte by hys only worde, *quia dixit et ffacta sunt*, and putt them be hym in that precious place of paradise. þan þat good lorde of hys goode grace to the cowmfforthe, solace and recreacion of Adam toke a ribbe frome the syde of Adam, he

PRAYING AND BELIEVING

beynge of slepe; god blyssyd itt and fformyd a woman theroff to be helper, he unto hym seynge: *Crescite et multiplicamini et replete terram, dominamini piscibus marls et volatilibus celi* &c: encrese, multiply and replesche ze the erthe; be ye souereyns and lordys ower all the ffysches off the see, ffowles and byrdys off þe eyre, and all þat berythe lyffe vpon erthe (Genesi primo). And qwhan þis was doo by the wyll and the handwarke off god, than bothe adam and eve obediauntlye consentyd to thys matrimonye qwhan adam seyde: *Hoc os ex ossibus meis et caro de carne mea* (ffor thyse wer the sacrament wordys in tho deys quoþ Reymundus ca de matrimonio): This bon off this woman is off my bonys and this fflesche off thys woman is off my fflesche; so thei wer ii sawles and one fflesche.

And like as it was the plesure and thee wyll of allmyzty god to make them one fflesche and ii sawles ryghzt soo it is the effecte nowe off the sacrament of matrimony in all holy churche. Ferthermore it is to wete þat euery man and woman þat be maryed and knytt by the sacrament of matrimony þei must be vnder the bonde and yoke off god on iii maner wyses. Ffyrste, vnder the bonde of honeste and worschep in workynge; the secunde vnder the bonde of true luff and ffeythfull in lyvynge; and the iiide vnder the bonde of obediens and continuall abydynge. Fyrste I seyde weddyd [glossed to *maryed*] man and woman must be undre the bonde of honeste and worschep in werkynge, þat is to sey þei shall do ryghzt noghzt that be azenste the oneste and ordyr disteynynge the sacrament off matrimonye nor displesyng god in noo Wyse. Secondly, thei must be under the bonde of true luff and feythfull in liffynge, þat is to sey þat with all theyr hertis effectually to luff them togedyr withinfforthe by inwarde affection, withowtefforthe with gode acorde, pees and quiete by dileccion, and bothe withinfforthe and withowtefforthe by goode werkynge and frutffull operacion. And ffor this cawse is the ryng putt and sett by the husbonde vpon the iiiite finger off the woman, ffor to schewe þat a true luff and precordiall affection must be betwyxe hem. Cawse qwhy, as doctours sey, ther is a veyne cummyng ffrome the herte off a woman to the iiiite ffinger; and therfore (The significacion of þe

THE CRAFT OF LOVE

Ryng) the Ringe is putt on the same fingar, that sche shulde kepe unite and luff with hym, and he with hyr. The iiide, I sey weddyd [glossed to *maryed*] man and woman muste be vnder the bonde of obediens and continuall abidynge, that is to sey that eyther off them shulde supporte, help and cowmforthe oon another in sekenes and in helthe as longe as thei lyff togedur to the worschep and plesure off allmyghzty god.

More ouer, ffor iiii [four] cawses we owe [glossed to *owzzhte*] grettly to have thys sacrament of matrimony in reuerens and worschep. One cawse is ffor god hymselff was ffyrst fownder and maker off the sacrament of matrimonye. The secunde, ffor it was made and ordeynyd off god in the most precious place that he wroghzt vpon erthe, ffor it was in *paradiso terestre*. The iiide cawse, for it was the ffirst sacrament that god ordeynde; and the iiiite, ffor holy chyrche hathe admyttyd it to be one of the vii sacraments off holy chyrche. And for thys cawse is the palle holden ouer theyr hedys in the messe [glossed to *communen*] tyme; ffor the palle representethe the (of þe pall þe significacion) dignite of matrimony. Also it is to wyte that this holy sacrament off matrimony muste be reseyvyd with devoute herte, a clene sawle, and a pure entente. Therffor holy chyrche exorteth, cownselythe, and ordenythe þat bothe man and the woman be reconcylyd to clennes of lyffe by conffessyon befforne the matrimony is solemnesyd ffor thee encresynge and augmentynge off grace. For he that reseyvethe it with a sinffull sawle and a corrupte entente he reseyvethe not the holy goste, and he that reseyvethe not the holy goste he reseyvethe no grace nor owre lorde god þat is grownde of grace. Qwherffor we all þat be present here shall beseche owr lorde mercy þat þise ii persawnes may be worthye to reseyve this holy sacrament of matrimonye with devowte hertys, clene sawles, with pure entente, and duly to kepe þeir charges and behestes [glossed to *commandes*]. Amen.

The preaching is at one with theology and liturgy

In these sermons, which were preached or *read* immediately prior to the exchange of vows, may be recognized the several themes, ideas, and images we have encountered in the contemporary theology, moral manuals, and the nuptial rite itself. Marriage is frequently referred to as "blessed" or "holy", with no suggestion that it might be inferior to any other way of life.

We are given in one of the sermons four of the commendations of marriage we will encounter in the moral manuals and in other preaching. There is the recollection that marriage is a "religious order," and a royal estate: in one sermon the word "order" to designate marriage is used, in the other bride and groom are referred to several times as "sovereigns", "worshipful sovereigns", and with Adam and Eve they are "lord and prince ... lady and princess" of all on earth. There is the idea, tactfully but unreservedly developed, of the full and intimate love, carnal and spiritual, between husband and wife—a love that is of "two souls in one flesh," an apt way of suggesting the need of each to respect the distinct personality of the other while also reverencing their carnal oneness in love. As did St. Thomas (and also the poet John Gower, as we shall see), one of our preachers speaks of love as "the ground and beginning of all virtues," and, as do all our theologians, as "the beginner and ground of this blessed sacrament of matrimony." There is the common theme of the magnitude of conjugal love: one must love one's spouse "above all other creatures next to almighty God." There is the equally common exegesis of the rib birth of Eve: the woman is taken from the side of the man "not far from man's heart" in token of the loving equality that must be between them.

Our preachers are careful to adapt their sermons to the liturgy about to be enacted. One explicates for the couple the symbolism of the ring ceremony as designating the "true love and cordial affection that must be between them," and he reminds them that the placing of the *gallium* is a sign of the dignity of marriage. The other homily suggests why the nuptial Mass is that of the Holy Trinity by dwelling on the intimate love between Father, Son, and Holy Spirit as the model for conjugal love. As in the liturgy and theology, here also marriage is presented as being principally for the man and woman who are giving themselves to each other in full and perfect love. Offspring is mentioned as a purpose of marriage, but briefly and as a kind of distant, background purpose. Even in the order of finality, our preachers are more concerned with the couple themselves. Marriage is spoken of as a

THE CRAFT OF LOVE

safe refuge for them against sin and, in the words of one of the preachers; it has been ordained "unto the confirmation and noble increase of moral virtues."

Such was the Church's doctrine of love and marriage as it was presented to the fourteenth-century and fifteenth-century English faithful—the countless numbers of rich and poor, nobles and peasants, learned and unlearned, scholars, poets, butchers, bakers—who had been married themselves or had attended, perhaps frequently, the weddings of others. That the faithful understood the message *as given* seems likely, since it is clear and forceful enough.

CHAPTER 7

THE MORAL MANUAL

The expressions of medieval Church doctrine were manifold. There was Holy Scripture, the written word of God, which the Church professed to guard, interpret, and proclaim. There were the definitions and anathemas of the great ecumenical councils from Nicaea forward; the canonical legislation for the whole Church; papal decrees and pronouncements addressed to the universal Church.

Also in a given period there were the speculative theologies of that period which would attempt to bring together, harmonize, explain and apply the general teaching as contained in Scripture, council, canon, and papal decree. Here was to be found the teaching of the Church at large. On a purely local level there were the decrees of particular synods of bishops, diocesan legislation, and the proclamations of the territorial bishop. But these, it must be noted and stressed, were not the teaching of the Church as such. They could embody, in one way or another, the universal ecclesiastical teaching, but of themselves they were limited in authority to the particular diocese or territory in which and for which they were originally ordained.

But there was more. In the Middle Ages, only relatively few Christians, even among the literate, would have known directly what the great councils or the popes or theologians like Augustine, Thomas Aquinas, or Duns Scotus had taught or were teaching on a given matter. Such high and specialized formulation and speculation had to be brought down to the level of the common understanding and interest; and in an age when books, as well as literacy, were rare, the Scriptures themselves had to be declared in public since they could not easily be read in private.

THE CRAFT OF LOVE

The Church had been aware of the problem from the beginning and had instinctively provided for "ordinary people" in two ways. First she provided through her liturgy—her official prayer—*Lex orandi lex credendi*, that is, as the Church prays so she believes. This formula is quite early, appearing, in a slightly different version, in the *De gratia Dei* of St. Augustine's contemporary and disciple, Prosper of Aquitaine who died in the year 463.[1] The phrase as it appears in Prosper of Aquitaine reads: "*legem credendi lex statuit supplicandi.*"[2] There, in the liturgy—the Mass, sacramental rites, the Divine Office (wherein the layperson might in some measure participate)—were brought together readings from the Scriptures and the Fathers, theological hymns, prayers, formularies, gestures, which were meant to instruct the mind and touch the heart of every Christian, learned or unlearned, and give him or her a sense of what the Church (and so Christ) taught; and part of the liturgy, of course, was the Church building itself, its art and architecture and stained glass with their lessons of Faith. Secondly, there was the Church's preaching, often apart from the liturgy as well as a part of it, wherein those who knew, or supposedly knew, their theology interpreted and illustrated it for the people. The preaching might also be included as part of the medieval drama as it is likewise part of the liturgy.[3] Accordingly, it was in and through the liturgy and preaching that most medieval Christians found the doctrine of the universal Church most readily and easily, and perhaps exclusively, available to them.

Manuals for morals

In the later Middle Ages still another source of inspiration and instruction sprang into being: books or manuals of Faith and practical morals. At first intended and written for the less learned parish clergy as an aid and encouragement toward more and better preaching and sounder counseling, they gradually came to take the form of books of instruction and devotion to be read directly by the laity, and with the advent of printing, came almost to supplant, as the laity's source of faith and piety, the preaching they were originally meant to support.

W. A. Pantin sees the fourteenth century as a development and flowering of things begun in the thirteenth century.[4] One of his chief examples is the multiplicity of handbooks for priests and catechisms

THE MORAL MANUAL

for the faithful that were the end-product of the reforms dictated by the Lateran Council of 1215 and the immediately susequent synodal constitutions of the English bishops enforcing the decrees of the Council. W. Nelson Francis says in his introduction to *The Book of Vices and Virtues,* "The principal reason for the multiplicity of translations of this text [the *Somme le Roi*], as well as the wealth of similar works produced during the fourteenth and fifteenth centuries, is to be sought in the Church's requirements concerning lay education during that period. The most important, though not the earliest, formulation of the matters in which parish priests should instruct their people is contained in the Constitutions of the Council called at Lambeth in October of 1281 by the Franciscan archbishop of Canterbury, John Peckham."[5]

Now, in the privacy of their own homes, Christians could grow in the knowledge of their faith simply by studying in their native tongue the pages of one or other of the hundreds of manuals and books of devotion which, in the centuries following the General Council of 1215 that had launched the project, had made their way into every corner of Western Christendom. As G. R. Owst says "... whatever has to be said about the decline of notable preaching as the Reformation approaches, the pulpit reference-books have a career which only flourishes the more as later years increase the power and efficiency of the printing press. Nevertheless, it is not hard to understand why, as an independent art, preaching well-nigh perished, overwhelmed with such a surfeit of written material." And as a contemporary witness to the superabundance of moral and devotional hand-books Owst cites the *Orologium Sapientiae*: "Ther beth so manye bokes and tretees of vyces and vertues and of dyvers doctrynes, that this schort lyfe schalle rathere have en ende of anye manne, thanne he maye owthere studye hem or cede hem."[6]

I have centered upon two of the moral manuals. First consider that of Guillaume Peraldus. His *Summae virtutum ac vitiorum* seems to have been the root source of the many other manuals, including the popular *Somme le Roi* of Fr. Lorens that followed both in England and on the Continent. Also considered will be the English Midland *Book of Vices and Virtues* which, like its Kentish counterpart, the *Ayenbite of Inwit*, appears to be a near translation of the *Somme* of Lorens.[7] Concentration, then,

THE CRAFT OF LOVE

on Peraldus's manual and the English Midland translation of the *Somme le Roi* should yield a fair idea of what many of the English as well as continental moral manualists had in mind when they came to write their chapters on conjugal love.

G. R. Owst gives the following genealogy of the chief moral treatises.

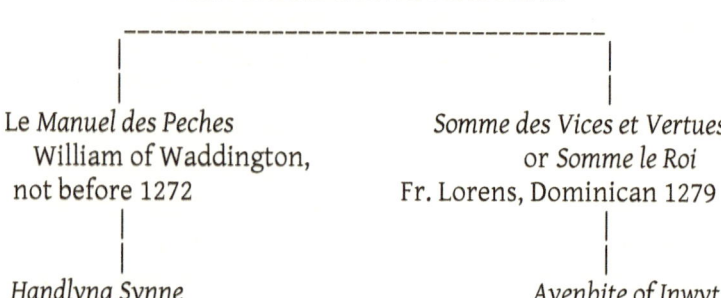

Summae de Viciis et Virtutibus
Gull. Peraldus written before 1261

Le *Manuel des Peches*	*Somme des Vices et Vertues*
William of Waddington,	or *Somme le Roi*
not before 1272	Fr. Lorens, Dominican 1279

Handlyng Synne	*Ayenbite of Inwyt*
Robert of Brunne,	Dan Michael of Northgate
translation 1303	c 1340

This gives a bare-bone simplification of a very complex genealogy with many more manuals involved. And perhaps it is not quite accurate even as to these key manuals. That, for instance, Peraldus's *Summae* is the direct source of Lorens's *Somme* is not altogether certain. R. Morris (*Ayenbite*) says that Lorens based his work on *Le Miroir du Monde*, while W. Nelson Francis *The Book of Vices* (p xii) claims that the *Miroir* is a "later version of the *Somme*." But whatever the details and complications of the genealogy, the importance and influence of Peraldus's manual can scarcely be disputed.

Two other kinds of "popular" manual treatment of marriage morality will be considered. Each is different from the other and from the ordinary manuals. The first is Nicole Oresme's commentary on the *pseudo-Economics* of Aristotle. "Of all the learned clerics who contributed to the remarkable flowering of scholarly productions under the encouragement of Charles V. by far the most distinguished and certainly the most competent was Nicole Oresme."[8]

THE MORAL MANUAL

John Noonan had argued that Martin Le Maistre, a late fifteenth-century layman of the University of Paris, was the first Catholic theologian to make, as he says, the "modern" breakthrough, offering reasons for conjugal intercourse other than procreation.[9] But here in Oresme, an even more prestigious University of Paris don a full century prior to le Maistre, we find the primacy of the love relationship between husband and wife at the core of marriage including its sexual expression. Furthermore, Oresme was not a maverick in his conjugal views but had found them in abundance in the liturgy and accepted theology of his day. Renee Mirkes also considers Oresme's views and finds them anticipated by yet an earlier theologian—the twelfth-century Hildegaard of Bingen.[10]

Oresme was in his own day authoritative in politics, economics, physics, and astronomy, and, after leaving the court of Charles, became bishop of Lisieux. One would suspect, then, that Oresme's reputation, if not his works, was also established in England among his contemporary theologians, mathematicians, and scientists of Oxford and Cambridge. And it is not unlikely that such English intellectuals as Gower and Chaucer, both of whom had personal contact with the court of Charles V, had met Oresme and knew something of his scholarly work.

As far as I am able to determine, Oresme's treatment of conjugal love is unique among the professional theologians, not in doctrine but in the expression of doctrine. First, he writes in the vernacular. This is an indication that he intended his commentary to have a wider circulation than simply among the clergy, theologians, and learned laity. A. D. Menut says, "Nicole Oresme was a notable precursor of the movement to disseminate learning through the medium of the vernacular languages. His translations from the Aristotelian corpus enriched the culture of his contemporaries and enjoyed wide circulation thereafter for nearly two centuries"[11]

Secondly, his treatment of marriage is much more homely and concrete than the technical and abstract argumentation of his professional contemporaries or even of his fellow manualists who also wrote in the vernacular. He has not, to be sure, the informality of a priest in the parlor. He is still very much a philosopher, but here in his commentary on the *pseudo-Economics* he is less a philosopher, a technical scholastic theologian, than we have thus far met in our study. Again Menut says, "... Oresme was motivated primarily by his desire to reproduce Aristotle in such a manner that the complex ideas could be easily and readily grasped and understood by French readers previously unschooled in such highly intellectual exercises. Therefore, although he followed his principle [to stay close to the text] in general, his translations cannot rightly be called literal; the exceptions are too frequent and too notable." [12] And for this reason, as well as for his *matter*, he deserves and will repay our attention.

LE LIVRE DE YCONOMIQUE D'ARISTOTE

Oresme prefaces his commentary on the *pseudo-Economics* with these words: "Here begins the book called *Economics*, which Aristotle composed and which determines the government of the household."[13] Such was economics for Aristotle and for the Middle Ages. It was the "science" of household management. We are presently concerned, then, with a book which is directly and only about married life. The commentary is divided into two smaller books, which are subdivided into several chapters each. The first book "examines broadly all the parts of the household and all the interrelated divisions of a household." The second book "considers particularly and more fully married life or marriage." Actually both books are concerned mainly with the relationship between husband and wife, and the last book almost exclusively so. Thus the sheer weight of the attention given to husband and wife and their mutual relations suggests what the commentator (Oresme) and text ("Aristotle") alike considered to be most important in marriage. But of this we can have no doubt as we begin to consider what is actually said. In the third chapter of the first book, for instance, after a general introduction has been made in chapter 1 and the material elements of the household outlined in chapter 2, the first of those elements and their interrelationship are discussed at length. The first concern of every man, says Oresme quoting and elaborating upon his text, must be for his wife who is his companion (*compaigne*); after her come the children, and after them the servants, etc. Oresme lists six reasons for the primacy of concern for one's wife. First, the union between man and woman is "natural", for, he explains, the begetting of children is natural, and for this living

THE MORAL MANUAL

together is necessary. But among human beings this union, specifically as realized in the sexual act, is not only natural; it is also reasonable (*par raison*) and deliberated (*dearticulee*).

Oresme then presents his view of human sexual love in general, that is abstracting from whether it is marital or extra-marital. Such love, he repeats, is natural and is also a product of understanding and freedom (*bar election*). Thus love in the human being is even more natural (*taus naturele*) than it is in the beasts. If one lacks understanding and approaches another only to satisfy one's appetite (*sans autre amour que pour accomplir sa concupiscence*), this is a beastial sin (*vice bestial*). But if the love is human, that is accomplished by reason (*ovegue usage de raison*), the implication is that it is good, even though it "sometimes" happens to be without correct reason.

I say "implication" because Oresme is not altogether clear at this point as to his moral evaluation of sexual love. He mainly describes such love—the kind of love he feels Ovid was talking about and which we often observe in the young who love with joyous heart (*olaisance de cuer*). Sometimes, he says, this love is chaste and prepares for marriage. It would seem that in this case Oresme regards the love as good, otherwise he would not call it "chaste." He then says that "if" there is sin in the love that is of reason (though not according to "right" reason), it is a human failure (*vice humain*)—as if to say that the sin does not destroy the fundamental worth of such love.[14] And this appears to be the meaning warranted by the tenor of the whole passage.

Oresme's sympathies seem definitely to be with the young joyous lovers and with their kind of love (chaste) prior to marriage; and so, *a fortiori* it may be said that he approved of such love within marriage. The only thing that seems to worry him is a love that is inhuman, merely animal (*bestial*). If such in fact is his doctrine it is not noticeably different from that of Alexander, Thomas, and Scotus—though now it is expressed less by a technical precision of thought and language than by the general drift and feeling of an entire context.

The other reasons that make for the primacy of the spousal relationship are that it is tender and loving (*amiable*), profitable, divine, and harmonious. By *amiable* Oresme implies "friendship", "love", "delight", and so much more, as his long and engaging explication of it makes clear. His *text* reads that men and women marry not only that they might survive and live but also that they might *be* more fully (*bien estre*) and live better lives (*bien vivre*). His gloss here is worth quoting at length:

> Married friendship ... includes all the causes and kinds of friendship as stated in [Aristotle's] Ethics VIII, 17. For this friendship comprises at once the good of usefulness, the good of pleasure and the good of virtue; and double enjoyment—that is, both the carnal and the virtuous or the sensual and the intellectual pleasures. This friendship exists between two individuals only; for it concerns but one man and one woman as we have said and this is clear from the reasons indicated in Ethics VIII, 17. This friendship is, moreover, permanent and stable and is not to be broken, as pointed out in Politics, VII, 14. It accords with the injunction of Scripture: "Whom God has joined together let no man put asunder" (Matt. 19:6). Such a friendship is extremely great, as the Scripture notes in the Book of Kings, where it says that Jonathan was more loveable than women .... And Solomon states it thus: "The beauty of woman brightens the countenance of her husband and excels every delight of the eye ..." It is said of this love of which we are now speaking that Jacob served seven years for the love of Rachel and the time seemed short because of the greatness of his love ... And the Scripture states that a man will leave his father and mother for this love of woman and cleave to his wife ... And the Apostle Paul commands that each man love his wife as himself .... This is also clear from the fact that nature granted carnal pleasures to the animals only for the purpose of reproduction; but it accorded the human species this pleasure not only for reproduction of its kind but also to enhance and maintain friendship between man and woman. This is implied in Pliny's statement that no female, after she has become pregnant, seeks sexual union, except woman only (Nat. Hist., VII, 5). And this greater unity is a cause of greater friendship. This explains the statement in Politics II, 1, that two friends desire to become a single being. Thus we may say that husband and wife are more nearly a unit than the male and female of other species because the first woman was formed

THE MORAL MANUAL

from a rib of her husband and this was not the case of the other animals. For this reason, Scripture says that a married couple is two persons in a single skin (Gen. 2, 24). Thus we may now perceive how this life of husband and wife together is based upon friendship.

In this exposition of conjugal love, which Oresme seems to take for granted is the common Christian tradition, all the concern is with the relationship between husband and wife. Their love is said to be most intimate and of the greatest (*telle grande*) friendship, which embraces "all the causes and kinds of friendship." It is useful (*bien utile*), pleasureable (*bien delectable*), virtuous (*bien de virtu*), and of double satisfaction (*double delectation*) since both body and spirit are rejoiced therein. Sacred Scripture and profane texts are cited and multiplied in proof that love and friendship between man and woman is the greatest there is, and it is seen as having its source in, as well as being expressed by, the act of love: two friends desire to become a single being (*une chose*), and so they join in carnal union; and out of this union grows a greater friendship still, for "*la plus grande unite est cause de plus grand amiste.*"

Oresme explicitly declares that human sexuality is for something more than procreation, for carnal pleasure is there to maintain and enhance the friendship and, unlike the female of other species, even when the woman has conceived she still longs for sexual intercourse. In other words, the act of love has finality in the lovers themselves.

In the chapters in which he outlines the rules that ought to govern a man (he is writing for men not women) in his relations with his wife, Oresme nicely advises the husband as to his sexual conduct. He does not establish a timetable of sexual performance and abstinence. Rather he suggests the need to develop an *art of love*. The husband, he says, must take good care to satisfy his wife's desire, such that she will not be tempted to look for love elsewhere. But he must not over-engage her in sexual love lest she become unduly restless in his absence or when he is sick; and he must perform the marriage act decently such as befits its generative purpose. Courtesy (editor Menut's translation of *moult grande honesté*), modesty, and self-restraint are advised. The husband must be sensitive to his wife's feelings, must come to her only when she is well disposed (*bien composee*). He must not abuse her as though she were a harlot (*tole femme*), treating her roughly (*trop hardiment*) and in a debauched way with dirty speech (*paroles dishonnestes*). In short, his love-making must be refined (*de bonne maniere*) as well as licit and honorable.

But the husband's art of love must extend further than the sexual act. By his general attitude toward his wife and daily treatment of her he must constantly prove his love and esteem for her. Thus in the husband's rules of conduct the very first rule is that he must not wrong his wife and must treat her not as a servant but as his partner: "The wife is his companion (*compaigne*) not his servant." Another rule is that he must demonstrate his love and respect by limiting his sexual activity to her alone, and if he does not he does wrong—does wrong, it is noted, because he thereby violates the love he should have for his wife. Not so much the fact of the wrong, but the reason why there is wrong is what Oresme seems to be stressing.

Robert de Sorbon, in a sermon preached in mid-thirteenth century, likewise stresses the violation of love as the reason for the evil character of adultery. The unfaithful husband, he says, sins in many ways. One way by betrayal (*traditio*), "when the man shows his wife a sign of love but already has given his love to another"; another is by robbery (*iatrocinium*), "because he has given his body in love to his wife, and afterwards takes it from her and gives it to another..." Note that Robert thinks of the *conjugal act* in terms of love: it is a "*signum amoris*", the husband gives his body "*in amore*" to his wife. The "*redditio debiti*" is quite definitely seen to be "an act of love."[15]

In *Le Livre de Yconomique d'Aristote* both the author (pseudo-Aristotle) and his commentator are one with the tradition of the centuries in holding that the husband is master of the household and head of his wife. He is to rule and instruct her, and she is to obey. But Oresme insists that the wife's obedience and goodness will be secured only to the extent that her husband proves his love and reverence for her. So in the fourth chapter of the second book which proposes to show "how and by what rules the husband should act so that his wife may be good," the first rule is fidelity:

THE MORAL MANUAL

> Text: For an honourable woman it is a very great honour if she sees that her husband keeps chaste for her sake ...
>
> Gloss (Oresme): For he is obliged to do so, as has been said, and in this he does her very great honour.
>
> Text: And if he cares for no woman as much as he cares for her and holds her above all others as his very own (*propre*), his beloved (*amie*), and his loyal and faithful spouse ...
>
> Text: For if the wife knows and sees that her husband loves her and is for her, and that he treats her loyally and justly, she in turn will study to be loyal and just with him.
>
> Text: And nothing does a woman value more from her husband than his honourable and faithful companionship.
>
> Gloss: And thus if she is robbed (defraudee) of it she becomes sorrowful and troubled and cares less about other things, and thus the home falls to ruin.

Both text and gloss are heavy with the demand for male fidelity, which, it should be noted, is treated as a matter of both justice (*loialment, justement, defraudee*) and love (*amie et loiale. amiable*); and the husband's fidelity is required precisely that the wife's honour and esteem and her own fidelity might be preserved.

Oresme continues to the chapter's end his insistence upon the husband's fidelity as the fundamental rule in the training of his wife, and concludes with an interesting reversal of an ancient bias:

> Gloss: It is a very great villainy that is done to a man when one can say that his mother was not chaste. But a man must be more virtuous than a woman. Thus, according to truth and reason, it is an even greater reproach when it can be said that one's father kept neither faith nor loyalty with his mother, but was promiscuous (*un ribaut*).

However, Oresme is really not much interested in whose virtue or fall from virtue is the greater. His chief concern by far is the nurturing of the love and equality between husband and wife; and if grades of perfection are to be measured then each should regard the other as the better:

> Gloss: For it is possible that one surpass the other in some virtue and is surpassed in another. Therefore, let each consider the other as the better; and let the man think that his wife does him the greater good than he does her, and let her think the same with respect to him.

This is, of course, the same idea expressed in the thirteenth-century note in the Worcestershire nuptial rite, where it is prayed that the spouses "each prefer the other to oneself." Here, then, is Nicole Oresme's teaching on the love that is set on marriage and fulfilled within it. As suggested above, there is very little if any substantial difference between it and the doctrine of Thomas Aquinas, Bonaventure, Duns Scotus and the Franciscans of the *Summa of Brother Alexander*. If his doctrine seems to us to be softer, more liberal, more sympathetic toward love and lovers, more "secular," it is only because he is writing in terms less formal, less technical and coldly scientific, in an easier, freer style, indeed in a language more like that of the medieval vernacular romances and close to our own present day language of love. And he writes directly for those who are married or destined for marriage, that is the laity. Thus he himself remarks in preamble to his *Livre Ethiques*: "Because the Aristotelian books on moral science were originally written in Greek and we have received them in Latin very difficult to understand, the King has desired for the common good to have them translated into French, so that he and his counselors and others may understand them better."[16]

Aquinas and our other theologians had written for ecclesiastical specialists in a language the meaning and "tone" of which they would have understood. The manualists wrote for priests in a less technical language to help them in confessional and pulpit. Oresme wrote for the laity in a manner they would understand and appreciate. But the doctrine was all one; and it is likely that the interested world of that time was aware of it.

THE MORAL MANUAL

SUMMAE VIRTUTUM AC VITIORUM

In his *Histoire de l'Occident* (c. 1225) Jacques de Vitry appears to have inaugurated a marriage theme which in the course of the thirteenth century and continuing into the sixteenth century became widely circulated and exploited throughout western Christendom. The theme was that marriage is an order similar to, and in some respects surpassing in dignity, the religious orders of the Church.[17] De Vitry himself seemed bent on popularizing the idea, for he used it in a sermon on the marriage feast of Cana in which he declared that while the various religious orders were founded by men, God established the order of marriage.[18]

Reasons for the surpassing dignity of marriage quickly multiplied, as evidenced in these enthusiastic words of a thirteenth-century Dominican preacher:

> The order of marriage ... is an order whose statutes are not of yesterday; it has existed as long as human kind. Our order [that of Dominicans] and that of the Friars Minor have been recently established; just as all other religious orders, they are of the era which begins with the Incarnation. But the order of marriage is as old as the world. I will say more: our order is the work of a simple mortal, a Spaniard, as that of the Friars Minor is the work of a Lombard; but it is God who himself instituted the order of marriage from the beginning of time. I shall say still more: at the moment of the deluge, the Lord saved by preference those who were married. Finally, the Queen of Paradise, the Blessed Virgin, was married, and God did not will to be born of her womb until she was.[19]

And with sustained enthusiasm, our preacher goes on to offer marriage, not virginity, as the model and ideal for God's people, outlining in detail its properties and duties.

The same theme was further propagated by another thirteenth-century Dominican, William Peraldus, in both his *De eruditione principum* (often attributed to St. Thomas) and his widely circulated *Summae virtutum ac vitiorum*. In the latter work, indirectly influential in England through the fourteenth-century English translations of its derivative, the *Somme le Roi*, the reasons for the superlative worth of marriage have increased to twelve. Besides those mentioned above they are: it was instituted in Paradise; it was instituted in the state of innocence whereas the other orders are *post peccatum*; it is the order in which the Blessed Virgin was a member; God, his Mother, and his disciples graced it with their presence at the marriage feast of Cana; God worked a great miracle at Cana to demonstrate the power of marriage, for there God changed "vile water" into "precious wine," thus showing how "the sexual act (*opus carnale*) without marriage is something vile but within marriage is precious"; the Church blesses the newly-weds during Mass while they are near the altar in the presence of the Body of Our Lord; marriage produces children who become the adopted children of God, and it is the source of virgins; it is one of the seven sacraments; its great power is multiple: it changes what otherwise would be mortal sin into venial sin or no sin at all, it prevents such evils as sterility, abortion, etc. which often result from sex practiced outside of marriage, it establishes peace by uniting families, and it defends man there [in his sexual appetite] where the devil's attacks seem most formidable.[20]

This is high praise for marriage, and for marriage in its totality including the conjugal act, which is likened to the "precious wine" made by God at Cana. No contemporary of Peraldus reading this passage from his *Summae* or hearing the likes of it preached from the pulpit, would have felt that marriage was at all evil or being offered as a poor substitute for some nobler Christian calling. The whole drift of the passage is toward establishing the superiority of marriage above the other orders; and if some special esteem is reserved for the state of virginity, Peraldus offers the reminder that it is the married who are the source of virgins.

The woman herself, in and for herself, seems to have profited through such exaltation of marriage. So A. Lecoy de la Marche in his history of the French medieval pulpit: "... the preachers render honor to the woman in gladly exalting the dignity of marriage, in presenting it not only as a sacrament, but a religious order, having its distinctive rule and its particular genre of holiness."[21] Robert de Sorbon's reference to marriage as a religious order is in the sermon quoted: "There is the example of the married burgher who thought stupid him who said to him: 'Hail, monk,' not realizing that he was thinking of the order of matrimony..." And Robert proceeds to advise the married to learn well the rules of their order "as novices in some [religious] order."

But womans' reflected glory becomes all her own as the preachers praise her in her own right. Thus a preacher of such prominence as Robert de Sorbon, one of those who praised marriage as a religious order: "... note that God made woman of more beautiful material than man, because he formed woman from the bones of Adam, but Adam from the slime of the earth. Likewise, he made woman in a nobler and more beautiful place than man, because he made man upon earth, but woman in Paradise. And perhaps it is because God has given such honor to women that they honor God more than do men. The man, therefore, must love and honor his wife greatly."

Medieval theologians in general seemed to be aware of the complexity of the motivation that leads to marriage. Besides the principal motives of *proles* and *remedium* and just wanting to be together in and through the *sacramentum*, other secondary motives were recognized, such as beauty, wealth, familial or political peace, some of which were honorable (*honestae*), others not. Much earlier Hugh of St. Victor had noted the worthiness of marriage motives other than the essential three, but he saw that, for a marriage in which these "other goods," such as "love" and peace, were to thrive, one or other of the essential goods had to be present.[22]

But Peraldus brings these secondary motives into the foreground, stresses their importance, and offers as the guiding principle in calculating their moral worth the "equality" that must exist between the spouses. The equality of those who love toward marriage, he says, is symbolized by the wedding ring: a perfect fit for the ring, a perfect match for the couple. Let the young marry the young, the beautiful the beautiful, the noble the noble. Otherwise, he warns, there will be trouble. "When the young and beautiful marries the old and ugly she holds him in disgust, and takes to adultery."[23] One cannot help recalling here the poet's preachment of the same wisdom: Chaucer's old, hoary Januarius is simply not the man for wild young May; but if he should insist on marrying her, we must suppose it was not for any advice he might have received from a confessor who knew his Peraldus.

For the rest, Peraldus seems simply to echo the other theologians whom we have considered. The conjugal act must be other-directed if it is to be entirely without sin and meritorious. It is other-directed if one is moved to it by the desire for children or to satisfy the needs and desires, even when unspoken, of one's spouse. Sin enters when self-satisfaction becomes the dominating motive, the *raison d'etre* of the act. And the only case of mortal sin (besides contraception and perversion) is when the husband is prepared to satisfy his lust with *any* woman. As with other theologians, here and here alone is the *vehemens amator*, the *ardentior amator* of his own wife: not the husband who loves his wife passionately, romantically, but rather with brutish unconcern and a heart set totally on himself and his private gratification. As for the pleasure that attaches to the marriage act, Peraldus agrees with the Catharite that it is always "immoderate," but, corrects Peraldus, such immoderation is not a moral evil or sin (*malum culpae*) but one of the inconvenient leftovers from original sin (*malum poenae*) for which we, as individuals, are not responsible. Still, Peraldus would have the pleasure kept "within its limits." It is difficult to determine what he visualizes here. If he means that spouses even when centered upon each other must nevertheless restrain their passion and pleasure, he differs from the "naturalism" of his brother Dominican, Thomas Aquinas, who, as we have seen, taught that, on the contrary, in this case the more passion (and pleasure) the better. If he means simply that spouses must take care to keep their love and pleasure within the bounds (limits) of their own marriage then he is in agreement with Thomas and our other theologians.

Noticeably absent from Peraldus's treatment of marriage in his *Summae* is any explicit mention of love, whether as *amor*, *delectio*, or even as *caritas*. The relationship between husband and wife is referred to solely in terms of *pietas* and *iustitia*, though the former word may legitimately be translated as "love." But if we turn to one of Peraldus's sermon outlines for the marriage feast of Cana, we find that, as in the case of St. Thomas and other scholastics, underlying his concepts of justice and piety was that of genuine tender and gracious love; and he is not at all shy about using the word itself. In marriage, he notes:

THE MORAL MANUAL

Gentleness (*mansuetudo*) is necessary, for hardness (*duricies*) in a man is often the cause of adultery in the woman. Colossians. 3: "Men, love your wives and do not become a source of bitterness for them." It is inhuman that a man behave in an evil way with her who for him has left mother and father and the rest of her relatives... Ecclesiastes 26: "Happy the husband of a good wife, etc." For a man must love his wife. Eph. 5: "Love your wives as Christ has loved the Church, and handed himself over for it..." The same for Eph. 5: "Men must love their wives as their own bodies." The same: "Whoever loves his wife loves himself." Likewise: "Let each love his wife as himself."[24]

And once again the marriage act is likened to the precious wine at Cana, only now rather than marriage "act," it is called conjugal "solace" or "comfort" (*solatium*): "As precious wine so is the solace of a woman to a husband who behaves properly" (*habenti se ordinate*) within the marriage." The three cases in which the marriage act can be performed "entirely without sin" are: the desire children, the rendering of due love (*iustitia movet*), and the avoidance of fornication (*pietas movet*). Peraldus's word for this last, "*pietas*", suggests love, a concerned love. It is said to obtain when the wife (out of embarrassment, shame) cannot bring herself to ask for intercourse. Then the husband should be moved (by his love, *pietas*) to take all the initiative.[25]

But if the *Summae* of Peraldus is wanting in explicitness with regard to the word "love," the lack is well-supplied when we turn to the English vernacular offsprings of his work.

THE BOOK OF VICES AND VIRTUES

The Book of Vices and Virtues is, as already noted, a fourteenth-century Midland translation of the thirteenth-century *Somme des Vices et des Vertus*, or *Somme le Roi*, by the Dominican friar Lorens d'Orleans, whose book in turn derives from Peraldus's *Summae*. It is a sister, therefore, to at least eight other English versions of the same French original, beginning with the *Ayenbite of Inwit* in 1340 and ending with Caxton's print of his *Royal Book* around 1486. Of all these English manuals *The Book of Vices and Virtues* seems to have attained the widest circulation; it has, at any rate, survived in three manuscripts while the others are extant only in single manuscripts. But whatever the relative circulation of the several versions, they were all much alike, being close literal translations of the French original; and taken together they must have formed the common reading and indoctrination of considerable numbers of the fourteenth-century English clergy and a few of the more learned and theologically minded laity. What, then, did *The Book...* have to tell them about love and marriage?[26]

Surprisingly, *The Book* treats of marriage not as an instance of the active life but, along with widowhood and the various states of virginity, in the section on the contemplative life under the general title of the "Gift of Understanding." Marriage appears as the third branch of the tree of chastity, while widowhood is the fourth branch and simple virginity the fifth, the sixth and seventh branches being reserved for Holy Orders and the religious life respectively. It is important to bear this total context in mind, for it demonstrates that marriage is definitely conceived as an integral part of the Christian life and at the summit of its perfection which, for the medieval Christian, was contemplation.[27] As usual, marriage is ranked below widowhood and virginity, receiving "thirty-fold fruit", while widowhood receives "sixty-fold" and virginity a "hundred-fold." But just as simple virginity does not seem to be demeaned by being placed in a lower category than Orders and religious life, and as the merely ordained are not thereby regarded as inferior to religious, so marriage would not, at the time, have appeared to suffer from the comparison. Together with the others it is a vocation within the highest vocation (the contemplative) of the Church, it has a dignity of its own, and is itself a way to further perfection. Lest some be tempted to think otherwise, our author is quick to add that if virgins receive a "special crown" which widows and the married do not, still there are many of the married who will enjoy a higher place heaven than many a virgin:

> and þeizh it be so þat in þe state of mariage and in þe state of widowhode men mowe wel wynne þe coroune of ioye, and more þanke haue to-fore God þan haue many virgines. For of suche ben fele [many] in paradis, þat ban lyued in mariage & widowhode, pat ben wel nere [nearer] God þan many virgines; neuer þe later þe virgines han a speciale coroune aboue þe coroune of ioye þat is comune to alle þe halewen...

THE MORAL MANUAL

But this is what is said directly of marriage:

> þe þridde braunche is þe staate and þe bonde of mariage, for þei shulle kepe hem eueriche for oþer, clenliche and truliche, wiþ-out any wrong doynge þat on to þat oþer, and þat askeþ þe lawe of mariage þat þat on holde trewþe and feiþ to, bat oþer of his body. For after þat þei ben knytte to-gidre flescheliche, þei ben al on body and on soule, as holi as þei ben on bodi, þed schulde ben of on herte be trwe loue, ne neueremore to departe of herte ne of body while þei lyuen; wherfore þei schulde kepe here bodies clenliche and chastliche, wiþ-out here owen harme, and þerfore seiþ seynt Poule þet wommen schulde loue here hosebondes and honoure, and kepe here bodies from alle oþere þen from here lordes; sobre in etyng & drynkyng, for of to moche etyng and drynkynge comþ moche quekenyng of þe fier of lecherie. And also scholde men kepe here bodies chast, þat þei ne zeue nouzt to a-noþer womman þan to here owen.

Here is clear and forceful proclamation of the intimacy of the union that must be between husband and wife. They are to be one in body, soul, and heart, and are to keep themselves (in their love) from all others that they might remain clean and chaste for each other. And if marriage is thought of in terms of justice (*trewþe, feisþ*), it is a justice that is quite evidently compatible with and rooted in love (*trwe loue*). This passage, it should be noted, is our author's introduction to his discussion of marriage; it is, then, what he considers marriage to be first and foremost, at heart and in essence. The word is not used but the reality is there: it is the *sacrament*.

After listing some of the commendations of marriage which we have already seen in the *Summae* of Peraldus, the author of *The Book...* turns to the marriage act itself. Again, the doctrine appears identical to that of our scholastic theologians, though, as with Nicole Oresme, its expression in the homely, more familiar vernacular may now enable us to "feel" as well as understand its meaning:

> Wherefore þe staate of mariage is so holi and so honest þat þe dede þat was erst dedly synne wiþ-out mariage is wiþ-oute synne in mariage, and not onliche wiþ-out synne, but in many caas grete þanke-worþi of God to wynne þi þe lif wiþ-outen ende....

THE CRAFT OF LOVE

Peraldus had written in praise of marriage that "without it the carnal act would be gravely sinful, but within it, it is only venial sin or no sin at all." *The Book* adds, what also the earlier scholastics taught, that it could also be meritorious, but it expresses the idea concretely and with simplicity and charm: the act of marriage is most worthy of "God's thanks" and "wins" life without end.

The Book goes on to say that there are three ways in which "you may do the deed of wedlock without sin and have great merit to the soul." The first, as in the theology generally, is when offspring is the motive, for which marriage was first made and "principally ordained." The second, again as usual, is when one spouse looks to the fulfillment of the sexual needs and desires of the other whether they are expressed "by mouth or by sign"; and if the husband should not read his wife's needs (or she his?) wrong is done, for "that is hers by right, for the one has right over the other's body." The third instance of merit is the traditional *vitatio fornicationis,* where the one spouse is anxious to secure the other's fidelity, to keep him/her from looking elsewhere for love.

As to the possibility of sin in the marriage act, our author's clear and precise vernacular presents a doctrine that conforms in the main to that of the greater theologians. The act is venially sinful "when men and women want nothing in such activity except only their pleasure and lust and lechery," yet limit their desire to their own spouse. It is mortally sinful "when the pleasure and the lechery for his wife is so great that reason and justice are blinded so that he would do as much to her even though she were not his wife." This last is the case of those who "put God so far out of their hearts and thoughts that they intend nothing but the satisfaction of their lechery." They copulate "as doþ an hors or a mule."

There are other instances of sin in conjugal love-making that *The Book* mentions, and there are times of abstinence which it recommends; but all is governed by principles of consideration and decency and respect for more fundamental and wider demands of Christian living. Thus the sexual act is considered to be gravely sinful if it is performed in an "unnatural" way. It is also sinful (the gravity of the sin is not specified) if it is forced in times of sickness, because of the harm it

THE MORAL MANUAL

might do to the sick spouse and also because of unhappy, unhealthy consequences to the child who might be conceived in such times. Likewise it is wrong to force oneself on one's wife when she is in childbed, "for shame, and for peril that may come thereof." One should not make love in "holy places," for such places are ordained exclusively for the service and worship of God. And in holy times—feasts and fasts—sexual abstinence is counselled, but only counselled,

> for to be þe more besy and entendaunt to serve God and praie goode praiers... not for þe synne þat it is to do suche þing in suche tyme—in suche entente may a man do it—but oþerwhile schal a man forbere þing þat he may do wiþ-oute synne for to purchase of God þe bettre þat man wolde, as seynt Austen seiþ.

Penitential books

Other moral manuals and penitential books were in circulation in late medieval England as elsewhere in Europe that according to our contemporary tastes were not as gentle with marriage and the married as those presented here. This is especially true of the "penitentials" which, as their name suggests, were concerned not with the good that people do but the bad.[28] Their fixation was upon sin and the ways to atone for and overcome it. They were not written for the laity but for confessors who, as physicians of the soul, had to know the range of spiritual ills, just as our medical doctors must know and understand the possible failures of the body—not from morbid curiosity and the desire to inflict pain, but that health might be secured or restored. But when it is a question of searching out the positive in marriage as in other matters, our medieval manualists—those instanced in this chapter and many others imitative of them—were as good at finding and encouraging it as the *ex professo* theologians we have considered in the preceding chapters.

The penitentials flourished from around the sixth century to the twelfth but continued to surface in various parts of Europe until the sixteenth century. Though they may seem severe to us, they may be regarded, and were so regarded in their own time, as mitigations of the earlier severity and shame of "public penance." Now the sacrament of reconciliation was a private affair, exclusively between a penitent and his/her "soul-friend," who used the penitential as one aid among several in his spiritual direction. The detail with which the penitentials discuss the many possible sins, and the feeling of gloom and doom that results from this, disturbs scholars such as Brundage.[29] But as some have noted the penitentials "are codes, comparable to the criminal codes of later times, and that such documents must perforce deal with unpleasant things. Defective as they are when viewed from the standpoint of modern ideals, a sound historical judgment will ascribe to them a civilizing and humanizing role of no small importance." At any rate, the penitential, whether good or bad, had all but vanished from the scene long before the period we are studying, and in its place stood the moral manual with its much broader and more positive approach to Christian living.

Though the moral manuals, catechisms, and books of devotion that proliferated in the last centuries of the Middle Ages were closer to the laity than the great academic theologies, closer still was the liturgy which, by word, gesture, song drew the faithful in general into the teaching and life of the Church. The laity, then, if they would know the mind of the Church on love and marriage, need only to have experienced the weddings of their day, their own and those of family and friends. Granted that many were married outside of any public ceremony in the forbidden but valid clandestine marriage; still during their lifetime they would have witnessed more than a few church weddings, and so would have heard the belief and teaching that underlay them.

CHAPTER 8

LOVE IN SECULAR MANUALS AND POETRY

THE BOOK OF THE KNIGHT OF LA TOUR-LANDRY

Another 'special' treatise which we will consider is the very popular fourteenth-century and fifteenth-century book *The Book of the Knight of La Tour-Landry*. The Knight tells us in his prologue that in writing his book he employed two priests and two clerks, whose work, the editor T. Wright, says, "appears to have consisted in collecting illustrative examples and anecdotes from different writers." Since it was written by a layman with the help of the clergy and shows literary as well as moral pretensions, it may serve as an apt transition piece from ecclesiastical doctrine to that of the poetry we will be considering.[1] What is said therein about love and marriage is definitely from a layperson's point of view, but the Church's teaching, as we shall see, is quite visibly present. *The Book of the Knight of La Tour-Landry*, accordingly, is offered as an instance (though only that) of what the educated and literary laity of the late Middle Ages understood of their Church's teaching on love and marriage, and of their reaction to it.

It is, or purports to be, a book of instruction compiled by Geoffroy de la Tour for his daughters in 1371-72, and translated into English from the original French in the reign of Henry VI (1422 ff).[2] Speaking of the original French book, Wright says, "*The book...* appears to have been extremely popular. Nearly a dozen copies of the original text are known to exist in manuscript, of which seven are in the Bibliotheque Imperiale in Paris, and one in the library of the British Museum. One or two of them date at least as far back as the beginning of the fifteenth century, and two are adorned with illuminations... The popularity of this book soon extended to foreign lands, and it was translated into several languages."

THE CRAFT OF LOVE

Beginning with the Prologue to *The Book of the Knight of La Tour-Landry*,³ it would seem that in our study we have moved away from theology, from ecclesiastical thought and practice, into the purely secular world of the late medieval laity and its poetry:

> In the year of the incarnacion of oure Lord Mle iijc lxxj, as y was in a gardin, al heui and fulle of thought, in the shadow, about the ende of the monthe of Aprille, but a litelle y reioysed me of the melodie and song of the wilde briddes; thei sang there in her langages, as the thrustille, the thrusshe, the nytinggale, and other briddes, the whiche were fulle of mirthe and ioye; and thaire suete songe made my herte to lighten, and made me to think of the tyme that is passed of my youthe, how loue in gret distresse had holde me, and how y was in her seruice mani tymez fulle of sorugh and gladnesse, as mani lovers ben. But my sorw was heled, and my seruice wel ysette and quitte, for he geue [me a] fayr wyff, and that was bothe faire and good, (who had knowleche of alle honoure, alle good, and of fayre mayntenynge,) and of all good she was bell and the floure; and y delited me so moche in her that y made for her loue songges, balades, rondelles, virolayes, and diuerse [other] thinges in the best wise y couthe. But dethe, that on alle makithe were, toke her from me, the whiche hathe made me haue mani a sorufulle thought and gret heuinesse. And so it is more than xx yeere that I haue ben for her ful of grete sorogh. For a true loveris hert forgettith neuer the woman that enis he hathe truli loued.

Geoffroy de la Tour was a layman of fourteenth-century England with a definitely secular interest; and though the form of his book is prose, its prologue is so obviously rhythmical that even had he himself not told us, we might easily have guessed at his original intention of writing in verse. All the feeling and conventions of the love poetry are there: the happy, springtime month of April, the joyous melody of the "wild birds," the forlorn lover "in great distress," the heaviness of heart, the long service of love finally rewarded, the pathos of the death of the beloved, the lasting fidelity of the true lover who survives.

But immediately after so romantic a beginning our "poet" returns us to theology, specifically to the fourteenth-century manuals of practical

LOVE IN SECULAR MANUALS AND POETRY

morality. For, he says, with the help of two priests and two clerks, it is his intention to write a book for the moral instruction and correction of his daughters, having previously written a like book for his sons.[4] He recalls the time when as a youth he went about with his fellows. He remembers how they tried to seduce every woman they would meet and caused the women who fell prey to them to lose their good names. He would say to them: "Seris, ye shulde loue, nor be aboute, to haue but one." But they would not listen. And so he would put his daughters on guard. He would write them a book in which they might learn how to conduct themselves in the world so as to end up honorably, handsomely, and happily married.

He begins with God, or rather with the good things the service of God is likely to win. He tells his daughters in good burgher style: "y haue gret desire that ye turne youre hertis and thoughtis to drede and to serue God; for he thanne wol sende you good and worship in this world, and in the other."[5] All that follows is mainly anecdote and example of this principle—stories of virtue rewarded and vice punished, especially in the matter of love. Many of the stories are from the Bible and lives of the Saints. Some are fabliaux—of the kind we would hardly expect a proper father to tell in the presence of, much less directly to, his daughters. Some of the stories are of his own experiences, as is the one concerning a would-be bride of his who had lost his young (and seemingly prudish) love and later her reputation because she was "so pert and so light of maners."[6]

J. T. Noonan writes, "It is typical that the knight La Tour-Landry warns his daughters that a girl who spoke to him in a friendly fashion when he was a young bachelor seemed too forward to be a decent bride." Noonan offers this anecdote to illustrate his claim that in medieval society there was no structure provided "in which persons could know each other before marriage.... In the social context provided by medieval institutions it was difficult to believe that personal love often motivated those who wanted to wed."[7] But what, then, should we make of the Knight's prologue to his book which features prenuptial romance as prelude to marriage? Apparently the society in which he lived did not prevent his finding a woman to his taste and did not obstruct his falling deeply in love with her, courting her, marrying her for love, and remaining married to her in love. Also,

THE CRAFT OF LOVE

much of our discussion in our preceding chapters—especially with regard to freedom of choice and therefore the presence of mutual love in the contracting of marriage, and the ecclesiastically blessed sponsalia (engagement rite)—argues rather to a social milieu that did in fact permit, and encourage, personal knowledge and love prior to marriage. To what extent people of the time took advantage of the Church's teaching here, as also whether the Knight's book reflects actual practice, is moot. But that a structure for courtship, freedom of choice, and love prior to as well as within marriage was provided by the Church and, at least in some of the literature, talked about, would be difficult to deny.

Toward the end of *The Book of the Knight* there is a pause in the storytelling. His wife (second wife?) enters upon the scene as he records a debate he once had with her over the desirability of love *peramours* (romance).

The Knight is obviously no theologian and makes no pretense of writing a theology of love or any other matter. He is a cultivated gentleman of the world who is principally concerned, in this book, to secure the good reputation and happiness of his daughters. But he is also an informed Christian, or fancies himself one, who would not dream of contradicting any of the teachings of his Church. Whatever else he may be, he is definitely not the kind of man who would deliberately overstep the bounds of the strictest conventional orthodoxy. What he says then about love—the chief burden of his book—we may rest assured he believed to be the teaching of his Church or, at least, in safe conformity with it.

Indeed, throughout the book there are echoes of ecclesiastical teaching as we have found it. The Church vigorously condemned sexual love outside of marriage, at least when it terminated, in act or desire, in fornication and adultery. The Knight says "amen" to this with fanatical intensity. So, as we have seen, his principal motive in writing his book was to preserve his daughters from the seductions of lascivious, promiscuous lovers such as he himself had known in his youth. And so incensed is he at the thought of adultery that he leaps beyond the harshest vituperations and condemnations of the severest preacher: he expresses the wish that England and France might have the law that

LOVE IN SECULAR MANUALS AND POETRY

still (he says) obtains in other countries whereby adulterers have their throats cut or are burned or buried alive.[8]

But if the Knight is opposed to sexual love outside marriage, he is graciously liberal in his attitude toward a love that is oriented to marriage and fulfilled within it. The prologue quoted above might alone stand as fair witness to this. The Knight himself had experienced the beauty and worth of an innocent love *peramours*. It had climaxed in a tender, sweet marriage, had lasted all through the marriage, and was still alive in his heart though his beloved wife had been dead now for twenty years, "for a true lover is hert forgetith neuer the woman that enis [once] he hathe loued." But there is further evidence of his kindly attitude toward romantic conjugal love. Much later in the book, in the debate with his "second" wife—and perhaps in the recollection of his own first-love—he deliberately takes up the cause of love *peramours*.[9] If, he says, some good knight happens along and wants to love and take a woman to wife, "why shalle she not loue hym?" He goes even further and argues that a *married* woman should be allowed to have a love *peramours* with a man other than her husband. The Knight's present wife who, significantly perhaps, is allowed the final word in the debate, dissents. The chief fruit of her dissent is the emergence of what she believes to be the ecclesiastically canonized doctrine of the fullness and exclusivity of love within marriage:

> And for certayne a woman may not haue two hertes, no more than a grehond may renne after two bestes. Therefore impossyble is that she myght loue her peramour of trewe loue and her lord also withoute faute or deceyuance. But God and reson naturell constrayneth her. For, as the clerkes say and the predycatours [preachers], God beganne the world by maryage of man and woman; and God hymself, whanne he came in to this world, he spake and treated at a sermon that he made of maryage, sayeng that maryage is a sacrament ioyned and annexed of God to the man and the woman, & how they be but one body, and that they oughte to loue eche other more than fader ne moder ne other creature... And therefore at the dore where as the preest maketh them to swere that they shalle loue and kepe eche other bothe seke and hole, and that they shalle not gwerpysshe [forsake] or leue eche other for none other

THE CRAFT OF LOVE

better or wors, and therfor I saye... how thenne shold the wedded woman gyue her loue ne do ony oth to some other withoute consent of her lord?[10]

"As the clerkes say and the predycatours," and also the priest at the church door—this was the wife's belief concerning love and marriage as she received it from the theology, the preaching, and the nuptial liturgy of her day. There were not to be two kinds of love, as the Knight seems to be suggesting—one for the lady's husband and another for her lover—but the one great love which she was to give entirely and exclusively to her husband who was to be her one and only lover. The same is implied for the husband: his one and only beloved is to be his wife.

But surely the Knight, with tongue-in-cheek, was merely egging his wife on, teasing her into an emphatic declaration of a truth he himself most assuredly believed. For much earlier in his book he had presented the same argument under a different form. There the story is told of a married woman who had got leave of her husband to go on pilgrimage but whose real motive was to be with a young squire of her fancy. She dallied with her lover, and then fell sick. When the fever was on her she had a vision of her mother and father. The mother showed her her breasts and told her that as she had once loved these breasts she should now love her husband. On awaking from the vision she asked a priest if he would interpret it for her. The priest summoned a holy man, who offered the following explanation:

> Furst, God hathe sheued you youre fader and youre moder, and that youre moder saide, "doughter, loue and worship youre husbonde as ye haue loved these brestis that have norisshed you;" that is to menying that ye shulde loue and doute [fear, reverence] youre husbonde, as ye loued youre moderes brest whanne ye were norrished therof. For the child louithe of all thinge the pappe... and so aught eueri good woman do after Goddes lawe, to loue her husbonde aboue all other loues, and to forsake worldely loues that be unlefull. For oure Lorde saithe with his mouthe that woman shulde leue fader, moder, brother, and suster, for her husbonde. For they are not diuerse, but two flesshes that God hathe ioyned in one, and that no man shulde

putte betwene hem no thinge that might seuere the loue that God and the churche hathe ioyned in hem. Yet youre moder saide you that ye toke youre norisshinge and waxing of the suetnesse of the milke, the whiche signifiethe the swetnesse that shulde be in trew mariage, and grace with loue of God... And also ye are suoren to God and to youre husbonde atte the chirche dore afore witnesse that ye shalle neuer breke it [the marriage] while ye leue togedre.[11]

Love *peramours* prior to marriage, perhaps. The Knight, though cautious concerning it, seems to have looked kindly upon it as long as marriage was its term. Even his present wife conceded, though reluctantly and with serious qualification, its legitimacy when the man was honorable. The Knight insists: What of the good knight, trusted as such? Should he not receive grace and worship from his *peramour*? The wife answers that "there be many maners of loue, and, as men saye, the one is better than the other." And so if a knight or a squire loves a lady or a damsel "by worshyp and honoure only... wythout prayer or request," such a love is good. The Knight then asks about kissing. The wife answers never, for it is father of the deed.[12] And neither gives any indication that the Church disapproved of it. But both agreed, without argument or thought of argument, that love *peramours* between husband and wife was not only legitimate but was the perfect way of marriage—the way, moreover, that was not simply recommended but was demanded by "God and reson naturell," by preacher, clerk, and nuptial rite.

This love *peramours* between husband and wife, this "sweetness that should be in true marriage," can and sometimes should, says the Knight, express itself even in jealousy. Seemingly aware of the theology on the subject, he distinguishes two kinds of jealousy: one which is rational, the other based only on suspicion. as noted above for both Aquinas and Bonaventure. The Knight echoes Aquinas in justifying a jealousy inspired by *amor amicitiae*, i.e. the love that is other-centered, while he conforms to Bonaventure in proposing the justice of a jealousy that proceeds from the desire to keep one's own for one's self (*amor concupiscentiae*).

THE CRAFT OF LOVE

Nevill Coghill speaking of the *De Amore* of Andreas Capellanus says: "Andreas affirms that love and jealousy are the same thing, and in this opinion declares that he has the backing of the Countess of Champagne, with her dictum that a man incapable of jealousy is incapable of love."[13] Then he proceeds to place jealousy among what, he says, C. S. Lewis called the "base" things of life. But perhaps Andreas and the countess were closer to the truth in this matter than either Coghill or Lewis. At any rate, for Bonaventure, Aquinas, and the Knight of Tour-Landry jealousy was not all bad. It could be vicious and base, but it could also be a virtue and a necessary part of love—even, as Bonaventure explicitly affirmed and Aquinas implied, when the love was *caritas*.

The rational jealousy, the Knight believes, is often a proof of love: "For the wise man saithe that ielosye is a great ensaumple of loue, for he that louithe me not, rechithe [cares] neuer whedir y do well or euelle; but my frende is sori whanne y do euelle, and therfor ielosie is neuer withoute gret loue." And so the woman should not love her husband less for a little jealousy on his part, "for she aught to thinke that he dothe it for the feruent loue that he hathe to her, and for ferde that ani shuld haue the loue of her sauf he hym selff, and that yef so be that an other man might haue her loue, he shal neuer haue her loue... and that the ioye of her [their] mariage is done, and her housholde lost."[14]

The Knight does not treat in any detail the sexual act within marriage. Outside of marriage the act is condemned as "that orible synne of the delyte of the flesshe," and the Knight warns his daughters to marry in good intent and not "only for flesshely delite."[15] In light of the contemporary theology reviewed in past chapters, we should by now recognize that such strong language against sexual pleasure sought outside marriage was by no means meant as disapproval of sexual pleasure within marriage. Peraldus and other manualists and preachers had spoken of "vile water" becoming, through the miracle of marriage, "precious wine," and all our great speculative theologians had insisted on the goodness of carnal conjugal love and the passion and pleasure experienced therein; and we should by now fully realize the vast difference in medieval theological thinking between marrying and making love for pleasure as one of several other deeper considerations, and marrying and making love *only* for pleasure. It is against this last, exclusive motivation—"only for flesshely delite"—that the Knight admonishes his daughters. As to the rest he will not trouble them. Backed by the authority of the Church as well as by a solid secular prudence he has sufficiently indicated the general direction love must take. It must move toward marriage and be fulfilled only in marriage, and within marriage it must aim at complete fulfillment, all of one's love centered exclusively upon one's spouse.

LE MENAGIER DE PARIS

In the England of the fourteenth century the moral manual was not an isolated instance; rather it was part of a context involving the laity in general, whether in England or elsewhere in contemporary Europe. For example, across the waters in France—always closely linked, whether in war or in peace, with the England that often dominated it while learning from it—another similar book was enjoying equal popularity with that of the Knight: *Le Menagier de Paris*.[16] The *Menagier* (Householder), like the Knight, is meticulously orthodox in his Catholic faith. He is a very old man who marries a very young woman. She asks him for counsel on how to be a good wife, and so he writes her a book on the subject, outlining her duties toward God (prayer, Mass, confession, etc.), toward himself in his old age, toward herself (games, recreation, clothes, etc.), and toward the household (servants, cooking, etc.). What is most remarkable is that much of what he says is to prepare his wife for her second marriage after he is gone and when she will have a husband nearer her own age. Especially when he advises her concerning love, it is usually with this second husband in mind. That it is a fullness of love—indeed, a love *peramours*—that he recommends is clear enough:

> In God's name... I believe that when two good and honorable people are wed, all other loves are put off, destroyed and forgotten, save only the love of each for the other. And meseems that when they are in each other's presence, they look upon each other more than upon the others, they clasp and hold each other and they do not willingly speak or make sign save to each other. And when they are separated, they think of each other and say in their hearts, "When I see him I shall do thus and thus to him, or say this to him, I shall beseech him concerning this or that." And

THE CRAFT OF LOVE

all their special pleasure, their chief desire and their perfect joy is to do pleasure and obedience *one to the other* [emphasis mine]... Fair sister, if you have another husband after me, know that you should think much of his comfort ... Wherefore cherish the person of your husband carefully, and, I pray you, keep him in clean linen... and assuaged with other joys and amusements, privities, loves, and secrets, *concerning which I am silent* [emphasis mine]... Certes, fair sister, such service maketh a man love and desire to return home and see his good wife and to be distant with other women.

That the husband and wife are to do "obedience one to the other" recalls the prayer of the Hereford marriage rite: "Each should obey the other." The *Le Menagier de Paris* makes it quite clear that the wife is to do much more of it! He unabashedly uses the analogy of a faithful, domesticated dog to illustrate and encourage a wife's loving obedience to her husband; and, even when her spouse is severe with her, she is to remember patient Griselda; though the Menagier is careful to add that he himself is no Marquis (Griselda's husband), that he would never be so foolish as to try his own wife so, and that in any case it is all just a story, though one worth pondering if only to be able to converse about it in social gatherings. So much for Griselda!

The above quotation, as indeed the whole of the *Le Menagier de Paris* text, is in accord with *The Book of the Knight of La Tour-Landry* as also with the ecclesiastical teaching we have considered: central to the life of husband and wife is their mutual love, intimate in body as well as spirit and productive of innocent joy and pleasure. And here, as in *The Book of the Knight of La Tour-Landry*, it is the spouses alone and their love for each other that seems sufficient for honest love-making. Children appear in both books, they are to be loved and cared for, but the procreative intent is not mentioned when the intimacies—the "amusements, privities, loves, and secrets"—of marriage are referred to. It would seem that both Menagier and Knight, both knowledgeable of and faithful to the teaching of their Church and anxious to secure the same fidelity on the part of their wives, found no cause in that teaching to scruple over conscious motivation for the act of love. The underlying love bond, the *sacramentum*, that was theirs seems to have

LOVE IN SECULAR MANUALS AND POETRY

been motive enough and, if faithfully lived, would manage the rest. In this they are at one with Duns Scotus and Albert the Great.

Love and marriage in fourteenth-century poetry

We shall now look to the secular poetry proper and compare its treatment of love and marriage with that of the Church. But first, there must be a cautionary word of preface. The theologians were *ex professo* teachers, they—especially the medieval scholastics—dealt directly with abstract ideas meant to be discussed as such and, where warranted, applied to concrete situations. These ideas could be isolated from a total work, put into other words, and summarized for the purpose of economy, comparison, and debate, with little if any loss in meaning, providing, of course, that all was done with respect for their overall context. But how to do this with a poem, or a statue, or a painting, the idea of which is the work itself in its totality apart from which a segment of it has little if any meaning or appeal?

Granted the poet, especially the medieval poet, may intend to teach—he or she has a meaning, a *sententia*—but the prime intention is to "please" or, if you will, disturb: to raise—through image, idea, music of rhythm and rhyme—feelings and awareness to another level wherein other truths, even those unknown to the poet, may stand revealed; and this is done by the poem *as a whole*. Here in fact is the teaching or "sentence" of the poet: not so much what is expressly said (content or matter)—though this also—but the way in which it is said (form or style). Thus poetic truth, differing from theological or philosophical truth, requires a different methodology for discovering and "experiencing" it. Further, the theologians were concerned about the *letter* of their writing: the literal meaning of their text was their sole objective. Whereas the poets often had objectives beyond the letter in what were designated as the allegorical, moral, and anagogical meanings that the letter was to suggest.

The "teaching and pleasing" work of the Christian poet ultimately derives from St. Augustine, *De Doctrina Christiana*, Book IV: There Augustine says, the task of the one practiced in speech *(eloquentem)* to teach *(doceat)*, to please *(delectet)*, and to persuade *(flectat)*. Keneim Foster and Patrick Boyde finds these elements harmoniously united in

THE CRAFT OF LOVE

Dante's poetry, with beauty (form and structure) being supreme.[17] They say:

> the stress, when Dante is discussing poetry, falls on form and structure, in particular on sound-structure. And this means that the poet has an overriding concern with beauty. He is a maker of beautiful objects; not only this, but very definitely this. His motive in 'making' is what we would now call aesthetic ... But it combined, of course, with other non-aesthetic motives which, setting aside that of mere vanity, can be roughly classified as moral, political, and religious.

Dante could, and did in much of his rhyme separate his meaning from the beauty of his poetry. For example, he did this all through his *La Vita Nuova*. But Foster notes, "in writing this exposition Dante was conscious that he was leaving the beauty behind—in the poem where it belonged."[18]

However, it is not our purpose here to consider the poetry as such, but rather to get behind it to some of the cultural background thought and attitude that helped, if only in a modest way, to shape it. This in fact is what those who have raised and pursued the question of the relationship between Church and poet have tried to do. They have looked to the content or "letter" of the poetry, the kinds of things the poets explicitly talked about and what they expressly said about them. Fixed upon this—the literal meaning of the poetry—they have found, for the most part, love doctrine opposed to that of the Church. I treat the matter here in like manner, looking simply or mainly to the "letter" and what it may reveal about the theological thinking and sympathies underlying the poetry. Rather than that of analysis, therefore, our procedure will be largely expository, placing before the reader what the poets expressly said and comparing it, when warranted, to the ecclesiastical teaching that we have examined.

It should be noted, however, that such a literal reading also has its importance for the poetry in and for itself as well as for our knowledge of its cultural milieu. In a good poem the letter works with all its other elements toward overall meaning and beauty. The thing to do is to get the letter of a poem straight before moving on to other, less obvious meanings. St. Thomas speaks of the several "spiritual" senses of Sacred

LOVE IN SECULAR MANUALS AND POETRY

Scripture presupposing and being based upon the literal sense, though, he adds, in some cases the spiritual is the literal. This, *servatis servandis,* should be true also of our poetry.[19]

Judson Boyce Allen points up the complexities of late medieval literary, as distinct from scriptural, exegesis.[20] He discusses at length the fourteenth-century poet's use of the spiritual sense, whether moral or allegorical, but cautions against searching for it in all the literature of the period. Though a mental set had been created to search out the spiritual or tropological in the Bible and in the classics of antiquity, this did not oblige the poet to place such meaning in his poem. At any rate, writes Allen, "we must never forget the letter. In a sense, the claim of the exegetes that the Bible was spiritually meaningful because it was literally true must be respected ... as the basis for our valuation of the letter of any text which is said to have a spiritual sense, whether fiction or not." For Allen, then, a given poem may have a meaning beyond the literal story or character or description, but these may also be of worth, in and for themselves as well as vehicles for the spiritual message. Thus Allen challenges D. W. Robertson. He quotes Robertson's treatment of Chaucer's *Miller's Tale* as not being "the reality of an individual, nor even that of a type; it is the harsh reality of discord nourished on gluttony, vainglory, and avarice ...."[21] Allen agrees that this may be some of the meaning of the *Miller's Tale,* but he says, "to discover it is to discover the man as well, and his realism is no rival of his possible significance either as moral example, figura, or myth."[22]

But we are not proceeding here as literary critics trying to measure and appreciate the poetry in and for itself. We will simply try to see its letter—though in ample context and with sensitivity to what spirit seems to break through it—in relation to the Church of the time, and hope that in addition to clarifying this relationship, our findings will also be of some help in future aesthetic analyses and evaluations of the poetry.

CHAPTER 9

CHAUCER'S CRAFT OF LOVE

> Bitwixen hem was mad anon the bond
> That highte matrimoigne or mariage,
> By al the conceil and the baronage.
> And thus with alle blisse and melodye
> Hath Palamon ywedded Emelye.
> And God, that al this wyde world hath wroght,
> Sende hym his love that hath it deere aboght...
>
> Chaucer, *The Knight's Tale*, I, 3094-3100

There are three large segments of the writings of Geoffrey Chaucer (c. 1342-1400) in which ecclesiastical doctrine of love and marriage is explicitly and prominently featured: *The Wife of Bath* (*Prologue* and *Tale*), *The Merchant's Tale*, and *The Parson's Tale*.[1] Here we find that Chaucer in addition to knowing the fundamentals of his Church's teaching on marriage was also familiar with some of the detailed and specialized theology on the subject. But underlying much of the remainder of his writing is an understanding and appreciation of loving in general and conjugal love in particular that accords well with the contemporary ecclesiastical teaching as outlined in our previous chapters. We will consider first this more implicit and generalized appreciation, and then we will be able to gauge more accurately the specifically theological presentations of Wife, Merchant, and Parson.

Since George Kittredge's famous article there have been debates about the "marriage debate" in the *Canterbury Tales*. But few who have disagreed with Kittredge on the precise nature and extent of the debate have failed to recognize Chaucer's preoccupation with the subject of marriage. The *Wife of Bath's Prologue* and the tales of *Merchant* and *Parson* are also evidence enough that Chaucer's interest had a theological bent. Jiro Takimoto, some seventy years later, and in view of many diverse opinions, found Kittredge's fundamental thesis to require little if any

THE CRAFT OF LOVE

revision. Donald Howard sees the marriage debate as a reflection of Chaucer's inner struggle following the death of his wife Philippa. In trying to decide whether or not he should remarry, Chaucer weighs the pros and cons of marriage and writes them into the Tales.[2]

George Kittredge argued that in the *Franklin's Tale* we have Chaucer's own solution to the marriage debate:

> It was the regular theory of the Middle Ages that the highest type of chivalric love was incompatible with marriage, since marriage brings in mastery, and mastery and love cannot abide together. This view the *Franklin's Tale* boldly challenges. Love can be consistent with marriage, he declares. Indeed, without love (and perfect gentle love) marriage is sure to be a failure. The difficulty about mastery vanishes when mutual love and forbearance are made the guiding principles of the relation between husband and wife.[3]

Donald Howard opts in favor of the *Wife of Bath* as holding Chaucer's final evaluation:

> what the tale shows about her fantasy is its uncertainty: she wants to dominate and she wants to submit. She wants her husband to obey her, but then she wants to obey and please. This may express Chaucer's idea—a man's idea—of what women really want: they want it both ways... And of course it expresses something about human nature itself—we all want to demand our way as we did when we were little children, and at the same time want to be passive, nurtured, and cared for. It may express au fond Chaucer's own confusion about his own desires..., his desire to remarry or remain single.[4]

A METAPHYSICAL VIEW OF LOVE

As in the great *summae* and theological commentaries of the age, so in Chaucer's "enditynges" human sexual love is seen as part of a much larger love created by God, reflective of him, and forever moving toward him. Love, sexual or otherwise, may in Chaucer's vision become ingrown and isolated, but then it is depicted as dark and sad and sinister. Our poet's two major romances—*Palamon and Arcite* and the

CHAUCER'S CRAFT OF LOVE

Troilus—are clear instances of his cosmic view of love. Chaucer was early recognized as, as his contemporary, Thomas Usk, referred to him, a "noble philosophical poete," whose "mater" William Caxton noted in the fifteenth century "is ful of hye and quycke sentence." Chaucer's *weltansicht* has since often been noted and described.[5]

Palamon and Arcite as later incorporated into *The Canterbury Tales* (as *The Knight's Tale*), was provided with the broad and sweeping setting of a Christian pilgrimage moving, as toward its ultimate term, to "Jerusalem celestial": but even within itself the cosmic element is dominant. It is the godlike Theseus who, as a kind of providence, brings lovers and beloved into one place, arbitrates between them, and in the end effects the proper union. And at the climactic moment of marriage he proclaims the "First Mover" and his "fair chain of love," but also the "boundes" or laws imposed on every individual thing. Each thing is itself with its proper limitations, but it is also part of the whole, derived from it and at home only within it:

> Thanne may men by this ordre wel discerne
> That thilke Moevere stable is and eterne.
> Wel may men knowe, but it be a fool,
> That every part dirryveth from his hool;   (its whole)
> For nature hath nat taken his bigynnyng
> Of no partie or cantel of a thyng,   (portion)
> But of a thyng that parfit is and stable
> Descendynge so til it be corrumpable.   (corruptible)
>   (3003-10)

For Judson Boyce Allen the ultimate goal of the pilgrimage is not the shrine in Canterbury but "a banquet in Harry Bailey's public house."[6] True enough! And so the Tales are regarded not as a divine but a human comedy. Still, the pilgrimage in point of fact does aim toward and ends with Canterbury and the Parson's reminder of the Celestial Jerusalem as our final end. The human comedy is none the less so for also being divine.

At the end of the *Troilus* Chaucer's metaphysical view of love again emerges. This time as he, together with his hero, is so absorbed in the

THE CRAFT OF LOVE

source of love, that the part of love that is specifically human, is along with the rest of the world, almost totally lost from sight:

> In hevene and helle, in erthe and salte see
> Is felt thi [Love's] myght, if that I wel descerne;
> As man, brid, best, fissh, herbe, and grene tree
> Thee fele in tymes with vapour eterne. (feel) (effluence)
> God loveth, and to love wol nought werne; (deny)
> And in this world no lyves creature (living)
> Withouten love is worth, or may endure.
>
> (III, 8-14)

In the *Troilus* God and his chain of love are likewise celebrated, once again as the poem to a union of lovers; and we are made to feel keenly the power of, and universal need for love:

> And down from thennes faste he gan avyse (began) (view)
> This litel spot of erthe, that with the se
> Embraced is, and fully gan despise
> This wrecched world, and held al vanite
> To respect of the pleyn felicite (in regard to)
> That is in hevene above.
>
> (V, 1814-19)

R. A. Pratt notes (after W. C. Curry) how, "in paraphrasing the *Teseida* [of Boccaccio], Chaucer discarded ancient mythological machinery and substituted as motivating forces Boethian destiny and the planetary influences of medieval astrology." Pratt also notes the similarities and differences between Arcite's death in Boccaccio and that of Troilus in Chaucer. Both go toward the eighth heaven and are alloted a place by Mercury, and both laugh; but it is only Chaucer who goes on to bring in Dante and the Christian perspective.[7]

This same sweep upwards, from concentration upon sexual love to sight of the universe as a whole, is also found in Chaucer's House of Fame. It is the high-soaring eagle who snatches "Geffrey" up and away from the desert precincts of the temple of Venus, wherein he had viewed sad tales of love, and carries him into the heavens. This is the beginning, says the eagle, of Chaucer's "recompense" for having written so much and so faithfully of love. The journey is to the house of the goddess Fame where he is to receive further "tidings" of "Love's folk." But in flight love is all but forgotten. The earth with all that is in and upon it appears as it did to Troilus's "light ghost," also looking down upon it from on high: a minute affair, a "prick" scarcely visible; and the poet is directed to look upwards:

> "Now," quod he thoo, "cast up thyn ye.　　(then) (eye)
> Se yonder, loo, the Galaxie...
>
> 　　　　　　　　　　　　　　　　　　(935-936)

Once arrived at Fame's house, and afterwards at the house of Rumor, the poet is made aware of tidings "As well of love as other things" (1739), and more, much more of other things than of love:

> Of werres, of pes, of mariages,　　　　　(peace)
> Of reste, of labour, of viages,　　　　　(voyages)
> Of abood, of deeth, of lyf,　　　　　　　(home)
> Of love, of hate, acord, of stryf,
> Of loos, of lore, and of wynnynges,　　　(fame)
> Of hele, of seknesse, of bildynges,
> Of faire wyndes, and of tempestes,
> Of qualm of folk, and eke of bestes....　(plague)
>
> 　　　　　　　　　　　　　　　　　　(1961-76)

We have little assurance that were the poem completed it would have returned to "love," at least for long. Chaucer's interest seems to have broken out of any incipient intention (if such there was) to write mainly of love and moved into larger areas of life.

"In the house of tidings and Aventure," writes J. A. W. Bennett, "he [Chaucer] had glimpsed the possibilities of a narrative art that could range far beyond the classical and the courtly; and it had even suggested the ideal vehicle for accommodating a medley of stories false and true: the tale of a journeying company 'Of sondry folk, by aventure yfalle/In felawshipe -- and pilgrimes were they alle.'"[8]

In The Parliament of Fowls human sexual love is the theme but once again it is viewed in the full context of the universe. The poet begins with his astonishment at Love and Love's "wonderful workings," but at once plunges into the story of the dream of Scipio. While in bed he

THE CRAFT OF LOVE

reads how Africanus had appeared to Scipio in sleep, carried him high into a starry region, showed him Carthage and "this earth that is so small/ compared to the heaven's quantity" (57-58), and bade him

>   syn erthe was so lyte, (since)
>   And dissevable and full of harde grace, (deceiving)
>   That he ne shulde hym in the world delyte.

>   (64-66)

The subject of love is reintroduced as Africanus now comes to the poet himself in sleep, and leads him to a park wherein all Love's children sport and play, and where stands the temple of Love's goddess, Venus. Within the temple, "in sovereign place," reigns Priapus, the god (now) of introverted sexual love, while off in a dark corner sits Venus with two solitary lovers kneeling before her; and all about, painted upon the walls, are lovers' histories, all of them failed and sad. Priapus does not seem here to appear as god of "love and fertility at its most natural," as C. McDonald claims he "certainly" does.[9] Chaucer's reference to the story of Priapus and the ass, where the ass' braying awakens the household to Priapus ridiculously exposed in the act of fornication, would more surely have suggested to Chaucer's audience mere lust and lechery.[10]

But once more our poet moves beyond "love": he leaves the dark and stifling confines of the temple and wanders into the broad, open field, "so sweet and green," where the "noble goddess Nature" sits and rules, with all the chirping, singing birds crowded about her, anxious to receive at her bidding their mates. We are still very much with love, for love is Nature's work at the moment. But it is Nature's kind of love: not isolated and hidden, as in the enclosed temple of Venus and Priapus; rather, it is out in the open, in accord with the loves of others, reaching beyond itself and ruled by laws other than its own, that is, by Nature in all her vastness and comprehensiveness:

>   Ne there nas foul that cometh of engendrure (was not)
>   That they ne were prest in here [Nature's] (presence)
>   To take hire dom and yeve hire audyence. (judgment)

>   (306-08)

CHAUCER'S CRAFT OF LOVE

And it is Nature, as ordering and measuring love, who reigns supreme till the end of the poem. Not that Dame Nature stands completely apart from Venus and *her* kind of love (romantic, physical, passionate). For before Nature the noble, "romantic" eagles also stand pleading their cause, and Nature treats them as tolerantly and kindly as the other, more earthy fowls. Also, Love's garden, Venus's temple, and Nature's land are all of a piece. Not one fenced off from the other, but each *shading* into each. It is as though, as one student of the poem has written, the poet wanted to show "that *courtoisie* [romance] is meet and commendable if regarded not as an end in itself but as part of the preparation of Youth for adult life and marriage."[11] Love must not be suffered to turn in upon itself (Priapus, Venus), at least not for long, but rather heed its own dynamism and continually reach out to the other. We are to be led by Venus into the care of Nature and thence, as Chaucer advises at the end of his *Troilus* into the loving arms of God.[12]

In the poetry of Chaucer, then, as evidenced in his great love poems, there is no trace or shadow of Manichaean dualism. As in the theology of the time, sexual love appears as natural and therefore fundamentally good, as an integral part of a vast order of being and of love, and as sanctioned and blessed by a God who "loves and from love will not turn away." But neither is his poetry pantheistic. As clearly as any medieval churchman, Chaucer was aware of the limitations of human love. It was part of and in tune with the one great, all-pervasive Love, but it was not identified with it. It could then fail, and could ultimately not satisfy. Thus the association of love with the vicissitudes of fortune in the *Troilus* and elsewhere in Chaucer's poetry.[13] Thus also the ready recognition that love together with every other creature is "corruptible" while the Creator alone "stable is and eternal" (KnT 3003-10), and the realization that in contrast to the joy of consummated heavenly love which "has no contrariety of woe or grievance" (ParsT 1077), the one "who has to do with love has sorrow more often than the moon has changes" (Mars 234-35). It is this acute awareness of the infinite distance between God and God's world, between divine and human love that sharpens the dramatic tensions in much of Chaucer's poetry, that often sends the poet high into the heavens whence he looks down upon the littleness and brittleness of earthly life and love, and that is explanation enough for his final retractions. Though one

THE CRAFT OF LOVE

may still allow that this awareness was intensified and deeply personalized at the close of his life by a special conversion or crisis of piety, leading him now to occupy himself only with God and, in the words of the Parson that "preface" the retractions, to secure his "salvacioun" by "grace of verray penitence, confessioun and satisfaccioun." Not that this life and human sexual love in themselves are not good and worthwhile and necessary, but that "with regard to the heaven's quantity ... with respect to the full happiness that is in heaven above," and in the prospect of "Jerusalem celestial," this world and all within it must seem "but a fair" and "vanity."

If viewed within this general context, this *weltanschauung*, human sexual love receives high marks, but only as it moves toward and is fulfilled within a true, exclusive, and lasting bond of mutual fidelity—an *obligatio viri ad mulierem determinatam*, as St. Thomas had expressed it, "which makes for marriage." Fornication, infidelity, adultery, wherever they appear in Chaucer's poetry, are severely censured. In *The Parliament of Fowls* Africanus declares that "lecherous folk" together with "breakers of the law" in general, "Shall whirl about the earth in pain,/ Till many a world be passed ..." (78-81). In *Anelida and Arcite* it is clear that Arcite stands condemned because he "was double in love and nothing plain./ And subtle in that craft more than anyone" (8788). Throughout *The Legend of Good Women* in spite of its occasional impish ironic twists, the condemnatory attitude toward adultery and fornication is clear. In the legend of Cleopatra we read how Anthony, in addition to being "Rebel unto the town of Rome," abandoned his wife, the sister of Caesar:

> He lafte hire falsly, or that she was war,   (before)
> And wolde algates han another wyf;   (of course)
> For which he tok with Rome and Cesar stryf.
>
>   (593-95)

Jason, who was "false to two," is more directly and severely castigated:

CHAUCER'S CRAFT OF LOVE

> There othere falsen oon, thow falsest two!
> O, often swore thow that thow woldest dye
> For love, whan thow ne feltest maladye   (sickness)
> Save foul delyt, which that thow callest love!
>
> (1377-80)

In the legend of Lucrece, an equally severe judgment is pronounced against the lustful, adulterous Tarquinius who:

> And caughte to this lady swich desyr   (such)
> That in his herte brende as any fyr   (burned)
> So wodly that his wit was al forgeten...   (madly)
> His blynde lust was al his coveytynge.
>
> (1750-56)

The *House of Fame* also carries its judgment against infidelity together with a sharp warning against surrendering to the mere appearances of love. And though here in Chaucer's source, Virgil's epic, Aeneas is excused because of the demands of his high destiny, in our English poem no such excuse is offered. "All of Chaucer's sympathies, even while he shows her folly, are with Dido; all of Virgil's power goes to vindicate his hero."[14] Chaucer is concerned only with the bond between the man and the woman that was meant to endure. Some of the fault was Dido's: she should have looked more deeply before giving herself in love. But Aeneas in his infidelity was most to blame:

> Allas! what harm doth apparence,
> Whan hit is fals in existence!
> For he to hir a traytour was;
> Wherfore she slow hirseif, allas!
>
> (265-68)

In *The Man of Law's Tale* several times Chaucer exercises his rhetorical skills in denunciation of lust (*luxurie*). The passages denouncing lust are found neither in Trivet's *Chronicle*, Chaucer's primary source, nor in Gower's Constance, of which Chaucer probably made use. His denunciations, as those of the Church, cover not just the foul deed but the "foul affection" as well:

THE CRAFT OF LOVE

> Sathan, that evere us waiteth to bigile,
> Saugh of Custance al hire perfeccioun,
> And caste anon how he myghte quite hir while   (repay her)
> And made a yong knyght that dwelte in that toun
> Love hire so hoote, of foul affeccioun,
> That verraily hym thoughte he sholde spille,   (die)
> But he of hire myghte ones have his wille.   (once)
>
> (582-88)

Providence, as usual in the story, preserves the holy woman and destroys the sinner, but once again Constance is assailed by a lecher, who is also destroyed. And now the teller of the tale must pause to vent his personal indignation:

> O foule lust of luxurie, lo, thyn ende!
> Nat oonly that thou feyntest mannes mynde,   (enfeebles)
> But verraily thou wolt his body shende.   (ruin)
> Th'ende of thy werk, or of thy lustes blynde,   (deed)
> Is compleynyng. Hou many oon may men fynde
> That noght for werk somtyme, but for th'entente
> To doon this synne, been outher slayn or shente!
>
> (925-31)

There is, then, in Chaucer's poetry, an uncompromising negative condemnation of extra-marital or contra-marital sexual love. There is also an abundance of positive appreciation of the love that intends and is fulfilled within marriage. In fact, all of Chaucer's happy loves are conjugal, and there are many of them. *The Knight's Tale* ends in the joyous marriage of Palamon and Emily presided over by god-like Theseus. At the wedding of Constance and Alla in *The Man of Law's Tale*, "They eat, and drink, and dance, and sing, and play," then "They go to bed, as it was right and proper" (707-08). *The Clerk's Tale* is also of a marriage that begins and ends happily, however unhappily it fares in between. *The Franklin's Tale* is of a definitely happy marriage; and in *The Tale of Melibee* we again find husband and wife central; and they are faithfully, piously, and happily married. *The Book of the Duchess* begins with Ovid's tale of Seys and Alcyone who are presented as devoted and loving husband and wife, and it is reasonable to believe that the lamenting knight and his lost duchess who feature in the poem were recognized by Chaucer and his audience as spouses as well as lovers.

In *The Legend of Good Women* it is Alceste, the faithful wife, who appears as the star of the prologue and the ideal of womankind; and she is depicted as walking hand-in-hand with Love. In *The Parliament of Fowls,* a poem of detailed and complex tapestry, the love of what seems to be marriage—the mating of the birds under the inspiration and guidance of Nature toward the "common good" *(commune profyt)* of procreation *(engendrure)*—is presented as right and happy. Certainly it is much more highly esteemed by our poet than are the hot and sighing loves of "lecherous folk" depicted in the closed, dark temple of Venus and the lascivious Priapus.

In regard to *The Book of the Duchess* B. H. Bronson remarks, "Despite the commentators, there is in the poem no overt suggestion that the knight is describing wedded love." But Bronson, along with Kittredge and the other commentators, does not doubt that in fact the Knight was John of Gaunt and the duchess his wife Blanche, and that Chaucer's audience recognized this. His point is simply that in this particular poem the question of marriage "does not and should not arise" since it is a poem presented "within the terms of courtly love" in which "it would have been incongruous to mention marriage."[15] In light of more recent evaluations (and denials) of "courtly love," Bronson's critique here may appear outmoded. Besides, it may be argued that if for Chaucer and his audience there was such an incongruity between marriage and the courtly aspects of love, it would have been unseemly for the poet to have described as "courtly" lovers those who in fact were married, especially in a poem intending to eulogize the dear and virtuous wife and console the bereaved husband.

True, some of Chaucer's poetry,—as the tales of *Miller, Reeve,* and *Merchant*—deals with objectively unhappy and even tragic marital situations. But in such poetry Chaucer is abstracting from the worth of marriage as such; or rather he is capitalizing on its worth and social acceptance in order to create a naughty, shocking, and therefore (given the other necessary ingredients) comical situation. If there is any moral or *enseignement* in these farces and comedy pieces (as there appears to be in *The Merchant's Tale),* it is directed against the given participants in a marriage rather than against marriage itself: old fools who marry young wild things, as in the *Miller's* and *Merchant's* tales, or, as in *The Reeve's Tale*, ridiculously proud and "deynous" parents who would keep their daughter spotless in order "to bestow her high/ Into some worthy blood of ancestry" (3981-82). Neither for Chaucer nor for the Church of his day was marriage automatically good and holy and happy. It was prey to the same corruption and same tragedies that all finite love was subject to; and its worth depended largely on the worth of those involved in it.

The *Troilus* may appear as an exception to the general respect for marriage and consequent distaste for extra-marital sex generally manifest in Chaucer's poetry. For here we have a non-conjugal, secret love fully and blissfully consummated, and, apart from the perhaps anomalous palinode, it would appear to have the poet's approval as well as his sympathy. But there are indications that Chaucer's "moral" intentions may have been otherwise. In *The Legend of Good Women* the poet is accused of having discouraged love *paramours,* for in the *Troilus* (or *Crisseyde,* as it is there entitled) and in his translation of the *Roman de la Rose* he wrote of unfaithful love while ignoring the multitude of "clean maidens... true wives... steadfast widows" (G 282-83). The poet, in the presence of Cupid (love) and Alceste (faithful marriage), replies that whatsoever "my author meant" (i.e. the source of his "translations"), it was his intention to offer the *Roman* and *Troilus* as an example "To further truth in love and the cherishing of it,/ And to be wary of falseness and vice ..." (G 462-63).

The bibliography on the relationship between the *Troilus* and the Christian conception of love is a long one, containing many diverse opinions, suggesting the complexity of the poem or, perhaps, the complexity of the minds of the critics! For the *Troilus,* A. Denomy claims in its "palinode," a rejection of "all human love, licit and illicit, as worldly vanity... in favor of the love of Christ."[16]

But within the poem itself there are reminders that love's proper home is not the secret liaison but marriage. Thus as the love affair begins, the poet suggests its impropriety by protesting that his story is of another time and place and that "each country has its laws." He will have, he says, "neither thanks nor blame of all this work," for he writes only "as my author said" (II, 18). And even within their own country of Troy, according to their own "laws" and "usages," Chaucer's characters seem to be aware that love properly belongs to marriage. Criseyde by her anxiety to keep the affair secret in order to preserve her good name betrays her misgivings about the honesty of her and Troilus's love. Troilus in face of the mounting inevitability of his separation from Criseyde comes to realize that the only way he might lastingly possess his beloved is through what seemingly is meant to be marriage. "For the love of God," he cries:

> if it be may,
> So let us stelen privelich away;
> For evere in oon, as for to lyve in reste,
> Myn herte seyth that it wol be the beste.
>
> (IV, 1600-03)

And Criseyde's dissembling reply may well have been intended by Chaucer to suggest the marriage that should have been: "Mistrust me not without reason, for mercy's sake,/ Since to be true I have plighted my troth." (1609-10).

These phrases—"Forever in one" and "plight my troth"—need not have pointed only to marriage, for they were used, even by Chaucer, in other contexts. But their special prominence in the nuptial liturgy of the day makes it unlikely that in the matter of sexual love they would not have suggested the idea of marriage to Chaucer's audience.

As noted in the liturgy the phrase "plight my trouthe" and "For evere in oon" is the central idea through the whole of the nuptial rite. Chaucer uses the former phrase even in a potentially adulterous situation, as when Aurelius, with adultery in mind, reminds Dorigen that "in myn hand youre trouthe plighten ye/ To love me best" (*FranT*, 1328-29). But he is also aware of its connection with marriage: "For unto Phillis hath he sworen thus,/ To wedden hire, and hire his trouthe plyghte" (*LGW*, 2465-66). Note the use of the phrase relative to marriage in the mid-fifteenth-century poem *The Weddynge of Sir Gawen and Dame Ragnell*, an analogue to the Wife of Bath's Tale: "Arthoure, kyng, lett fetche me Sir Gaweyn.../ That I may nowe be made sekyr,/ In welle and wo Trowethe plyghte vs togeder..." (525-28). Examples might be

THE CRAFT OF LOVE

multiplied. Whatever other uses the phrase may have been put to, certainly in the context of love it would have at least suggested marriage.

At any rate, soon after this final meeting between Troilus and Criseyde the idea of marriage as the only proper fulfillment of love explicitly emerges. Diomede, charmed by the beauty of Criseyde, and "on the make," wonders "why her father tarieth so long/ To wed her to some worthy fellow" (v, 862-63). Criseyde thinks back on her dead husband. Her reply is at once a miniature encomium of conjugal love and the faithful wife, and (indirectly) a sad and pointed commentary on her unwise, illicit affair with Troilus:

> "But as to speke of love, ywis," she seyde,
> "I hadde a lord, to whom I wedded was, till that he deyde;
> And other love, as help me now Pallas,
> Ther in myn herte nys, ne nevere was."   (is not)
>
> (V, 974-78)

Here, our poem seems to imply, is the kind of love that should have been between Troilus and Criseyde: wedded love in which one's whole heart is given exclusively to one's beloved until death, and further if possible. It is against the contrasting background of such "honest love" that the de facto "feigned" love featured in the poem—that which Criseyde's uncle Pandarus, true to his name, had craftily arranged—is viewed. Thus when we reach the poem's final stanzas, the so-called palinode, we are not surprised. We have been prepared for them, however subtly, and we find they are in harmony with the rest of the poem, both in emotion and idea. They simply bring to the surface, though with powerful eloquence, warnings latent in the poem from the beginning—warnings, it is to be noted, not against all sexual love but only against that which the *Troilus* has been directly concerned with: the kind of love, we might say, that has become trapped and enmeshed in the temple of Venus/Priapus. True, at the poem's magnificent ending the "young fresh folk" are advised to "return home from worldly vanity" and fix their hearts "all wholely" on Christ. But in the context of the nuptial liturgy and much of the theology of the time this need not be understood as a recommendation for a life of celibacy. It may have been so taken, but it may just as well have been received by

CHAUCER'S CRAFT OF LOVE

Chaucer's audience as an invitation to the *sacrament* of *conjugal* love, outside of which fornication, or "feynede loves," was deemed an insurmountable temptation for the great majority of Christians (and so marriage as *vitatio fornicationis, remedium concupiscentiae,* as we have seen), and within which a man and woman precisely by being intimately, lovingly faithful to one another were regarded as mirroring and achieving the love of Christ (marriage as *sacramentum*). Laying their hearts wholly on each other they were, as our poem's conclusion would have it, laying them wholly upon Christ.

CHAUCER'S CONJUGAL UNION

The conjugal union is a prominent aspect of Chaucer's poetry. It can be seen that this union bears all the essential features required or sanctioned of the sacramental union by contemporary ecclesiastical teaching.

1. Marriage is a product of love and freedom

Chaucer's marriages are not bargained for or dictated by parents or guardians; rather are they formed by the free choice of the couple involved according as their "heart is set" (PF 627). So in *The Knight's Tale,* though Theseus uses his powers of persuasion to draw Palamon and Emily together in marriage, he does not force the marriage. He offers Emily reasons why she should *choose* Palamon, why of her "grace" she should "take pity on him/ And take him for husband and for lord" (3080-81); and to Palamon, so eager for his beloved, he says simply: "I believe there is little need of sermoning/ To make you *assent* to this thing" (3091-92). In *The Clerk's Tale* the great Marquis tells his people that if he is to marry he himself will choose his bride, and choose her, it is emphasized, of his own free will:

> Wherfore of my free wyl I wole assente
> To wedde me, as soone as evere I may...
>
> (150-51)
>
> Lat me allone in chesynge of my wyf,
> That charge upon my bak I wole endure.
>
> (162-63)

THE CRAFT OF LOVE

The Marquis then asks Griselda's father for his daughter's hand, but he recognizes that the decision is Griselda's own:

> For I wol axe if it hire wille be
> To be my wyf, and reule hire after me.
>
> (323-27)

The Franklin's Tale tells us that for love of Dorigan, Arveragus wrought "many a labor, many a great venture" before finally she:

> Hath swich a pitee caught of his penaunce   (such)
> That pryvely she fil of his accord
> To take hym for hir housbonde and hir lord.
>
> (740-42)

The knight in *The Book of the Duchess* having finally proved to the duchess his love for her receives "The noble gift of her mercy" (1270). And in *The Parliament of Fowls* liberty of choice in matters of love and mating is so strongly stressed that it may be regarded as a major point of "doctrine" in that "philosophical poem" of love and marriage.[17]

2. Marriage endures in love

In the ring and dowry ceremony of the Sarum nuptial liturgy in Chaucer's day, there was the reminder that the love between husband and wife must be "always new" (*dilectio... semper... recens*). This belief and these very words appear as the Black Knight reveals his promise to the duchess that he would "love her always fresshly new" (BD 1228); and, having been accepted by her, he kept his promise for "full many a year," even to the death of his beloved. In this same poem the conjugal love between King Seys and his Queen Alcione, which foreshadows the love between the knight and the duchess, is presented as tender, deep, and enduring. When, because of his death, Seys fails to return to his wife,

> She longed so after the king
> That, certes, it were a pitous thing
> To telle her hertely sorowful lif
> That she had, this noble wif,
> For him she loved alderbest.   (best of all)

CHAUCER'S CRAFT OF LOVE

(83-87)

And when her husband's death is finally confirmed, she dies upon the spot from excess of grief. The marriage of Palamon and Emily, we are told, having been formed in liberty of love, endures in love to the very end: they live together "in bliss, in luxury, and in health," and "Thus endeth Palamon and Emelye" (3102, 3107). The same is true of the marriage of Dorigan and Arveragus: it begins in a love *peramours,* continues "in bliss and in joy" for "a year and more," survives a severe trial, and continues on in bliss and love "for evermore." The marriage between Alla and Constance, begun so happily, is, through no fault of husband and wife, ruptured for *a time,* but when Alla finally recovers "his holy wife so sweet" there is joy in love once again:

> I trowe an hundred tymes been they kist,
> And swich a blisse is ther bitwix hem two
> Ther is noon lyk that any creature
> Hath seyn or shal, whil that the world may dure.　　(seen)
>
> (MLT 1074-78)

3. Marriage is also a matter of justice

Marriage is an unbreakable bond, it gives husband and wife strict rights over one another, and it is a social as well as private affair. Thus there is the sense of a social formal contractual element in the love marriage of Palamon and Emily:

> Bitwixen hem was maad anon the bond
> That highte matrimoigne or mariage,　　(is called)
> By al the conseil and the baronage.
>
> (3094-96)

There is the subtle interplay between love and justice suggested in the marriage of Arveragus and Dorigan, with no diminution of love implied:

THE CRAFT OF LOVE

> Here may men seen an humble, wys accord;   (wise)
> Thus hath she take hir servant and hir lord,—
> Servant in love, and lord in mariage.
> Thanne was he bothe in lordshipe and servage.   (service)
> Servage? nay, but in lordshipe above,   (all the more)
> Sith he hath both his lady and his love;   (since)
> His lady, certes, and his wyf also,
> The which that lawe of love acordeth to.
>
> (791-98)

As we have seen, infidelity and adultery, both instances of injustice, are fiercely condemned wherever they are found. Even the great Aeneas is considered to have sinned against justice as well as love. To Dido he "swore so deep... to be true,/ For well or wo, and change her for no one new" (LGW 1234-35), and she "took him for husband, and became his wife/ For evermore, while that they had life" (1238-39). It is for having violated this bond of *justice* that Aeneas stands condemned: not simply because he "Is weary of his craft [love] so soon," but because in spite of the fact that he "has so deeply sworn" he will nevertheless from his "wife thus foully flee" (1286, 1285, 1307).

Even the conjugal act is viewed as a matter of justice as well as love—a reflection of the ecclesiastical doctrine of the *redditio debiti*—husband and wife have the *right* to one another's body. So Dorigan replies to the ardent Aurelius who would seduce her that a man should not "love another man's wife,/ That hath her body whenever it pleases him" (V, 1005). In one poem. Dido, having given herself to Aeneas in what the poet seems to regard as a marriage, is said to "let him do/ All that belongs to marriage" (HF 243-44); and in another poem "She hath her body and also her realm given/ Into his hand" (LGW 1281-82). Even the virtuous Constance, along with other "holy" wives, is duty bound to cooperate in her husband's sexual love:

> For thogh that wyves be ful hooly thynges,
> They moste take in pacience at nyght
> Swiche manere necessaries as been plesynges
> To folk that han ywedded hem with rynges ...
>
> (MLT 709-12)

CHAUCER'S CRAFT OF LOVE

4. Marriage intends a union of bodies

Besides the passages just cited there are other instances in Chaucer's poetry of the innocent and spontaneous attibution to "weddynge" of the sexual fulfillment which "longeth too" it. In *The Legend of Good Women* Cleopatra loves Anthony, and the poet makes a long story short (as usual) by saying simply: "She became his wife, and had him as she pleased" (615). In the same poem we read of Jason and Medea:

> That Jason shal hire wedde, as trewe knight ...
>
> And hereupon at nyght they mette in-fere,   (together)
> And doth his oth, and goth with hire to bedde.
>
> (1636-44)

And of Demophon and Phillis:

> For unto Phillis hath he sworen thus,
> To wedden hire, and hire his trouthe plyghte,
> And piked of hire al the good he myghte...
> And doth with Phillis what so that hym leste.   (desired)
>
> (2465-69)

True, these are portraits of false lovers of innocent women, but the falseness is considered to have resided not in the sexual embrace but in the infidelity to that embrace. So of Jason it is said: "as a traitor he is from her *gone*/And with her left his two young children" (1656-57).

This union of bodies that is proper to marriage is, as in the contemporary ecclesiastical teaching, directed ultimately to procreation (*engendrure*). The immediate purpose of love is to unite the lovers in personal union, but this union is to be a fertile one, moving beyond itself into the common good. Thus as the springtime of natural fertility, when Flora and Zephirus—"They two that make flowers grow"—cover the earth with "many flowers" (BD 400), stirs our poet to a joy that overleaps the conventional, so the winter, "with his sword of cold," causes a sadness that is genuine. In *The House of Fame* the time is "Of December the tenth day,/ When it was night" (111-12), and this bleak, melancholy setting is in accord with the kind of love the poet is about to consider: ruptured love of self-interest and self-indulgence

THE CRAFT OF LOVE

which precludes fertility. As the poet emerges from the mournful temple of Venus in which he saw portrayed the false love of Aeneas for Dido and bethought himself of other false lovers such as Demophon, Achilles, and Paris, his vision is of a sterile desert in which there is nothing "That is formed by Nature" (490). In *The Parliament of Fowls* there is a complex background of contrasts between fertile and sterile love. There is Africanus's exhortation to Scipio to be "well-moraled" and to love the "common good," to avoid lechery and keep the law (47, 78-79). There are the two gates before the garden, Love's park: through the one "men go unto the well of grace. There green and lusty May shall ever endure," while through the other men go:

> Unto the mortal strokes of the spere
> Of which Disdayn and Daunger is the gyde,
> Ther nevere tre shal fruyt ne leves bere.
>
> (129-37)

Again, in the *Parliament,* there is the near blatant contrast between the somber temple of Venus/Priapus with its tales of woeful broken loves and the gay blossoming garden of Nature. And while Venus sits in a "private corner" of her temple in almost total darkness, Dame Nature, who conducts the mating of birds toward "engendrure," is enthroned in full and joyous light "upon a hill of flowers" (302-308).

In The Knight's Tale there is the likelihood that the marriage of Palamon and Emily, though presented mainly as a personal union, is to be a fertile one. Nothing, says Theseus, in his speech which introduces the marriage, is eternal, except God, but "species of all things and natural processes/ Shall continue by succession" (iv, 3013-14), i.e. by procreation. But Emily herself, unwittingly, had long since prognosticated her double role within marriage: "to be a wife and be with child" (iii, 2310). And in Chaucer's other great romance—even there where the tale is of a private, introverted affair—we find that our poet when he thought of marriage must likewise think of children, however silent his "source" may have been concerning them. With reference to Criseyde's first marriage he observes: "whether that she children had or no,/ I read it not, therefore I let it go" (i, 132-33). Other instances of love's fertility abound. Alla and Constance after their wedding go to bed and "On her he got a male child anon" (MLT 715).

CHAUCER'S CRAFT OF LOVE

Walter is begged by his people to "take a wife" lest his "lineage should fail" (CIT 135-37), and "Not long time" after his marriage with Griselda "she a daughter hath borne," and later a male child too. The very first line of Chaucer's "own" tale (Melibee) on the way to Canterbury is of procreation: "a young man called Melibeus ... bigot upon his wife, who was called Prudence, a daughter who was called Sophie." And the poet's manifest, unconventional tenderness toward children who appear in his poems—Griselda's children, those of Ugolino (MkT), the "little clergeon, seven years of age" of *The Prioress's Tale*—is added confirmation of his respect for the procreative dimension of human sexual love.[18]

But however significant in the Chaucerian "philosophy" procreation is, more important still is the personal relationship between husband and wife. As in the liturgy and theology of the time, this is what is in the foreground of Chacuer's poetry. So in the marriage of Palamon and Emily, as in the whole of *The Knight's Tale,* our attention is directed almost exclusively to the romance of love and to the "Living in bliss, in comfort, and in health" of husband and wife, with the natural fruitfulness of marriage simply by way of promise or suggestion. In *The Franklin's Tale* the poet is silent concerning "engendrure"; all his interest is in the romantic, faithful love of husband and wife. The same is true of the double love story in *The Book of the Duchess.* Only the love of Seys and Alcyone and that between the Knight and his Lady are explicitly considered, with no mention of offspring. Both in Ovid and Gower, Seys and Alcyone, transformed after death into birds, joyously propagate their kind. Chaucer, for the purpose of his elegy, ends the story with the sad death of bereaved Alcyone. But he does not neglect to remind his readers that there is more to the narrative than he has time to tell: "But what she sayede more in that swow/ I may not telle yow as now;/ Hyt were to longe for to dwelle..." (215-17).

And perhaps the clearest expression of the superiority of the personal relationship between husband and wife over the procreative purpose of love lies in that Job-like response of Griselda to her husband after he has threatened to separate her from her child. As much as she loved her daughter, she apparently loved her husband more:

THE CRAFT OF LOVE

> Ther may no thyng, God so my soule save,
> Liken to yow that may displese me;   (pleasing)
> Ne I desire no thyng for to have,
> Ne drede for to leese, save oonly yee.
> This wyl is in myn herte, and ay shal be;
> Ne lengthe of tyme or deeth may this deface,
> Ne chaunge my corage to another place.   (heart)
> (CT 505-11)

5. Marriage intends a union of hearts

Physical sexual love, whether in its procreative intention or as personal fulfillment of husband and wife, is by no means the dominant in the Chaucerian perspective. The main purpose of marriage is rather to secure a union of hearts, of spirits. In *The House of Fame* the warning is sounded against love-unions for superficial reasons, for "looks, or speech, or for friendly manner," because "There may be under seeming goodness/ Covered many a wicked vice" (274-78). In other words, not physical appearance and the delight in it, but spiritual and moral virtue must be the ground of marriage. In harmony with some of the theology of the day, Chaucer evidently agreed that beauty may be a legitimate consideration for marriage, but it ought to be far from primary. One must wait, love must be tested, and mere passion must grow into a fineness of courtesy, tenderness, and "gentilesse" (nobility). So Palamon and Arcite are in love with Emily for many a year before marriage even becomes a possibility for them. Arcite even as he lies dying, though he has never physically possessed Emily and realizes he never shall, loves her to the end. Palamon must wait still longer. "By process and by length of certain years" the mourning for Arcite was brought to term, and only then was Palamon's desire fulfilled; and in the resulting marriage "Emily him loveth so tenderly,/ And he her serveth all so gently." It is worth noting that in Boccaccio's *Teseida*, of which Chaucer's poem is a "translation", only several days transpire between the death of Arcite and the wedding of Palamon and Emile.

Arveragus endured "many a labor, many a great trial" before he won his lady, and it was only "for his worthiness\ And namely for his meek obedience" that she "at last" accepted him for her spouse (FranT 732-

42). And in that marriage also all was "gentilesse," patience in love, and mutual obedience and service. The Black Knight loved his fair and virtuous lady for a long time before he even ventured to tell her of his love, and when "at the last" he did tell her, she said "no," and he had to wait still another year; till finally:

> ... she wel understood
> That I ne wilned thyng but god, (good)
> And worship, and to kepe hir name honor)
> Over alle thynges, and drede hir shame (fear for)
> And was so besy hyr to serve...
>
> (BD 1261-65)

And this love union too continues in virtue and courtesy until the beloved dies.

The finest expression in Chaucer's poetry of the need for love to be grounded in moral virtue and reason rather than in beauty, riches, pleasure, etc. comes unexpectedly and from an unexpected source, thus emphasizing the truth all the more. With little if any reason that may be found in the poem, at least on its surface, Criseyde on the eve of her departure and the beginning of her "treason" says to her lover:

> For trusteth wel, that youre estat roial,
> Ne veyn delit, nor only worthinesse (vain)
> Of yow in werre or torney marcial,
> Ne pompe, array, nobleye, or ek richesse (also
> Ne made me to rewe on youre destresse; (take pity)
> But moral vertu, grounded upon trouthe,
> That was the cause I first hadde on yow routhe! (mercy)
> Eke gentil herte and manhod that ye hadde,
> And that ye hadde, as me thoughte, in despit
> Every thyng that souned into badde,
> As rudenesse and poeplissh appetit, (vulgar)
> And that youre resoun bridlede youre delit;
> This made, aboven every creature,
> That I was youre, and shal while I may dure.
>
> (IV, 1667-80)

THE CRAFT OF LOVE

In the parallel passage in Chaucer's source, Boccaccio's *Il Filostrato*, which is spoken by Troilus rather than Criseyde, no mention is made of "moral virtue grounded upon truth" nor of "reason bridling delight," but only of "proud and noble bearing," of "high worth and courtly speech," of "manners more courteous than those of other ladies, and thy charming womanly scorn."[19] The former are Chaucer's additions, and they are significant. Our English poet continually moves beyond the pagan and the merely courtly to the contemporary Christian view of the universe and of love.

6. Marriage must be built upon equality and mutual sovereignty

We have seen that in the later medieval theology and nuptial liturgy husband and wife emerged as equals, with the husband, however, still holding a position of lordship or authority—not a tyrannical lordship, which was condemned, but one that was to be exercised in love. Here is yet another ecclesiastical prescription that Chaucer, in his ever charming, original manner, repeats and elucidates. It is expressed most clearly and forcefully, as though Chaucer himself were now priest and sermonizer, in *The Franklin's Tale*. In the Franklin's own comment on the happy marriage of Arveragus and Dorigan the ideas of liberty, love, and equality are presented as correlatives. You can't have one without the other.

> For o thyng, sires, saufly dar I seye,
> That freendes everych oother moot obeye,   (must)
> If they wol longe holden compaignye.
> Love wol not been constreyned by maistrye...
>
> Love is a thyng as any spirit free.
> Wommen, of kynde, desiren libertee,   (by nature)
> And nat to been constreyned as a thral;
> And so doon men, if I sooth seyen shal
>
> (761-70)

"Friends must obey each other." Here again are the very words of the nuptial liturgy—*"uterque alteri obnoxius"*—and the theologian's doctrine of the *"mutuum obsequium."* But the added ecclesiastical insistence—the husband's lordship—likewise appears. Each year, on Maundy Thursday, the faithful of Chaucer's day would have heard

CHAUCER'S CRAFT OF LOVE

Christ's words: "If I washed your feet, I who am teacher and lord, then you must wash each other's feet"; and would have recalled Christ's other similar declaration: "The princes of the gentiles lord it over them, but I have been among you as one who serves." So Arveragus would keep the name of lord in the marriage but he would be "Servant in love" (793). He promised his wife that he:

> Ne sholde upon hym take no maistrie
> Agayn hir wyl, ne kithe hire jalousie, (show)
> But hire obeye, and folwe hir wyl in al,
> As any lovere to his lady shal, Save that the name of soveraynetee,
> That wolde he have for shame of his degree. (honor)
> (747-52)

Yet in a desperate situation he could make effective use of "the name of sovereignty" and command his wife "on pain of death" to do his will. But that, he conceived, was for her good and "For very love which that I have for you" (1475-83). The equality was there at the root of the marriage, but essential to it was the *twin* sovereignty: the social, domestic authority of the husband which the wife was to obey, and the authority of the wife requiring the husband's service in love.

The same doctrine, though much less detailed, appears in *The Knight's Tale*. Theseus asks Emily to take Palamon "for husband and for lord" (3081). Here is recognition of the man's domestic authority in marriage. But again it is an authority that is to be exercised in love and service and that respects the basic, balanced equality in the conjugal relationship:

> And Emelye hym loveth so tendrely,
> And he hire serveth al so gentilly,
> That nevere was ther no word hem bitwene
> Of jalousie or any oother teene. (vexation)
> (3103-06)

In *The Book of the Duchess* the woman's sovereignty in love is stressed almost to the exclusion of the corresponding male authority—perhaps because this poem, after all, is an elegy on the death of the beloved and so it is her ideal beauty, virtue, and power that must be extolled. But

THE CRAFT OF LOVE

the equality demanded in a perfect love spontaneously emerges, as the Knight recalls their "marriage":

> Oure hertes wern so evene a payre,   (pair)
> That never nas that oon contrayre   (one)
> To that other, for no woo.
> For sothe, ylyche they suffred thoo'   (alike) (then)
> Oo blysse, and eke oo sorwe bothe;   (one)
> Ylyche they were bothe glad and wrothe;
> Al was us oon, withoute were.
>
> (1289-95)

And the fact of the male authority is not altogether forgotten even in this delicate eulogy of so beautiful a woman. It is quietly insinuated in and through the introductory tale of Queen Alcyone and her "lord" and "love," King Seys, who even in death knew how to gently but firmly command his wife:

> My swete wyf,
> Awake! let be your sorwful lyf!
> For in your sorwe there lyth no red.   (is no cure)
> For certes, swete, I nam but ded.   (am not)
>
> (201-4)

True, there appears in some of Chaucer's poetry a male sovereignty in marriage that is devoid of love and service, but the unhappy situations that it gives rise to are evidence enough that it in no way stands approved. It is out of her misery at the prospect of her "arranged" marriage that Constance cries: "Women are born to thraldom and penance,/ And to be under man's governance" (MLT 286-87). And it is in this same context that the *Man of Law* makes his ironic thrust at the domineering husband: "Husbands be all good, and have always been;/ That know wives; I dare say you no more" (272-73). In *The Clerk's Tale* Walter lords it over his much too patient wife but, we are given to understand, wrongfully. The Clerk himself must several times pause in his narrative to express his disapproval:

> But as for me, I seye that yvele it sit
> To assaye a wyf whan that it is no nede,   (test)
> And putten hire in angwyssh and in drede.

CHAUCER'S CRAFT OF LOVE

(460-62)

> O nedelees was she tempted in assay!　　　(trial)
> But wedded men ne knowe no mesure,
> Whan that they fynde a pacient creature.

(621-23)

And in a passage original with Chaucer over and above his source,[20] Griseld too must rebuke her husband and recall to his mind the kind of lordship he seemed initially to have promised:

> O goode God! how gentil and how kynde
> Ye semed by youre speche and youre visage
> The day that waked was oure mariage!
> But sooth is seyd --algate I fynde it trewe,　　(and)
> For in effect it preeved is on me—　　　　　　(proved)
> Love is noght oold as when that it is newe.

(852-57)

These are sad stories and sad realities our poet seems to be saying. But what is or may be does not alter what ought to be. And for the Church as well as for Chaucer the poet, as he apparently understood it, marriage ought to be grounded upon liberty and equality, and a love of mutual respect and service.

THE WIFE OF BATH

What Dame Alison, Januarius (and Merchant) in *The Merchant's Tale*, and the Parson say about marriage must be read in the context of their distinctive characters and aims. For whereas in some of the *Canterbury Tales*, narrative is of greater interest than the narrator, here interest is focused at least as much upon the character as upon his or her narration, and one of the main purposes of the latter is to delineate more closely and vividly the character in question. Thus if we are to discover the authentic ecclesiastical doctrine of love and marriage from which Chaucer seems to have drawn for the purposes of these particular narratives, we must disentangle it from the alterations it undergoes by reason of the individual characters expressing it. By so doing we will be able to form some idea of the Church's doctrine as it was explicitly known by Chaucer, and to judge its relevance to the

THE CRAFT OF LOVE

philosophy of love and marriage at work within his poetry. Let us begin, as she herself would demand (!), with the *Wife of Bath*.

The description of the Wife in the *General Prologue* to the *Tales* underscores her indomitable drive to master every situation and person:

> In al the parisshe wif ne was ther noon
> That to the offrynge bifore hire sholde goon;
> And if ther dide, certeyn so wrooth was she,
> That she was out of alle charitee.
>
> (449-52)

Her face, Chaucer tells us, was "bold", and she could "easily" ride her horse. In her own prologue she herself tells of a life dedicated to domination over men, and her tale exemplifies her personal history.

But her masculine drives are seasoned and softened by a gay sense of humor: she knows how to laugh and to laugh at herself. She does not want to be taken too seriously nor is she taken seriously either by Chaucer or the other pilgrims. Chaucer says of her that "in fellowship well could she laugh and joke" (GP 474). She herself asks the pilgrims not to be offended by what she says but to allow for her "fantasye," for "my intent is only to play" (WBT 192). At the end of her long preamble we read that "The Friar laughed, when he had heard all this" (829), and at the completion of her tale he congratulates her on having "said much thing right well" with respect to "school-matter" of "great difficulty." However, he thinks that she should "leave authorities ... To preaching and to the clergy's schools" (1270-77). We are thus given to understand that though there is some theological truth in what the Wife says, she is no professional theologian ("authority"), and her "theology" is to be viewed in light of her whimsical imagination and need for fun.

However, though the Wife may be loose in her morals she is not the heretic some suppose her to be.[21] Nor has she personally violated the sacrament of marriage, as has been claimed by D. W. Robertson. Each of her five marriages, as we are told in both the General Prologue and in her own, was blessed by the Church, and, as we have seen, both the medieval theology and liturgy provided for remarriages no matter how many times the party in question had been widowed.[22]

The "school-matter" of the *The Wife of Bath's Tale* prologue is the theology of marriage, which she applies to her personal conjugal history. Allowing for her deliberate exaggerations in the cause of "play" and the distortions due to her "likerous" (lustful) appetite, domineering temper, and her "fantasy," we find in her narration elements of genuine ecclesiastical teaching fully compatible with the philosophy of love found elsewhere in Chaucer's poetry.

1. Sexual love is not all

Though it certainly seems to be so for the Wife personally, she herself recognizes that "everyone hath of God a proper gift" (103). She even grants that the state of virginity, providing it be dedicated ("with devocion"—recall St. Thomas's *"pia" virginitas*), is a higher, more noble state than that in which sexual love finds fulfillment (95-106). She also concedes that except for virginity men would lose all care for chastity (138), as though she were aware that, as the Church taught, part of the vocation of the celibate was, simply by being such, to remind humankind of deeper and higher reaches of love.

2. Marriage is a vocation

But love, if it be fulfilled within the marriage bond, is still good, and very good. It is sanctioned by God, as is evident from the Scriptures, which the Wife duly quotes, and is blessed before the church door; and this same sanction and blessing obtains whether the marriage be the first, second, or, as in the case of the Wife's own history, the fifth, providing one's former spouse "is gone from the world" (47). Marriage in fact is recognized as something of a religious vocation, an "estaat" to which God calls us and in which we are to persevere (147-48); it is seen as a "proper gift" by which husband and wife may "do their Lord service" (101-3).

3. The marriage act is part of the goodness of marriage

The marriage act shares in the lawfulness and goodness of marriage itself. The command to "increase and multiply" is from God; the

THE CRAFT OF LOVE

Apostle bids a man "to yield his wife her debt"; and man and woman are *naturally* endowed for the act of "procreation." The Wife argues against her supposed adversary that the genitals are not only for purgation. The adversary in question would seem to be St. Jerome in his *Adversus Jovinianum*.[23] But here Jerome does not argue that the only use of the genitalia is for purgation and the distinction of the sexes but that apart from their sexual function they have these other uses which are reason enough for their being. Jerome is defending virginity, not condemning marriage. The Wife certainly exaggerates the intentions of the *redditio debiti*:

> Myn housbonde shal it have bothe eve and morwe,
> Whan that hym list come forth and paye his dette.
> An housbonde I wol have—I wol nat lette — (deny)
> Which shal be bothe my dettour and my thral,
> And have his tribulacion withal
> Upon his flessh, whil that I am his wyf.
>
> (152-57)

Neither does Chaucer's more sober writing (as *The Franklin's Tale* and *The Parson's Tale*), nor the Church's teaching, suggest self-indulgence or the enslavement of one's spouse, but, on the contrary, a generous giving, a true *redditio*, of one to the other. But the basic drift of the Wife's argument rings true in terms of contemporary belief and suggests what may have been the historic fact: the *redditio debiti* encouraged rather than discouraged conjugal love-making and served to fully exonerate the intimacies of husband and wife even apart from any further intention for procreation.

4. Sexual love can be evil

The Wife takes lechery, especially her own, lightly enough, but she does realize, however sadly, that it is wrong: "Allas! Allas! that ever love was sin..." And it is clear from the immediate context in which she utters her cry of regret the kind of love she had in mind:

> For God so wys be my savacioun, (certainly)
> I ne loved nevere by no discrecioun,
> But evere folwede myn appétit ...

CHAUCER'S CRAFT OF LOVE

(614-23)

Appetite with no discretion—the opposite of the virtue Criseyde claimed she had found in Troilus: reason bridling delight. It is the "blind lust," the "foul lust of lechery" so frequently castigated in Chaucer's poetry generally, and the "pleasure alone" (*cola delectatio*) condemned also by the Church and tolerated as venial sin only when the intention remains within the marriage bond.

5. Marriage is a state of mutual surrender

It is by way of contrast that the doctrine of conjugal equality and mutual sovereignty is suggested. The Wife's ambition for "governance of house and land," for mastery of her husband—"his tongue, and of his hand also" (813-15)—is plainly not being proposed as an ideal. It is an anomaly, a part of the comedy and the major part. But it suggests the belief in light of which the Wife's conduct may be judged anomalous and enjoyed as comic, and which, as we have seen, appears elsewhere in Chaucer's poetry, namely that marriage is not to be a power-game, an affair of "mastery," but a state of mutual love and worship and surrender—much, in fact, as is the marriage at the end of the Wife's tale in which the husband surrendered to his wife and she in turn "obeyed him in everything" (1255).

In *The Weddynge of Sir Gawen and Dame Ragnell* the same wifely obedience is promised following the husband's surrender: "Whilles that I lyue I shal be obaysaunt,/ To God aboue I shalle itt warraunt,/ And neuere withe you debate" (784-86). And Gawain answers: "My loue shalle she haue,/ Therafter nede she neuere more craue,/ For she hathe bene to me so kynde" (790-92). And note in this poem the clear indication, and appreciation of the marriage *debitum* as a matter of both love and justice: "A, Sir Gawen, syn I haue you wed,/ Shewe me your cortesy in bed,/ Withe ryghte itt may nott be denyed" (629-31). And finally there is, as at the conclusion of the Wife's tale, the innocent happiness husband and wife enjoy in bed:

THE CRAFT OF LOVE

> He made myrthe alle in her boure,
> And thankyd of alle oure Sauyoure,
> I telle you, in certeyn.
> Withe joye and myrthe they wakyd tylle daye,
> And than wold ryse that fayre maye.
> "Ye shalle nott," Sir Gawen sayd,
> "We wole lye and slepe tylle pryme..."
>
> (712-18)[24]

THE MERCHANT'S TALE

In *The Merchant's Tale* ecclesiastical doctrine on marriage is even more explicit and detailed than in the *Wife of Bath's* narrative. But here, too, it is artfully exaggerated and distorted to fit and illustrate the character in question, this time two characters: the cynical Merchant and the lecherous Januarius. There is a fusing of the two characters in the tale. The Merchant's paean on marriage is probably an ironic expression of his own cynical attitude toward marriage, but it is likewise meant to be the blissful exaggeration prompted by the lustful hopes of the lecherous Januarius.[25] "I have a wife, the worst that may be" (1218), bemoans the Merchant, and of the "hero" of his tale, Januarius, he observes:

> ... sixty yeer a wyfless man was hee,
> And folwed ay his bodily delyt
> On wommen, ther as was his appetyt.
>
> (1248-50)

If, then, we are to view in their pristine form the elements of ecclesiastical doctrine that Chaucer knew and apparently respected, and altered toward the making of his *sententia*, we must abstract from the cynicism and lechery that brood over our present tale. In doing so, we find, in summary:

1. Marriage is recognized as being good and holy

The Merchant says he does not know whether it was "for holiness or for dotage" that Januarius finally decided to marry (1253). He speaks of marriage as "that holy bond/ With which that first God man and woman bound" (1261-62). It is "a full great sacrament" (1319), "so virtuous,/ And so commended and approved also" (1348-49); and Januarius will marry "To live his life in ease and holiness" (1628). We may even catch an echo of the thirteenth-century and fourteenth-century preaching on marriage as a kind of religious order in Januarius's apostrophe: "O blissful order of precious wedlock" (1347). Whatever the irony here—and there is an abundance of it—such belief about marriage was apparently "in the air" and so Chaucer was able to draw upon it and, by way of contrast, accentuate the evil in its violation.

2. Marriage is a union in body and affection

Marriage is likewise presented, on ecclesiastical authority, as a state of most intimate union in love: a union in body and in affection. And we are reminded of St. Paul's admonition to husbands to love their wives as their very selves. Husband and wife, says Januarius:

> moste nedes lyve in unitee.
> O flessh they been, and o flessh, as I gesse,   (one)
> Hath but oon herte, in wel and in distresse.
>
> (1334-36)
>
> Love wel thy wyf, as Crist loved his chirche.
> If thou lovest thyself, thou lovest thy wyf;
> No man hateth his flessh, but in his lyf
> He fostreth it, and therfore bidde I thee,
> Cherisse thy wyf, or thou shalt nevere thee.   (thrive)
>
> (1384-88)

3. The reasons a man should marry

Januarius claims that he knows "For what causes man should take a wife," and he lists them:

THE CRAFT OF LOVE

> If he ne may lyven chaast his lyf,
> Take hym a wyf with greet devocioun,
> By cause of leveful procreacioun
> Of children, to th'onour of God above,
> And nat oonly for paramour or love;
> And for they sholde leccherye eschue,
> And yelde hir dette whan that it is due;
> Or for that ech of hem sholde helpen oother
> In meschief, as a suster shal the brother;
> And lyve in chastitee ful holily.
>
> (1446-55)

Almost the whole of the Church's teaching on the motivation for marriage is here in summary:

1. Marriage is to be undertaken "with great devotion," because, as the Church taught and Chaucer with his character(s) recognized, it is a "full great sacrament" (1319).

2. Marriage is not to be "only for paramour or love," that is, as the theologians warned, not only for self-gratification or pleasure (the apparent meaning of "love" in this context, as with the Wife of Bath above), but also for the "common profit," as in The *Parliament of Fowls,* that is for society and the Kingdom of God through "lawful procreation."

3. Marriage also requires the mutual surrender or *redditio* of the "debt" of the body.

4. Marriage is a safeguard against the sin of fornication, a *remedium concupiscentiae* whereby husband and wife "eschew lechery."

5. Within marriage there must be a *mutuum obsequium:* husband and wife are not to lord it over each other but are "to help each other."

6. Marriage might also be lived "in chastity full holy," in continence, as Januarius apparently means here; for in the following line he staunchly affirms that such marriage is not for him! The Church did bless celibate marriages—for such was the marriage of Mary and Joseph—providing, of course, *both* spouses agreed thereto.[26]

CHAUCER'S CRAFT OF LOVE

Some of Januarius's terminology is not that of the theologian (for example, "love" or "paramour" for *delectatio* or pleasure), but his statement may be seen to be accurate and complete in terms of the theology he set out to summarize. And it is a statement that is quite compatible, *mutatis mutandis,* with the love doctrine that appears elsewhere in Chaucer's canon.

4. Sin in the marriage act

As to the possibility of sin in the act of marriage, two views are expressed in the tale. Both uphold the fundamental goodness of the act, but one with qualification, the other without. For Januarius, as we might expect, conjugal love-making can never be sinful. On his wedding night he assures his bride:

> It is no fors how longe we pleye; (matter)
> In trewe wedlock coupled be we tweye; (two)
> And blessed be the yok that we been inne,
> For in our actes we mowe do no synne.
> A man may do no synne with his wyf,
> Ne hurte hymselven with his owene knyf;
> For we han leve to pleye us by the lawe. (leave)
> (1835-41)

The Parson in his tale will claim differently; for him a man may assuredly harm himself with his own wife. But we need not wait for his sermoning to learn the limitations of Januarius's theology, for as much is said in the present tale. Justinus, much more sober about marriage than Januarius, and more accurate in his theology, offers the following counsel to his old and doting friend:

> I hope to God, herafter shul ye knowe
> That ther nys no so greet felicitee
> In mariage, ne nevere mo shal bee,
> That yow shal lette of youre savacion, (keep from)
> So that ye use, as skile is and reson,
> The lustes of youre wyf attemprely,
> And that ye plese hire nat to amorously,
> And that ye kepe yow eek from oother synne.

THE CRAFT OF LOVE

(1674-81)

The Wife of Bath had loved "by no discretion." Januarius is warned here against such loving: he is advised rather to be "reasonable" and "temperate" in his love for his wife. He may please her amorously, but not *too* amorously. The theological dictum—*ardentior amator propriae uxoris*—is clearly recognizable and is explicated. As with the theology, not the man who loves his wife *very* much, but who loves her *too* much, that is from passion and pleasure alone, with no regard for her proper person and good. It is evident into which category Januarius falls. He is isolated in his own private lust; he does not love his wife, but only himself. He is, in short, a prize concrete illustration of the *ardentior amator* of the traditional theology, and seems to be deliberately offered by Chaucer as such.

5. The nuptial rite

In the present tale Chaucer, in addition to proving his near-professional knowledge of the formal theology of marriage, also manifests an easy familiarity with the nuptial rite. Cynicism, of course, colors the description of Januarius's wedding, for it is the Merchant, gravely disappointed in his own recent marriage, and not Chaucer, who is the immediate narrator of the story. We must also understand that this particular wedding, grossly motivated as it is, is in fact sacrilegious. But the ceremonies are there, briefly, mockingly summarized. The Merchant, referring generally to the various blessings of the wedding ritual and particularly to the climactic moment of the nuptial blessing itself wherein the virtues of the holy wives of the Old Testament are recalled, almost laments:

CHAUCER'S CRAFT OF LOVE

> But finally ycomen is the day
> That to the chirche bothe be they went
> For to receyve the hooly sacrement.
> Forth comth the preest, with stole aboute his nekke,
> And bad hire be lyk Sarra and Rebekke
> In wysdom and in trouthe of mariage;
> And seyde his orisons, as is usage,
> And croucheth hem, and bad God sholde hem blesse,
> And made al siker ynogh with hoolynesse.   (sure)
> Thus been they wedded with solempnitee...
>
> (1700-9)

Even the blessing of the bridal bed is mentioned and, as provided in the contemporary Sarum ritual, bride and groom seem to be within the bed as the priest imparts the blessing:

> The bryde was broght abedde as stille as stoon;
> And whan the bed was with the preest yblessed,
> Out of the chambre hath every wight hym dressed;   (left)
> And Januarie hath faste in armes take
> His fresshe May, his paradys, his make.   (mate)
>
> (1818-22)

6. Marrying for lust

The end that Januarius's marriage comes to is comment enough on the worth of his kind of marriage. If there is a moral to the tale, it is not against marriage as such, but against the particular kind of marriage wherein an old man marries a young maid, and marries her only for "blind lust." Such a moral is in full accord with the teaching of Chaucer's contemporary Church. Marriage, said the theology, may be secondarily motivated by considerations of beauty, pleasure, familial peace, and so on, but the primary motivation must run deeper, and must be grounded in a love that looks to the other and to the common good as well as to oneself. And as Peraldus had advised, marriage should be between equals—in beauty, riches, nobility, and certainly in age. What a fine and welcome *exemplum* for the preacher of the time would Chaucer's *Merchant's Tale* have been!

THE CRAFT OF LOVE

THE PARSON'S TALE

We might imagine that in the Parson's presentation of the ecclesiastical doctrine of love and marriage we should find what Chaucer considered to be an exact formulation of that doctrine uncolored by any bias of character. It is the Parson, after all, who is given the final word, not just on the question of marriage, but in the whole of the pilgrimage. We are about to enter the holy city of Canterbury, our journey's end; It is a solemn moment and a serious one. If we are to have the truth, therefore, it would be at this juncture. Further, the Parson is introduced in the *General Prologue* as an ideal priest, both good and learned. What he says, therefore, must have been intended to be the truth precisely as the Church proclaimed it.

But there are indications within the Tales and within the Parson's lecture itself that here again Chaucer proposed to present a particular point of view toward a particular end, true and good enough in substance perhaps, but not the whole truth in complete objectivity. Thus our high esteem for the Parson is slightly threatened when we encounter him in the epilogue to *The Man of Law's Tale*. Here he is accused by the Host and Shipman of Lollardry, a Wycliffite reform heresy strict and stern in belief and practice. And though in fact the accusation may tell more against his accusers than himself—for all he did was ask the Host to stop swearing—still we are put on guard: perhaps the Parson is too religious, too good and holy. At least we are aware that Chaucer, in the persons of Host and Shipman, recognized the possibility of an excess in religion. But even granting the Parson's complete orthodoxy, still his presentation of ecclesiastical doctrine seems to be an intentionally qualified one. The Parson himself tells his companion pilgrims that the meditation he is about to present he would put "always under correction/ Of clerks, for I am no theologian" (55-7). He takes "but the sentence" and *insists* that he "will stand to correction" (58-60). Further, at the beginning of his sermon he states that "Many be the ways spiritual that lead folk to our Lord Jesus Christ, and to the reign of glory" (79). He himself will speak of one way, that of Penitence. Our good priest, then, (and Chaucer with him) will have us understand at the start:

CHAUCER'S CRAFT OF LOVE

1. That though what he is about to say should be substantially true, we may find alterations and embellishments which may not accord with the exact truth;

2. That only one aspect or phase of Christian living is to be treated; and

3. That this aspect is the "full noble" but largely negative one of penance.

We are not, therefore, to read *The Parson's Tale* as a perfect representation of Chaucer's idea of the ecclesiastical teaching of his time. That teaching Chaucer evidently recognized to be broader and brighter than the Parson's particularized expression of it. The Parson would speak only of "Morality and virtuous matter" (38). But that is the Parson, not the Church as a whole as Chaucer apparently knew it; and certainly it is not Chaucer himself! Other members of the Church might have other more immediate interests and less severe intentions and still achieve "the reign of glory." But let us see what the Parson in the general context of his theme has to say specifically about our subject.

The Parson first mentions marriage when discussing venial sins that people generally neglect to confess, such as drinking more than the sustenance of the body requires, speaking more than is needful, failing to harken to the needs of the poor, etc. Among the examples given is that of the man who "useth his wife, without sovereign desire of procreation to the honor of God or for the intent to yield to his wife the debt of his body" (375).

The second "oblique" reference to the marital relationship occurs in the discussion of the sin of wrath. Here the Parson speaks of contraception and abortion as deadly sins of homicide; the "unkyndely" (unnatural) act of intercourse is also viewed as a type of homicide. It is likewise homicide when "a man approacheth to a woman by desire of lechery, through which the child is killed, or else strikes a woman witingly, through which she loseth her child" (579).

But marriage receives its direct and full treatment in the Parson's discussion of the sin of *luxuria* or lust. Lust is viewed as a sin that militates against marriage, and marriage is presented as a remedy against lust. Speaking of lust generally, the Parson repeats God's commands against it and cites the terrible punishments inflicted because of it in the Old Law. He then turns specifically to "that stinking sin of Lecherie that men call adultery of wedded folk" (840). Adultery, he argues, is wrong because the violation of the sacrament of marriage is "a horrible thing," since marriage is so great a sacrament betokening "the knitting together of Christ and holy church" (842-43).

He describes the "five fingers" of lust. The first is the foul looking, the second the villainous touching, the third is the foul words, the fourth is the kissing, and the fifth is "the stinking-deed" itself" (852-62). As if recalling the loose theology of both Januarius and the Wife of Bath, the Parson interjects into this discussion reference to the possibility of sin even when the sexual embrace is conjugal:

> As for that many men weneth that he may nat synne, for no likerousnesse [lust] that he dooth with his wyf, certes, that opinion is fals. God woot, a man may sleen hymself with his owene knyf, and make hymselve dronken of his owene tonne [barrel]... Man sholde loven hys wyf by discrecioun, paciently and atemprely; and thanne is she as though it were his suster. (859-61).

He then takes a closer look at the sin of adultery and enumerates the harms that proceed from it. First, adultery involves the breaking of faith, "and certes, in faith is the key of Christendom"; secondly, it is a sin of theft, for by it a woman steals her body from her husband and her soul from Christ, gives the former to a lecher and the latter to the devil; thirdly, it befouls the author of matrimony who is Christ; finally, the harm of adultery is like to that of homicide, "for it carves in two and breaks in two them that first were made one flesh" (875-88). And again we are reminded of the besotted Januarius as the Parson declares that adultery is "somtime between a man and his wife:"

> and that is whan they take no reward [regard] in hire assemblynge but oonly to hire flesshly delit, as seith Seint Jerome,/ and ne rekken of nothyng but that they been assembled; by cause that they been maried, al is good ynough, as thynketh to hem./ But in swich folk hath the devel power ... for in hire assemblynge they putten Jhesu Crist out of hire herte, and yeven hemself to alle ordure [filth] (905-6).

CHAUCER'S CRAFT OF LOVE

The Parson becomes more positive as he leaves the sin of lechery and considers its remedy, which "is generally chastity and continence" (915-48). He notes the traditional threefold division of chastity, that of the married, of widows, and of virgins, without, however, comparing or ranking them in the traditional hierarchy of good, better, best. Most attention is given to the chastity of marriage. The Parson begins by repeating his praise of it: it is a full great sacrament, was made by God himself in Paradise and was himself born of it, and He hallowed it at Cana where He worked his first miracle. The effects of marriage, he says, are that it "clenseth fornication... replenisheth holy church... changeth deadly sin into venial sin... and maketh the hearts all one of them that be wedded, as well as bodies" (920). He lists the reasons for monogamous marriage: peace between the spouses and sureness of one's offspring. A third reason is a switch on one that St. Thomas had given. Thomas had argued for monogamy because in it, as opposed to polygamy, the woman is more intensely loved: being his only wife she has all of her husband's love. The Parson thinks in terms of polyandry but, strangely, concludes that the wife "should be the less beloved from the time that she were conjoined to many men" (924). Whatever obscurity may be in his reasoning here, his intention, like that of St. Thomas, is to secure the most love possible for the wife.

He next treats of the conduct of husband and wife toward each other. The husband is to hold his wife "in sufferance and reverence," as is illustrated in the creation of Eve. Here the Parson repeats the traditional rib symbolism, but, charmingly, alters it in obvious reference to our domineering Wife of Bath. God, he says,

> he made hire [Eve] nat of the heved of Adam, for she sholde nat clayme to greet lordshipe./ For ther as the woman hath maistrie, she maketh to muche desray. Ther neden none ensamples of this; the experience of day to day oghte suffise. Also, certes, God ne made nat womman of the foot of Adam, for she ne sholde nat been holden to lowe; for she kan nat paciently suffre. But God made womman of the ryb of Adam, for womman sholde be felawe unto man (926-27).

Further:

THE CRAFT OF LOVE

> Man sholde bere hym to his wyf in feith, in trouthe, and in love, as seith Seint Paul, that a man sholde loven his wyf as Crist loved hooly chirche, that loved it so wel that he deyde for it. So sholde a man for his wyf, if it were nede (928).

The wife in turn is to be obedient to her husband, for she is under his authority. She should desire to serve him "in all honesty." She should strive to please him, though not by "fancy dress"; and

> aboven alle worldly thyng, she sholde loven hire housbonde with al hire herte, and to hym be trewe of hir body./ So sholde an housbonde eek be to his wyf. For sith that al the body is the housbondes, so sholde hire herte been ... (937-38).

The Parson concludes his little tract on marriage with a statement on the morality of the conjugal act. Husband and wife, he says, "flesshly might assemble" for three reasons:

> The firste is in entente of engendrure of children to the service of God; for certes that is the cause final of matrimoyne./ Another cause is to yelden everich of hem to oother the dette of hire bodies; for neother of hem hath power of his owene body. The thridde is for to eschewe leccherye and vileynye (939-40).

Intercourse for the first motive is meritorious, "the second also, for, as sayth the decree [canon], that she hath merit of chastity that yieldeth to her husband the debt of her body, ye, though it be against her liking and the desire of her heart." Intercourse for the third motive is venial sin, and, the Parson adds, "truely, scarcely may there any of these be without venial sin, for the corruption and for the delight" (941-42). This last smacks of the severity (and Lollardry) that the Host may have sensed in the Parson, for certainly such a surmise is not to be found in the greater orthodox theologians of the day. But note that the Parson does not suggest that every conjugal act may be a sin, but that scarcely may any be without sin. Perhaps the Parson had something of Scotus's thinking in mind, who as we have seen, held that even though there may be venial sin in a marital act this does not destroy the goodness and merit of that act, since venial sin neither takes away grace nor prevents its further influx.

CHAUCER'S CRAFT OF LOVE

The Parson notes a fourth motive, but this renders conjugal intercourse deadly sin. It is when husband and wife "assemble only for amorous love and for none of the foresaid causes, but for to accomplish that burning delight, they reckon never how often. Truely, it is deadly sin; and yet, with sorrow, some folk will trouble themselves more to do than to their appetite suffiseth" (943). Here also the Parson is stricter than the theology we have treated. Our theologians distinguished where the Parson does not. For them, to seek pleasure alone with one's spouse was only venially sinful providing one's desires were contained within the marriage bond. It was mortal sin only when one sought and experienced such solitary pleasure with one's wife while prepared to do the same with any woman.

No single ecclesiastical source has been uncovered for *The Parson's Tale,* and though several parts of the "tale" and its general form and style appear to be original with Chaucer, the teaching therein on marriage as on other matters seems to be a faithful expression of current theological doctrine, with modifications as suggested, due to the Parson's character and his somber and sobering theme of penitence.[27] And although the theme is such, and interest is not just in moral goodness but perfection, there is still alotted to marriage, and love and sex within marriage, a high and noble place. Even as they approach "Jerusalem celestial," of which Canterbury Cathedral is the symbol, and so are required to purify themselves to the hidden depths of their spirit, husband and wife are not to surrender their love and love-making. On the contrary, they are to be all the more loving and faithful to each other, to be truly "all one." This is further evidence for what has been argued above when discussing the palinode of the *Troilus,* namely that conjugal love was not among the "feigned loves" that our poet would have young folk avoid that they might fix their hearts "all wholly" on Christ; and it suggests Chaucer's awareness that his Church, even in its stricter moments, held the love of the married to be among the good and perfect things of life.

CHAPTER 10

GOWER'S CONFESSION OF A LOVER

So mikel love was hem bitwene	(much) (them)
That all the werd spak of hem two,	(world)
He lovede hir and she him so	
That neither other mighte be	
Fro other ne no joye see	(nor)
But-yif he were togidere bothe;	(But if)
Nevere yete no weren he wrothe	(angry)
For here love was ay newe...	(their) (ever new)
He geten children hem bitwene	(they)
Sons and doughtres right fivetene...[1]	

Havelok the Dane (c. 1300) 2962-71

Like Chaucer, his contemporary and friend John Gower (c. 1330-1408) was recognized in his time as a love poet, celebrating love in many a "rondeal, balade, and virelai." But his muse reached into other corners of human experience as well, both political and private. His major works are three long, very long poems, one in Latin *(Vox Clamantis)*, one in French *(Mirour de l'omme)*, and the other in his native English but with a Latin title, *Confessio Amantis*. According to Gower's own notation found in most manuscripts of the *Confessio Amantis*, the *Vox Clamantis* exposes the grave social and moral corruption that he personally witnessed during the reign of Richard II. The same notation refers to the *Mirour de l'omme* (also entitled *Speculum Meditantis* and *Speculum Mominis*) as treating the vices and virtues with the intention of leading the sinner back to God. The *Confessio Amantis*, written c. 1390, was his last and, reputedly, greatest poem. It is an anthology of stories or *exempla* charmingly framed by the confession of a failed lover to Genius, who is the Priest of Love.[2]

THE CRAFT OF LOVE

Whatever Gower's principal intent was in shaping the *Confessio,* he was certainly preoccupied with the matter of human sexual love and concerned to establish it within the scope and context of the entire universe.[3] So the poem begins and ends with the larger love that looks to the whole of society, and seeks the "common good" (Prol., 377) or "social justice" (VIII, 3023) and results in "peace between the lands" (Prol., 189). Often throughout the poem we are borne up into the "high God" (V, 1), the "high almighty providence" (Prol., 585), the "mighty god, who has no beginning/ Exists of himself and hath begun/ All other things at will" (VIII, 1-3); or we are reminded of a profound Christian mystery such as the "high almighty Trinity" (VII, 77) or the "great sin original" (VI, 1). All of Book VII, which stands near the end of our lover's confession and the beginning of the shift, is a discourse on education that touches on all things from the unseen mysteries of theology and philosophy to the visible functionings of "man, of beast, of herb, of stone ... of liver, of lung, of gall, of spleen" (139, 465). The confession itself is concerned with a lover's sins, but by no means just that. Genius, the priest of Venus and the lover's confessor, has wider interests than "love" alone. He is concerned about virtue and vice in general and claims a fuller priesthood than one circumscribed by the goddess of love:

> That thogh I toward Venus were, (for)
> Yit spak I suche wordes there,
> That for the Presthod which I have,
> Min ordre and min astat to save,
> I seide I wolde of myn office
> To vertu more than to vice
> Encline, and teche thee mi lore.
>
> (VIII, 2077-83)

The sins examined and illustrated are truly the seven capital sins and their various species as they emerge from and affect not just love but all of life, private and political, and the lover's sins are treated as real—not mock—instances of these. We have, therefore, in the *Confessio Amantis,* a presentation of human sexual love, but not as closed in on itself, a garden of delight shut off from the rest of the world, nor even as the most important thing in the world; but as part of the world, continuous with it, and opening out into it.

Sexual love is further viewed in the *Confessio Amantis* as an instance of both the love of "kind" (natural love) and, in a less explicit way, of "charity." In the Latin prologue to Book I, as also in the gloss to the first sixty lines, we read that the subject of the argument is to be *Naturatus amor* (natural love); the poem is to treat "of that love by which [to which?—*a quo*] not only human kind but also all animals are subject [*subiciuntur*]." And in the poet's "englissh" his intention to speak of *amor naturalis* is manifest:

> Fro this day forth I thenke change
> And speke of thing is noght so strange,
> Which every kinde hath upon honde,   (nature)
> And wherupon the world mot stonde,   (must)
> And hath don sithen it began,
> And schal whil ther is any man;
> And that is love, of which I mene
> To trete, as after schal be serve.
>
> (I, 9-16)

This love "which is according to nature" (V, 119) must in the human animal, whose "kind" is rational, be "in harmony with reason" (VII, 4564). When it is not, then it is "wode" or "rage," that is, madness, and ought not to be called love. Love is common to all, but the one who acts immoderately and in excess is not to be considered a lover *(non reputatur amans)* (VIII, Latin vs. ii). But when reason does guide and direct our natural instinct to love, the love is then true and "honeste," that is, morally sound and commendable.

St. Thomas uses the term *honestas* to designate one of the "integral" parts of the virtue of temperance: "*honestas*, through which one loves the beauty of temperance."[4] He also argues that the "honest" and the "virtuous" converge: "Honor is due to excellence. However, one's excellence is considered mainly in terms of virtue ... And therefore, properly speaking, the honest and the virtuous refer to the same thing."[5]

THE CRAFT OF LOVE

Such honest sexual love is never referred to explicitly as *caritas*. That title, appearing only in the prologue and epilogue, is reserved for the love that has to do *directly* with God and the service of humankind at large, which is the *caritas eliciens* of the professional theologian's vocabulary. Thus it is when Gower discusses clergy or religious—those dedicated by profession to God, world peace, and the poor—that he speaks explicitly of charity: such people, for instance, are not to go to war, for their work is "To make peace between the kings/ After the law of charity" (Prol., 256-7), and "of charity" they are to feed and clothe the poor (466-7); and they are to:

> ... praie and to procure
> Oure pes toward the hevene above,
> And ek to sette reste and love
> Among ous on this erthe hiere.   (us)
> For if they wroughte in this manere
> Aftir the reule of charite,
> I hope that men schuldyn se
> This lond amende.
>
> (VIII, 2995-3005)

And it is as our poet turns from "love," fingering his "black beads" in prayer for universal peace that he thinks specifically on

> ... thilke love which that is
> Withinne a mannes herte affirmed
> And stant of charite confermed...
>
> (VIII, 3162-64)

But Gower's conception of *caritas* is wider than his restricted use of the word. As we have seen, the later medieval theology was aware of a *caritas imperans* as well as *eliciens* charity, that is, that commanded other virtues, brought them into its service, sharing with them its proper dignity and merit. *Caritas eliciens* is the virtue of charity itself, which is the direct love of God and the love of others for the sake of God (*Propter Deum*). *Caritas imperans* is this love as the ultimate motivation of virtuous activity that has more immediate and particularized goals. Whether or not Gower had explicit knowledge of this teaching, he seems at least to have appreciated its *sens*, as in the last passage quoted where love is said to be "confirmed" by charity. In the *Confessio Amantis* all virtue, both public and private, is portrayed as working toward the common weal. Each class, in an ordered hierarchy, and each individual within a class, is conceived as having a proper function for the good of all. John Fisher says,

> Patristic authority and all medieval political theory supported the notion of a hierarchy of ranks and orders... What distinguishes Gower's views from those of many of his contemporaries, and places him among the progressive thinkers of his day, is his emphasis upon legal justice and regal responsibility for all the estates, defined in terms of 'le bien commune,' 'bonus communi,' or 'the comun good,' depending on the language in which he happened to be writing.[6]

Every virtuous act, therefore, is subsumed under the virtue of love, or charity that looks directly to the common good, universal peace, and to the ultimate source of these, the "High God." Here is "Love's orderly estate" (*Prol*, 148). Whatever individual, particularized form or forms love might take, it can and should be grounded upon, strengthened by, charity, the intended "imperating" force of all our loves.

That specifically sexual love is regarded in the *Confessio Amantis* as one kind of love that can and should be subsumed under charity need not be labored. Such love can, as we shall presently see, be "honeste," that is, virtuous; therefore, as any virtue, it can be strengthened and directed by charity. So in the epilogue where, as in the prologue, the larger love of charity is clearly evidenced, the king is counselled to "ammend himself/ Toward his god and leave vice" (VIII, 3070-1). But in the body of the poem one of the vices he is warned against is that of lechery. He is not asked to surrender desire, but to:

> ... tempre and reule of such mesure,
> Which be to kinde sufficant
> And ek to reson acordant,
> So that the lustes ignorance
> Be cause of no misgovernance.

(VII, 4562-6)

THE CRAFT OF LOVE

The king's measured or reasonable sexual desire is seen as relevant to his governance that is to his particular work of charity. But it is not the chastity, and so the charity, of only those in high places that is the concern of this particular section of the poem, for the story of the humble Sara and Tobias is also narrated, in which the latter's chaste love is contrasted with the lechery of Sara's first seven husbands (VII, 5344-63). Plainly, it was in the poet's mind that anyone's sexual love, if it be "according to reason," is a matter of charity as well as of the virtue more immediately involved.

But is there not at the commencement of the body of the poem an avowed turning away from the larger perspectives of charity—politics, religion, world peace, etc—in order to treat of human sexual love, the love that is "not so strange [remote, distant]?"

> I may nought strecche up to hevene
> Min hand, ne setten al in evene   (right)
> This world, which evere is in balance:
> It stant nought in my sufficance
> So grete thinges to compasse...
>
> Fro this day forth I thenke change
> And speke of thing is noght so strange...
> And that is love...
>
> (I, 1-15)

And at the poem's ending, the poet seems purposely to be abandoning this lesser love and returning to the claims of charity: he is about to "make a plain release of love" and "pray hereafter for peace" (VIII, 2912-14). It may seem then that the two loves are perceived as disjointed rather than harmonized. A close scrutiny of the poem, however, reveals otherwise. At the beginning of Book I the poet does not at all signal that he is turning from charity. He simply admits his inability directly to reform the socio-political world: his powers are too slender to compass these things "so great and high." But, as he indicates at the end of the prologue, he can still pray to Christ for the good and peace of the world (1090 ff); and, as J. Fisher observes, he will throughout the poem remain sharply aware of the commonweal, God, king, and government, though he will see them in and through personal amorous love.⁷

As for the poem's ending, as just noted there is here no blanket rejection of amorous love in favor of charity, but simply the plea that whatever love there may be should be grounded and confirmed in charity. If the poet himself will no longer have anything to do with sexual love, it is because, in the words of J. A. W. Bennett, he is now too old for it: "Bide" has caught up with him and at last he realizes it; he is in "the last stage of life, when man no longer has dues to pay to 'Kinde'."⁸

And, indeed, it is at the end of the poem that its unified conception of love is most forcefully brought home. Penetrating into the tradition of the good and celestial Venus Gower seems to move beyond her. *His* Venus points and directs to herself, but also to Nature, to Reason, and then to Charity itself in the formal sense of *caritas eliciens*. This goddess of love who stands "without law" introduces herself to the poet as she "who only my desires [lusts] seeks" (VIII, 2399). She is, then, instinctive love, mere appetite that wants fulfillment and satisfaction. But she would be subject to Nature who, she says, "is under the Moon/ Mistress of every living thing" (2330), and she will accept into her court nothing "but thing which is to nature due" (2348). She has a reverence for "reason" too, and for "charity" in its non-sexual manifestations. Thus she will grant the old would-be lover remedy, but:

> Noght al per chance as ye it wolden,   (would)
> Bot so as ye be reson scholden,   (should)
> Accordant unto loves kinde.   (nature)
>
> (VIII, 2369-71)

She begrudgingly admits that not all need to love. True, Nature is universal mistress, and so the urge to follow natural instinct and so to love and beget is universal. Still she may find "Some holy man that will withdraw/ His natural desires from her law." (2333). And there are some who *ought* not to love and, concludes Venus, the old hoary-headed poet kneeling before her is one of them. Finally, it is Venus herself who brings the poet back to the theme of charity and peace with which he began his poem:

THE CRAFT OF LOVE

> Bot my will is that thou besieche
> And preie hierafter for the pes,
> And that thou make a plein reles   (release)
> Of love, which takth litel hiede   (heed)
> Of olde men upon the nede,   (in need)
> Whan that the lustes ben aweie: (sexual prowess)
> Forthi to thee nys bot o weie,   (one)
> In which let reson be thi guide.
>
> (VIII, 2912-19)

St. Thomas, as we have seen, argued that every desire, every movement of love, is a real beginning *(inchoatio)* of one's total perfection, which is to be found in God; and in the *Summa of Brother Alexander* carnal love was seen to be good in itself while at the same time being a preparation for a still higher love. Is there not something of this same doctrine underlying and informing Gower's poem? Ideally, Venus, Nature, Reason, Charity all move in the same direction toward the one final goal, "the mighty god," who "hath begun/ All other things at will," and who is the source of universal peace. Venus, though she may begin the process, can, and sometimes should, be surrendered; but if so she is no less worthy for that. There is no end without a beginning, no high and great things without first bending toward that which is "not so strange." And carnal love itself has its own ways of bringing one to the realization that he or she is no longer in need of it and may be the better off without it.

Gower's conception of love as expressed in the *Confessio,* is not dichotomous. The same unbroken chain of love that appears in the poetry of Gower's friend and fellow poet is at work here. But, again as in the poetry of Chaucer, there is the sober recognition that love—human sexual love—can go awry. At the very beginning when Gower declares his intention to write of *Naturatus amor* a warning note is sounded:

GOWER'S CONFESSION OF A LOVER

> For loves lawe is out of reule,
> That of tomoche or of tolite
> Weinyh is every man to wyte,   (aware)
> And natheles ther is noman
> In al this world so wys, that can
> Of love tempre the mesure,   (observe)
> But as it faith in aventure.   (happens by chance)
>   (I, 18-24)

Yes, no one is so wise as to be able to love in proper measure, unless it is by chance. And throughout the poem we are given example after example of the various ways in which love can be "too much" or "too little." But as the excesses and defects of love are considered, there emerges a clear picture of the measure, or mean, of proper love and where it is to be found. As noted above, human sexual love is viewed in the poem as "honeste," or virtuous, when it is subject to both the law of nature and of reason. Time and again this truth emerges. It receives precise formulation in Genius's comment upon the story of Sara and Tobias:

> For God the lawes hath assissed   (appointed)
> Als wel to reson as to kinde,   (as)
> Bot he the bestes wolde binde   (beasts)
> Only to lawes of nature,
> But to the mannes creature
> God yaf him reson forth withal,
> Wherof that he nature schal
> Upon the causes modefie,   (with reason)
> That he schal do no lecherie,
> And yit he schal hise lustes have
> So ben the lawes bothe save
> And every thing put out of sclandre.   (disrepute)
>   (VII, 5372-83)

This twofold subjection—to "Kinde," or nature, and to reason—is considered to be realizable only in marriage. So every tale in the poem of a love that seeks fulfillment outside or against the marriage bond is an unhappy, tragic tale, and the love therein is openly condemned as "unreasonable," "madness," "blindness," or "folly." In the tale of

THE CRAFT OF LOVE

Mundus and Paulina the lecherous duke, in whom "Love put reason away," violates the faithful wife but is justly punished for his crime. The priests who cooperated in "that horrible sin" were executed, and the duke himself was banished: "For whoever violates truth,/ He may not escape vengeance" (I, 1058-9). In the tale of Canace and Machaire, where the latter "His love upon his Sister cast," again it is a case of tragedy resulting from unreasonable love that seeks fulfillment where there is no marriage, a love that "no reason can allow" (III, 156). True, the poet is evidently in sympathy with the poor young innocents, as he often empathizes with love even when it is unreasonable. Still, subjective innocence does not rectify objective disorder nor prevent consequent pain and disaster.

Much of the unhappiness of such tales is due not to any willfulness on the part of the lovers but to the wickedness of those who, like Canace's father, or like Tiresias who in the tale immediately following maliciously disturbs a pair of copulating snakes, do not respect the force of "the law of Kind." But it also results from the fact that the love in question cannot, in the nature of things and of society as it is, be given proper, lasting fulfillment. So in the tale of Iphis, where again we find an unreasonable love between two innocents—this time of the same sex—the poet's sympathy is with the love, but still the relationship is judged to be unnatural, unreasonable, and therefore wrong:

> For love hateth nothing more
> Than thing which stant ayein the lore   (teaching)
> Of that nature in kinde hath sett.
>
> (IV, 493-5)

This time, however, tragedy is averted and happiness results, but only because a miracle is worked which makes all natural and reasonable, and brings the love within the "lawe of mariage" [Cupide]:

> Transformeth Iphe into a man,
> Wherof the kinde love he wan   (natural) (won)
> Of lusti yonge Iante his wif;
> And tho thei ladde a merie lif,   (then)
> Which was to kinde non offence.

GOWER'S CONFESSION OF A LOVER

(IV, 501-5)

Many other tales might be cited which portray the terror and tragedy of the "firey rage," the "foul delight," the "madness" of extra-marital and contra-marital love: the tale of Orestes, for instance, which tells of the horror resulting from the "spousebreche" (adultery) of Clytemnestra who was "greatly to blame/ To love where it may not last" (III, 1910); and the tales of Arrons Tarquinius and Apius Claudius, both of whom by their "blind lusts," by their love which was "not reasonable," destroyed the one a marriage already happily fulfilled, the other a marriage yet to be realized (VII, 4754-5306). But it is in the tales of faithful conjugal love and in what is said directly and explicitly of marriage that we are "taught" that love has its lawful and joyous fulfillment only in marriage. There are the happy, quite obviously commended marriages of the tales of Constance (II, 587 ff), Ulysses and Penelope (IV, 147ff), Pygmalion (IV, 371ff), Iphis and Iante (IV, 451ff), Nauplus (IV, 1815 ff), Ceix and Alcione (IV, 2927ff), Lucrece (VII, 4754ff), Tobias and Sara (VII, 5307ff), Apollonius (VIII, 271ff). At the end of the poem there is the grand parliament in which appear those who loved apart from marriage or were perpetrators or victims of a faithless marriage; they are sad and grieving lovers (VIII, 2500ff). But in open contrast to them, in that same procession four women are introduced "Whose names I heard most commended" and by whom Venus's "Court stood all amended." They are Penelope, Lucrece, Alceste, and Alcyone—"the four wives:"

> Whos feith was proeved in her lyves: (their)
> For in essample of alle goode
> With mariage so thei stode,
> That fame, which no gret thing hydeth,
> Yit in Cronique of hem abydeth.

(VIII, 2615-20)

Midway in the poem, as Genius discusses the sin of sloth relative to love, he pauses to advise that men and women be not slow to give themselves to love, and, indeed, to a love "of paramours." As the priest of Venus, Genius is here simply acting in character. But, as so often in the *Confessio*, he moves beyond his "role" and qualifies the love he recommends. It is a love that is "set upon marriage," that is not hidden

THE CRAFT OF LOVE

or secret but "well at ease" and open for all to see. It is a "great wonder," exclaims Genius, that maidens do not hasten into "such a feast/ Wherein the love is all honest" (IV, 1476-84).

Finally, in the longest tale of our poem, and the last, the celebration of marriage reaches its zenith. Apollonius has the bride of his choice and she the groom of hers (VIII, 898-900), and the marriage is joyously consumated:

> This lord, which hath his love wonne,
> Is go to bedde with his wife,
> Wher as thei ladde a lusti lif,
> And that was after somdel sene,
> For as thei pleiden hem betwene,
> Thei gete a child betwene hem tuo,
> To whom fell after mochel wo.
>
> (968-74)

The "wo" that befell was the tragic separation of wife, husband, and child. But eventually all three are reunited. First, father and daughter, who is then wedded to a young nobleman. Then Apollonius recovers his wife:

> The king with that knew hire anon,
> And tok hire in his arm and kiste;   (knew)
> And al the toun thus sone it wiste.
>
> (VIII, 1859-61)

Apollonius returns with his wife to her country and the people there "crowned him together with his wife." Genius himself is overborne by the joy of the tale and breaks out in a paean of praise for marriage:

> Lo, what it is to be wel grounded:
> For he hath ferst his love founded
> Honesteliche as forto wedde,   (honestly)
> Honesteliche his love he spedde
> And hadde children with his wif,
> And as him liste he hadde his lif...   (desired)

GOWER'S CONFESSION OF A LOVER

> Lo thus, mi Sone, myht thou liere
> What is to love in good manere,
> And what to love in other wise...
>
> Forthi, my Sone, I wolde rede   (counsel)
> To lete al other love aweie,
> But if it be thurgh such a weie
> As love and reson wolde acorde.
>
> (VIII, 1993-2023)

Soon after this tale, as the poem concludes, Gower reintroduces the concept of charity in explicit form, but already it will have been firmly established that love "set upon marriage" is one with the love of charity; it is "well grounded" and "confirmed" in it, since it is in happy accord with both nature and reason. Extra-marital or contra-marital love should be "renounced" but not the love that intends and is fulfilled in marriage.

It may be gathered from the above quotations that what is regarded in the *Confessio Amantis* as fundamental to marriage is the love between husband and wife: a love that is intimate, single, and lastingly faithful. It is suggestive of the *sacramentum* of the traditional theology. When Apollonius's wife is at long last reunited to him she cries:

> Ha, blessed be the hihe sonde   (high decree)
> That I mai se myn housbonde,
> That whilom he and I were on.
>
> (VIII, 1859-61)

This oneness ("on") together with the joy experienced therein is what characterizes all Gower's "honeste" loves. It is a oneness of flesh, as we shall presently detail, but more deeply it is of heart and spirit. Thus, as we have seen, human love must not be merely physical, of "nature," but must take the direction offered by reason. When love seeks only physical satisfaction, as in the case of Sara's seven lecherous husbands, it is condemned as being contrary to the "law of marriage" (VII, 5351). But when physical appetite is purposely restrained and controlled, as with Tobias who is taught by the angel "how to be honest" (5359); when love abides in spite of long absence, as with Penelope, Apollonius, and Constance, whose tale, Genius tells us, points

THE CRAFT OF LOVE

up "the true meaning of love"; or when, as with Alceste, the lover willingly suffers death that the beloved might live or, as with Alcyone, gladly follows the beloved into death—then there is praise and commendation. All such cases argue the presence of a love that reaches far deeper than physical appetite that unites hearts even more than it "knits" bodies. Venus herself, the personification of physical desire, would have it so: the merely physical she rejects, admitting to her court only those of "noble love" (VIII, 2345); and, as we have seen, she respects "reason" and also "charity." At one point Genius lists the happy effects of love. They are, in part, those of the conventional courtly poetry: courtesy, "gentilesse," courage, generosity. But, as in Criseyde's praise of the virtues of Troilus noted in our chapter on Chaucer, their reach into the *spirit* is unmistakable:

> For evere yit it hath be so,
> That love honeste in sondri weie
> Profiteth, for it doth aweie
> The vice, and as the bokes sein,
> It maketh curteis of the vilein,
> And to the couard hardiesce
> It yifth...

> And overthis, mi Sone, also   (more than this)
> After the vertu moral eke   (according to)
> To speke of love if I schal seke,
> Among the holi bokes wise,
> "Who loveth noght is hier as ded";
> For love above alle othre is hed,
> Which hath the vertus forto lede,
> Of al that unto mannes dede   (deed)
> Belongeth...

(IV, 2296-2329)

Opposite the lines beginning "After the vertu moral eke" there is a gloss that reads: "Note concerning the love of charity" *(Nota de amore caritatis)*. The Christian *caritas* does seem to echo in these lines—what virtue other than charity is "head" of all the others?—infusing whatever other virtue is mentioned therein with its spirit, and, by way of *imperation*, "leading" the others to its own goals. Genius here assures us that the "honest love" he is forever commending is not soley a matter of flesh and physical appetite. It has its roots deep within the heart, and the high God himself as its ultimate end.

But if the emphasis in the *Confessio Amantis* is on marriage as a matter of spirit and a union of hearts; its worth and dignity as a union of bodies is also appreciated. Indeed, the carnal and spiritual are regarded as continuous and intertwined, each is the natural and spontaneous completion of the other. When in any of the tales two people are in love, marriage is sought that they might become "all," that is, entirely, one, and the resulting union is generally fruitful and is redolent of a joy that is both physical and spiritual. So after every marriage in the tales the couple are brought to bed and there, it is said, "at that feast" (VII, 5360) a "merry" (IV, 504) or a "lusty" (VIII, 970) life is led, or a child is begotten, or both; and always the chief interest is in the spouses and their fulness of love rather than in the generative results of love. In the tale of Florent, the Knight's bride says:

> My lord, go we to bedde,
> For I to that entente wedde,
> That thou schalt be my worldes blisse.

(I, 1769-71)

Once in bed, she prays him not to turn away but rather toward her, "For now, she saith, we be both one" (1793). And when he turns and finds "the old hag" now a sweet and fair eighteen, then between them "was pleasure and joy aplenty" and "Each with the other played and laughed" (1853-54). When Constance marries King Allee, the implication is that the king wasted little time abed, for:

> The hihe makere of nature
> Hire hath visited in a throwe   (at once)
> That it was openliche knowe
> Sche was with childe be the king.

(II, 916-19)

And that there was both physical and spiritual joy in the love of Allee and Constance is apparent in the description of their reunion after years of separation:

THE CRAFT OF LOVE

> ...whan he sih his wif, (saw)
> Anon with al his herteA lif
> He cawhte hire in his arm and kiste o
> Was nevere wiht that sih ne wiste (person)
> A man that more joie made.
>
> (II, 1439-43)

The joy that Pygmaleon experiences in his marriage is likewise of both body and spirit, and through it "engendrure" is realized:

> Lo, thus he wan a lusti wif... (won)
> And hadde al that he wolde abedde.
> For er thei wente thanne atwo (parted)
> A knave child betwen hem two (male)
> Thei gete...
>
> (IV, 424-33)

This same fullness of joy is found in the marriage of Alcyone; and here again, as in the marriages of Constance and Pygmalion, procreation is part of the joy. When the bereft wife finds her husband lying dead on the seashore, the gods—"for the truth of love,/ Which in this worthy lady stood" (IV, 3090-91) transformed both her and her husband into birds, and joyfully:

> Hire winges bothe abrod sche spradde,
> And him, so as sche mai suffise,
> Beclipte and keste in such a wise (embraced)
> As sche was whilom wont to do...
>
> and so fulofte
> Sche fondeth in hire briddes forme,
> If that sche miht hirself conforme
> To do the plesance of a wif,
> As sche dede in that other lif...
>
> Wherof into this ilke day (very)
> Togedre upon the See thei wone, (live)
> Wher many a dowhter and a Sone
> Thei bringen forth of briddes kinde.
>
> (IV, 3106-19)

GOWER'S CONFESSION OF A LOVER

Tobias, unlike Sara's former husbands, loves his wife temperately, but this did not preclude his experiencing joy enough, both of body and spirit, in his wife's love:

> Whan sche was wedded to Thobie,
> And Raphael in companie
> Hath tawht him hou to ben honeste,
> Asmod wan noght at thilke feste,
> And yit Thobie his wille hadde;
> For he his lust so goodly ladde,
> That bothe lawe and kinde is served.
>
> (VII, 5357-63)

The joy, carnal and spiritual, in the marriage of Iphis and Iante, as also the joy and fruitfulness of the marriage of Apollonius have already been noted. Cephalus, whom Genius presents as a model of watchfulness in love, prays Phoebus to withold for a time the day that he might longer abide in joy with his beloved:

> For I mi love have underfonge,   (received)
> Which lith hier be mi syde naked,
> As sche which wolde ben awaked,
> And me lest nothing forto slepe.   (desired)
>
> (IV, 3217-29)

That this is no mere "dawn song" of a light-hearted and transient lover but a prayer arising out of *conjugal* love is suggested by Cephalus's further petition to Diana that his love-union be blessed with children (3238-52). Full joyous love between husband and wife with offspring as its natural and welcomed term—this is the "honeste" love of marriage as it is presented in Gower's *Confessio Amantis*. The picture is, accordingly, not unlike that which we have found in Chaucer's "enditynges" and in the contemporary theology and nuptial liturgy.

That the physical union between spouses, together with the joy and pleasure experienced therein, is morally good is scarcely questioned in the *Confessio Amantis*. Our poet seems simply to take it for granted that conjugal intercourse is as right and good as marriage itself of which it is the natural and spontaneous completion. Some restraint, however, is necessary. This is the explicit message of the tale of Sara and her

THE CRAFT OF LOVE

intemperate husbands. The latter quite literally slew themselves with their "own knife," as Chaucer's Parson would have put it. Genius warns that there is "full great distress in marriage/ When poison mixes with the sweet," and "lust" (sexual excess) is one of the poisons (V, 2832-37). Sexual restraint is the implication of the teaching of both Venus and her priest that love be always "gentil" (noble, tender) and "curteis" (respectful) and according to the laws of nature and reason. There is even, perhaps, the suggestion of the ecclesiastical counsel of periodic abstinence for the sake of prayer. In the tale of Hercules and his beloved Iole we read that on a given night "they would not lie together/ Because that they would offer/ Upon the morrow their sacrifice" (V, 6872-79).

But whatever the restraint imposed upon or practiced by Gower's husbands and wives, it never seems to interfere with the joy and bliss native to the act of love. It is rather as though our poet thought of restraint as intensifying rather than diminishing joy in the *whole* of one's conjugal life. St. Thomas, as we have seen, had taught that there was greater ecstacy in the love of friendship, which requires a generous regard for the other and therefore a correponding self-restraint, than in that of simple concupiscence which looks primarily to oneself. Gower's honorable loves seem to be an illustration of this spontaneous and unpremeditated love.

The marriages of the *Confessio Amantis* are unions of love; they are also, as in the theology of the time, bonds of justice. The rape of Lucrece (VII, 4754 ff) and the violation of Virginia (VII, 5131ff) were sins against love; but they are also viewed as crimes against justice since they robbed what belonged or was promised to another, and society itself revolted against the villains. Conjugal fidelity is a matter of love, but also of justice since even in those cases (Jason, Demephon, Aeneas, Clytemnestra) where one of the parties ceases to "love," the infidelity is still to blame. Marriage, whether there is love or not, remains "The bond which may not be unknit" (V, 556).

It is the same for the marital act. It is definitely conceived as an act of love; but it is also referred to as an act of justice. As in the poetry of Chaucer, so also in Gower's poem the ecclesiastical doctrine of the *redditio debiti* is found, even the terminology itself. In the tale of Florent, for instance, the knight is loath to go to bed with the old woman he has just wedded:

> Bot yit for strengthe of matrimoine
> He myghte make non essoine (excuse)
> That he ne mot algates plie (assuredly submit)
> To gon to bedde of compaignie. (intimacy)
>
> (I, 1777-80)

In the gloss of the tale of Iphis we read (in Latin): "Since Iphis did not have the wherewithal to pay her debt *(debitum soluere)* to her spouse, god intervened to help her." Genius commends Cephalus's eager watchfulness in love "So that he mighte do the *lawe,/* In thilke point of loves *heste,/* Which cleped is the nyhtes feste"(IV, 3256-58), and adds:

> Bot Slowthe, which is evele affaited, (shaped by)
> With Slep hath mad his retenue, (service)
> That what thing is to love due,
> Of all his dette he paieth non.
>
> (IV, 3266-69)

In the tale of Echo, Juno may be reflecting the ecclesiastical prescription of the *vitatio fornicationis,* so closely linked with that of the *redditio debiti,* when she claims that Jupiter had no cause to go seeking love elsewhere, clearly implying that she, his wife, had taken care to satisfy his needs (V, 4591, 4629). In discussing the four complexions of the human being, Genius says of the sanguine:

> Of alle ther is non so good
> For he hath bothe will and myth
> To plese and paie love his riht.
>
> (VII, 424-26)

While of the coleric he says,

> Though he behote wel a day, (promises) (by)
> On nyht whan that he wole assaie, (try)
> He may ful evele his dette paie. (not at all)
>
> (VII, 438-40)

THE CRAFT OF LOVE

In all these instances there is an intermingling of the concepts of love and justice. Certainly no opposition between them is suggested. One must make love even when unwilling (as in the case of Florent), but again one may gladly pay one's debt out of love, as did Cephalus and Iphis (and Florent too at a later stage!). And it is interesting, and of moment, to note precisely how Gower apparently understood the *redditio debiti.* He seems to take the prescription as the unqualified right to make love within marriage. Some theologians, as we have seen, distinguished between asking for one's due, which was venially sinful, and rendering the other his/her due, which was meritorious. But qualifications were introduced whereby husband and wife were obliged to look for the "signs" of desire in each other and respond to them, and, by the law of *vitatio fornicationis,* were to insure that the other had no cause to seek sexual satisfaction apart from the marriage. Practically, this meant that husband and wife, if they truly loved and "worshipped" one another, had fullest liberty to make love, and do so with peaceful and happy conscience. At any rate, this seems to be how Gower understood the "law," for in the *Confessio Amantis* it is viewed only as encouraging conjugal love-making and in no way limiting it.

As to the social relationship of husband and wife, there is little if any question that in the *Confessio Amantis* headship belongs to the husband. In almost all the tales of love—those, for instance, of Constance, Penelope and Ulysses, Ceix and Alcione, Lucrece, Apollonius, Alceste—the man is dominant, and the good wife is submissive to her husband. Once the fact of this relationship is given explicit expression, when the husband speaks his will, says Genius, the wife "must forbear and to him bow:"

> For man is lord of thilke feire, (affair)
> So mai the womman bot empeireo (do harm)
> If sche speke oght ayein his wille.
>
> (V, 563-67)

But the context in which these lines appear suggests that more is required of the conjugal relationship than wifely subjection. For Genius here is referring to the jealous husband and his persecution of his innocent wife. He is by no means depicting an ideal arrangement. A tale of happier mood in which Genius proposes a different doctrine and one which seems to be more to his taste is that of Florent. As is usual in the various renditions of this tale, the man surrenders in obedience to his wife and is richly rewarded for it. But here in Gower's version a special emphasis is placed upon the worth of male obedience; and, claims Genius, it is the "clerks" who have formulated the doctrine:

> And clerkes that this chance herde
> Thei writen it in evidence,
> To teche how that obedience
> Mai wel fortune a man to love
> And sette him in his lust above,
> As it befell unto this knyht.
>
> (I, 1856-61)

If we consider the tale of Florent together with all the tales of conjugal love, and note the respectful attitude expressed toward women throughout the poem, we must conclude:

1. That the husband is assuredly "lord in the marriage";

2. He is to exercise his authority with "courtesy," i.e. with love and reverence for the person of his wife; and

3. As prayed in some of the liturgy of the day, he is to take care that the obedience be mutual.

Illustrations of such "courtly" authority abound. In the tale of Constance, the faithful wife, lying "abedde" with her lord, "beseeched him and also counselled," and he, without any hesitation, "graunteth all that she asked" (II, 1456-63). Lucrece, after being raped, kneels before her husband:

> And he, which fain wolde understonde
> The cause why sche ferd so,
> With softe wordes axeth tho,
> "What mai you be, mi goode swete?"
>
> (VII, 5026-29)

And when she tells him of her sorrow, "Her husband, filled with sadness,/ Conforteth hire al that he can." (5051-52). There is also the lover-poet's own exaggerated devotion to his beloved that is the warp

THE CRAFT OF LOVE

to the woof of the various tales, giving them unity and coherence. He assuredly does not regard her as in any way his inferior; on the contrary, in true courtly style he exalts her above himself, and there is no indication given that had he been successful in his suit his devotion would have terminated with the marriage. Indeed, whatever the authority given to the male in the poem, it is the woman who holds pride of place, precisely because she is superior in love. This is richly evidenced in the poem generally, but especially at its climactic conclusion, where the four faithful wives—Alceste, Alcyone, Penelope, and Lucrece—are singled out for special praise. It is not men but these women who are the representatives of "honest love" and who "redeem the court of Venus."

The reader will recall our discussion of gender equality in our preceding chapters. A further word on the subject may be of help. D. W. Robertson maintains that the conjugal equality described, for example, in Chaucer's *Franklin's Tale* runs counter to the medieval ecclesiastical doctrine of the sovereignty of the husband. He therefore denies that such was Chaucer's belief.[9] However, the letter of the tale is ironic, meant to emphasize the heretical character of the Franklin's words. Alan Gunn suggests that in the *Roman* Ami's instruction on the equality in love is Jean de Meun's innovation and is not found in the moralists of his or the preceding generations (thirteenth century and before).[10] But our study, including our present chapter on Gower's *Confessio Amantis*, should have made it clear by now that neither Chaucer nor de Meun nor Gower were saying anything new or startling in their day, and certainly nothing heretical. They were simply echoing a doctrinal tradition that had long been established within the Church. "You are my equal" says Adam to Eve in the early thirteenth-century mystery, *Mystere d'Adam*. And L. Gautier traces the theme to earlier poetry still and locates its ultimate source in the Sacrament of marriage.[11]

A passing statement of Genius—"To love is every heart free" (I, 752)—summarizes the belief implicit throughout the poem of the need for freedom in the formation of marriage. Certainly the poet's own lady-love is at liberty to accept or reject his proffered love. In all the true loves in the poem the love is mutual, implying thereby that both husband and wife have freely chosen each other. At least twice we are expressly assured that the woman is free as to the marriage itself and a given partner. Once, when King Allee proposes to Constance: he will, he says, become a Christian and marry her "if that she would" (II, 898). And once again, when the suitors of the daughter of the King of Pentapolim approach the king and present their suit. The king refers the matter to his daughter and says that she is to reply "Just as she in her heart discovered." She refuses them all, and replies:

> "Bot if I have Appolinus,   (unless)
> Of al this world, what so betyde,
> I wol non other man abide."

(VIII, 898-900)

Even here, where it is a question of a royal marriage, which in Gower's day was customarily arranged, our poet seems intent upon emphasizing what his readers (or listeners) should have known from their Church: that for a marriage to be not only right and proper, but also valid, both parties must choose it in freedom and in love.

As has been amply demonstrated, sexual love in the *Confessio Amantis* has its lawful fulfillment only within the bond of marriage. But the poem also implies the belief that such love may licitly and honorably have its beginnings prior to marriage. In other words, courtship is sanctioned, as it was by the Church of the time. So the poet-lover is in no way reproved by Genius for loving and wanting to possess his beloved; he is rebuked only for his faults in loving. And if in the end his love is censured, it is simply because, as we have observed, he is now too old for that sort of thing. But such happy tales as those of Apollonius and the virtuous Constance in which premarital love does feature, however briefly, are witness that the love of courtship stood approved. Let it simply be "set on marriage," be courteous and measured, be clean of all "fiery rage," "foul delight," "madness," and, like the full love within marriage, it too will be "honeste" and "wel at ese."

The *Confessio Amantis* is true to the theology of the time in ranking the state of virginity above that of marriage. In the Latin verse that prefaces the tale of Phyrinus we read: "As the rose prevails over the thorn out of which it has risen ... so virginity, which without sin brings forth eternal offspring, conquers marriage" (V, vs. x). In olden times,

THE CRAFT OF LOVE

Genius recalls, maidenhead and virginity were held in honor and esteem:

> Noght onliche of the wommen tho,
> Bot of the chaste men also
> It [virginity] was commended overal.

(V, 6367-69)

He concludes the brief tale of Phyrinus with high praise for virginity:

> So mai I prove wel forthi,
> Above alle othre under sky,
> Who that the vertus wolde peise   (weigh)
> Virginite is forto preise,
> Which, as thapocalips recordeth,
> To Crist in hevene best acordeth.

(V, 6385-90)

The tale is then told of the emperor Valentinian who had subjected kings and lands to himself, and yet his greatest boast was "That he his flesh hath overcome:/ He was a virgin, as he said" (V, 641415).

The virginity extolled is understood by our poet as involving more than mere sexual abstinence. As in much of the best contemporary theology (and the *Wife of Bath's Prologue*) it is given positive content. Its ultimate value lies in the service it renders to the Lord and to society. In the prologue of *Confessio Amantis* recalling "the days of old," our poet tells of the dedication of the clergy and speaks of it largely in terms of their celibacy *(their* kind of chastity):

> Thei were ek chaste in word and dede,
> Wherof the people ensample tok;
> Her lust was al upon the bok,   (Their pleasure)
> Or forto preche or forto preie...

(Prol. 228-31)

Though our poet apparently esteems virginity over marriage, the latter retains the high value placed upon it throughout the poem. To be sure, except for the Latin verse quoted above, there is no open comparison between the two. Virginity is lauded, but then so also is marriage, of which the entire poem might be regarded as a hymn of praise. There is no contradiction or muddle in the thinking here. It simply instances the world-view native to the poem, a view common to the great theologies and literature of the late medieval period. In the large and varied world created by the "high almighty Trinity," there are different institutions and all are meant to work in their own way toward universal love and peace. Let there, then, be priests, religious, virgins who do their kind of work; but let there also be kings and queens and knights and the married in general who do theirs. The world is large enough for all and needs all. From this perspective the lover in the poem may be seen to give to Genius's praise of virginity, referred to above, the balanced response we might expect from the thinking, believing Christian of the time:

> And natheles youre goode sawe
> Is good to kepe, who so may,
> I wol noght therayein seie nay.   (deny)
> Yee, fader, al this wel mai be,
> Bot if alle othre dede so,
> The world of men were sone go:
> And in the lawe a man mai finde,
> Hou god to man be weie of kinde   (by nature)
> Hath set the world to multiplie;
> And who that wol him justefie,
> It is ynouh to do the lawe.
>
>   (V, 6418-28)

CHAPTER 11

LYDGAT — LOVE-GOOD, LOVE-BAD

> Ich am of Irlaunde
> and of the holy londe
> Of Irlande.
> Gode sire, pray ich thee,
> For of sainte charite,
> Come and daunce wit me
> In Irlaunde.[1]
>
> Anonymous, earlier 14th c.

John Lydgate (c. 1370 - c. 1450) was a monk at the abbey of Bury St. Edmund's and, in his writing of verse, a self-proclaimed disciple of Chaucer.[2] His poetry was respected and popular in its time, but is today recognized not so much for its quality as its quantity, running to some 145,000 lines. His long poems, broad translations from Latin and French originals, include *Troy Book*, a recounting of the legend of Troy, and containing Lydgate's notable hymn of praise to Chaucer; and the *Siege of Thebes*, the story of the struggle between Oedipus's two sons for the kingship of Thebes. In its prologue, Lydgate offers the *Siege of Thebes* as his personal contribution to Chaucer's pilgrimage on the projected return journey from Canterbury. But reputedly the best of Lydgate's long poems is *Reason and Sensuality*,[3] a translation of the French *Les Echecs Amoureux* (Love's Game of Chess). It is a detailed allegory of love.

Reason and Sensuality is incomplete, but enough of an attitude toward human sexual love is revealed therein to permit a just surmise as to the poet's ultimate and full intentions; a surmise substantiated by a consideration of the original of the poem and Lydgate's other briefer poems of love, particularly the *Temple of Glass*.

The general setting of *Reason and Sensuality* is similar in its magnitude to that of the theology and other poetry that we have been considering. There is the joyous fullness and bride-like quality of springtime and generation (139-67). This is seen as part of the work and functioning of the vast world of Nature, and Nature herself is viewed as standing under the still broader, all-powerful aegis of God, "the Lord eternal" (253-389, 527-30). In the midst of this world and, because endowed with reason, supreme within it is humankind (394-406, 540-54). The human person stands at the crossroads of reason—which Nature commends as her "own friend" (722), her "sister dear" (874) and the way to virtue and heaven—and of sensuality, against which Nature warns the poet-lover, for it has "no other appetite/ But in bodily delight,/ All set on worldly vanity" (779-81). It leads to viciousness and destruction.

Into this universal setting specifically human sexual love, in the person of the goddess Venus, is introduced. The young lover, obedient to Nature's injunction to avoid "idleness" and go forth and "take good heed of all her works," begins to make his way through the wondrous world, but:

>   In a while, this is no nay,
>   I was disloggyd of my way,
>   That I left anoone ryght   (soon)
>   Therof bothe mynde and syght.
>
>   (927-30)

He meets Mercury in the company of the three goddesses, Pallas, Juno, and Venus. He is asked to comment upon Paris's judgment and make his own choice as to which of the three goddesses is most deserving of the golden apple. Juno represents riches, and if the lover chooses her, his reward will be wealth. Pallas, as both text and gloss remind us, is the goddess of wisdom and as such the daughter of "the true and highest god." She has the qualities that have been assigned by Dame Nature to reason: she stands for "prudence" and "wisdom," is against "idleness" and for living "virtuously"; she comprehends "Secrets that are divine," can make people "Like gods for to be eternal" and can bring them to heaven. Her primary concern is with the celestial and eternal, but she also alters her stature to consider earthly and temporal matters. If the lover should choose her, he will be made the wisest of men. Venus is the goddess of love; accordingly, if she

LYDGATE — LOVE-GOOD LOVE-BAD

should be the lover's choice, his reward will be love. The lover, "lightly" and "without reflection," chooses Venus, and as the other goddesses and Mercury depart, Mercury's farewell words are: "All this world goes the same way/ Everyone thinks alike" (2107-08). Venus remains behind to tell her young admirer that he will have as his reward the most beautiful of women, whom he will find in the garden of Deduit (pleasure). The lover asks how he might find the garden and is told he is already on his way; he will discover it shortly, and "Idleness," the portress, will let him in. He expresses some misgivings, since he does not want to violate Nature's charge to go the "true way" and avoid sensuality. Venus dispells his doubts by assuring him that she and Dame Nature are "fully of one accord" (2257-2306). The lover then, "With heart and all," becomes her man.

This particular section of the allegory (ll. 897-2700) is crucial for the purposes of our study for several reasons. The first concerns the lover. Here as elsewhere in the poem there are pointed indications that he is not behaving as he ought and as he had, under the inspiration of Nature, originally intended. He had, he says, become lost: like the great Dante before him, he was confused in mind, weak in spirit. In making his choice between the three goddesses, contrary to instructions he had received from Dame Nature he chooses lightly and hastily. In the Latin gloss that comments on his choice we read that of the three forms of life—the contemplative, the active, and the life of pleasure—"The young, because they follow their passions, choose the life of pleasure ..."; an observation later illustrated in the text itself when the lover remarks of Diana's forest of chastity that "It does not accord with my age" (4490). Nature had specifically and emphatically warned the lover against idleness, and he had found the warning freshly echoed in the presence and person of Pallas; yet "heart and all" he would remain Venus's man even though the first duty she imposes upon him is to familiarize himself with "Idleness," necessary, she says, for his entrance into the garden of pleasure. And when the lover asks for directions to the garden Venus replies that he is already on his way and very close to his goal. In short, the young lover's conduct, though it is recognized as universal ("All the world goes the same way") is being judged in our poem as mis-conduct.

THE CRAFT OF LOVE

Secondly, noteworthy also are the nature and characteristics of Venus as thus far presented. At the beginning of the poet's description of her, the gloss reads: "Venus is carnal concupiscence or the planet which inclines to concupiscence and signifies the life of carnal pleasure *(clue debetur carnalibus).*" It is an accurate description, for as the poem proceeds Venus appears as the sensual or physical appetite itself abstracted from, not of itself opposed to, possible direction from a higher source. As such it seeks only its own fulfillment, its own satisfaction, and if left to itself would eventuate in a life of carnal pleasure. Thus in the text Venus appears neither as love nor as pleasure. These are rather considered as gods apart from Venus though intimately conjoined to her: they are her sons, Cupid and Deduit (2373-2496). She is more basic, more primitive than they; her power is in the appetite itself which moves toward them:

> Enclynyng be fleshly appetite
> Folkys, for to haue delyte   (people)
> To serve love...
>
>   (1471-73)

Though she can and often does incline toward "sensuallyte" and other vices, there is a native goodness about her enabling her, whenever she so wished *(whan hir lyst),* to join with the forces of virtue toward virtuous ends: she can bring to accord those who are at war, make the avaricious generous, bend the proud to lowliness and humility (1490-1501). Like the Venus of Gower's *Confessio Amantis* (though scarcely to the same degree), Lydgate's Venus can and often does look to forces and values other and higher than herself. When, to cite another instance, she tells the lover, in order to quiet his scruples, that she and Nature are in complete accord, she is no doubt exaggerating; but more than a grain of truth is intended when she is made to say:

LYDGATE — LOVE-GOOD LOVE-BAD

> I take recorde of thise clerkys,   (the writing)
> That the forge of al hir [Nature's] werkys,
> Withoute me, in certeyn,
> Was nat waked but in veyn,
> For but I putte to my cure   (care)
> Hir forgyng myghte nat endure,
> To hyr I am so knyt by bonde
> Necessarie to hir honde.
> I make redy alle thing
> Pertynent to hir forgyng,
> And pleynly, lyke to hir desire,   (according)
> In hir forge I make the fire...
>
> (2283-94)

Opposite the lines (2491-93) where Venus insists that she serves Nature, the gloss seems to agree and simply defines, in scholastic terms, the sense in which she renders that service: "Venus is said to serve nature because she is [nature's] concupiscible power." Again, Venus appears to be open to higher forces—and an incipient morality is suggested—when she warns the lover not to seek pleasure apart from love, as though she recognized something of a larger context in which she, as physical appetite, must seek and find proper fulfillment:

> For Deduit, I warne the,
> Hadde lever exilled be   (rather)
> Than to twynne on any side   (separate)
> From presence of Cupide.
>
> (2529-32)

A third feature of this section bearing closely upon our subject is the person of Pallas. There is no hint given at this point that the goddess of wisdom was intended to reappear later in the poem, but had Lydgate completed his "translation" and continued to follow his original she would have returned with a vengeance, emerging as the most prominent of our poem's personages. For in the *Les Echecs Amoureux,* of the 144 folios of the now lost Dresden manuscript, over 100 were devoted to Pallas and her speeches (6v; 45v-144v); and had the *Les Echecs Amoureux* been completed she is likely to have been given much more additional space, since the text breaks off in the midst of her

THE CRAFT OF LOVE

encyclopedic exposition of the world and the life of humankind. Also, in the original poem it is Pallas who finally takes hold of love and places it within the ambit of marriage and the family.[4]

Pallas reappears in the *Les Echecs Amoureux* after the lover had met his promised lady in the garden of Deduit and had been given his instructions by Cupid. Now it is Pallas's turn to advise the lover. First, since he is presently on dangerous ground he must let reason rule him (47r) and should not lead the life of the *fol amoureux* (foolish lovers) who live only for *peliz* (pleasure) (47v-52v). She tells him that there are three ways of living: the "voluptuous life" of Venus, the "active life" of Juno, and the "contemplative life" of Pallas herself. The active life is a reasonable one, but the life of contemplation is best of all *(la plus suppellative)* (66r-66v). She advises the lover to abandon Venus and urges him to embrace the contemplative life, devoting himself to study in the schools of Paris (73v-74v). But if he is not able to support the burdens of the contemplative life, then he should at least choose the active life (74v).

From this point to where the text breaks off, Pallas lectures the lover on the active life, treating of the king and princes, councellors, judges, knights, the clergy, and others. The lover—it is said that he likes to hear her talk—asks her to speak of marriage (104r). Pallas obliges and embarks on a long disquisition on the subject. Nature, she begins, inclines men and women to marriage for three reasons:

1. That they might share each other's company;

2. That they might have children;

3. That they might be of mutual help in acquiring the necessities of life (104v-105r).

Marriage is divine, she says; and it must be monogamous, for it is the most perfect of terrestrial loves *(lamistie parfaitte... sur tout aultre amour terrestre)* and as such cannot be given to many (105r). Men and women are unlike, and from their differences is meant to come harmony (106r). Marriage is a very amicable thing, because husband and wife work together and help each other: they are like the birds that nest in the spring (106v). The friendship of marriage includes all possible kinds of love (107r). Those who wish to lead the contemplative life may not marry, but those who avoid marriage to practice fornication degrade themselves (107v). No reasonable criticism can be made of the marriage state (108r). No evil can be said of women that cannot be said of men; also, whatever good qualities men may have women may likewise have (108v). Pallas elaborates on the mutual relationship of husband and wife. A wife, she says, is not to be treated like a servant *(serve)* (115v). The husband should influence his wife toward virtue by moderating his desire and anger and setting a good example. He should be chaste and loyal, and should be clean and amiable of speech when talking with his wife, and should treat her according to her particular disposition (116v-117v). The husband should provide rules for the guidance of his wife, but they must be reasonable (118r). He should not be too jealous of his wife. The wife in turn should obey her husband and do his will in all reasonable matters (118v). As a true friend she should cherish and obey him in evil fortune even more than in good (119r-v). She should be chaste, shy, sober, etc. (120r-121r). Husband and wife have each certain rights and duties. The wife has charge of the *ostel* (home) and all that is in it (121v). The husband is master of the *ostel*, should see that all goes well within it, and should assume the tasks involving the heaviest labor (122v). He must be first to rise in the morning and the last to bed at night. He must respect and teach his wife, and show her what is to be done. She is next to him in authority (123v).

To sum up: for the Pallas of the *Les Echecs Amoureux* marriage is good and holy ("divine") and is a matter fundamentally of love; indeed, it embraces, as we have previously learned from Nicole Oresme, various kinds of love. It surpasses all other earthly loves. In it the husband's prime concern is to love his wife *(Laquelle it doit premierement/ Amer de cuer entierement)*, love her fully and from the heart, and lastingly and loyally as *bonne amistie* requires.[5]

We may suppose, then, that it was to be in and through the figure of Pallas, the virgin goddess of wisdom and daughter of the Most High, that Lydgate's version of the *Les Echecs Amoureux* was to include the positive side of a doctrine of love: it was to be from the vantage point of contemplation (and virginity!) that the true and full worth of marriage was to stand revealed. Prior to this second appearance of Pallas, the love doctrine of *Reason and Sensuality* was to be largely negative, a stern warning against the purely carnal love of Venus, Cupid, and Deduit. Pallas, however, would propose another kind, or mode of, sexual love, that of marriage, and would assign it an honorable place in God's great world. Yet the way had already been prepared earlier in Lydgate's poem by the description at its commencement of the blossoming, bride-like quality of spring, by the reverential presentation of Dame Nature who works the generation and regeneration of all, and by the recognition that Venus looks beyond herself for her proper fulfillment and is in fact indispensable for Nature's work. But it is especially adumbrated by the teaching of another of the poem's major figures, also a virgin: the goddess Diana. In Lydgate's translation as in the original, after the poet-lover has surrendered himself to Venus and has set out for the garden of Deduit, he comes upon a forest "full of trees," where:

> may no corrupcion
> Damage nouther crop nor rote   (root)
> Nor the holsom fruytes sote   (sweet)
> Corupte neuer, nor apayre...   (suffer harm)
>   (2742-45)

Diana, whose forest this is, soon appears to the lover. In some respects Diana seems to represent the virtue of chastity in its highest form which, for the time, was virginity. She appears all dressed in white and "wimpled," looking as "She was of some religious order" (2844); and at the end of her long argument in which she concludes that the youth should remain in the forest with her instead of moving on to Pleasure's garden, he replies that he would not "as yet be no hermit/ nor solitary of living" (4498-99). But this is Diana as the restless young lover sees her. That the chastity she promotes is not in fact restricted to that of virginity is evident in one long speech of hers where she looks back upon a golden age when, to the envy of Venus, she, Diana, "had of friends great plenty" (3157); and these friends were, surprisingly, those who "Loved the days paramours":

LYDGATE — LOVE-GOOD LOVE-BAD

> For love was tho so pure and fre,   (then)
> Grounded on al honeste
> Withoute engyn of fals werkyng   (contriving)
> Or any spot of evel menyng,
> Which gaf to knyghtes hardynesse,
> And amended her noblesse...   (their)
>
> The myghty famous werriours,
> Lovede the dayes paramours,
> Gentilwymmen of high degre,
> Nat but for trouthe and honeste...   (only)
>
> And al they mente in honest wyse,
> Vnleful lust was set a-syde.
> Women thanne koude abyde,   (wait)
> And loveden hem as wel ageyn   (them)
> Of feythful hert[e] hool and pleyn,
> Vnder the yok of honeste,
> In clennesse and chastite...
>
> Wher so as her sort was set   (fate)
> The knot never was vnknet...
>
> Of my scole they wer so lered   (taught)
> To love hem that wer preyed best...
>
>   (3167-3213)

She herself may have been a virgin, but evidently Diana recognized the worth of the chastity of sexual love as well as of virginity. Like the Pallas of *Les Echecs Amoureux* she believed in, and inspired ("Of my school they were so taught") a full and worthy love between a man and a woman, a reciprocal love which, while remaining clean and chaste, would also be chivalrous and romantic *(paramours)*, grounded in and promotive of virtue, and faithful to such a degree that its "knot" might never be untied. Venus conceivably might still have a place, but it would be subordinate; she would be "put under" (1. 3219). Such love, according to Diana's reading of the Arthurian story, once thrived but, laments our virgin goddess, it is no more, "for love now has no desire or appetite/ Except in what gives pleasure" (II. 3231-32).

THE CRAFT OF LOVE

In light of this exposition by Diana of love-past and love-present (love as it might and should be, and love as it generally is), we can recognize the kind and only kind of love against which our poem as a whole seems levelled: purely carnal love that is for pleasure alone. It is the kind of love censured in the theology and preaching at that time as well as in the poetry of Chaucer and Gower. But "honeste" love, single and faithful unto death, whatever its rewards or pleasures, was another matter entirely: it received highest marks from both wisdom (Pallas) and virginity (Diana). It ranked with the best of what the world, and God himself, had to offer.

In *Reason and Sensuality,* as we have seen, Lydgate got as far as describing the ways of "love-bad," with Venus as merely sensual, though open to higher values. Better things were to come as the poem moved toward completion, and Diana's long speech in praise of "love-good" was their herald. In Lydgate's other major love poem, this one completed, it is rather upon "love-good" that our priest-poet centers his attention. In *The Temple of Glass* Venus is presented as a gentle kindly deity who, while still representative of physical desire and love, is quite at home with reason and virtue.[6] Within her temple, near to her own statue, stands that of Pallas "with her crystal shield" (248-49), and "before" the one and "beside" the other kneels the heroine of the piece who presents her complaint of love. Venus is depicted as "meekly" inclining her head and "softly" replying (370-71). She counsels the fair and virtuous lady to have the patience of Griselda, Penelope, and Dorigan, and of the saints and martyrs, and to be constant like the hawthorn branch. She assures the lady that in time she will have "full possession" of her knight "in honest manner, without offense" (427-28). And since the lady is resolved "In virtue only his youth to cherish," Venus promises to "Make him to eschew always sin & vice" (447-50). The goddess of love is equally gentle and gracious with the complaining knight, also present before her, and equally moral in her demands. The knight is to ground his love "upon honesty" such that his beloved's reputation is always secure. He may expect nothing from her except what conforms to her womanly dignity *(womanhede).* He is to be patient and "let reason bridle his desire." If this be so, then:

LYDGATE — LOVE-GOOD LOVE-BAD

To forn all she shal the louen best:	(before) (thee)
So shal I here, withoute offencioun,	(her) (harm)
Bi influence enspiren in hir brest,	
In honest wise, with ful entencioun,	
Forto enclyne, bi clene affeccioun,	
Hir hert fulli on the to haue routhe	(thee) (mercy)
Bicause I know that thou menyst trouth.	

(869-89)

The *Temple of Glas* is concerned with the beginnings of a courtship and, apparently, an engagement rather than with love already realized and fulfilled within marriage. In the first part of the poem there is love between lady and knight but neither is aware that it is a mutual love. In the second, climactic part when Venus binds them with her chain of love they become thereby inseparably one—"in one forto perseuere,/ While that they live and never to separate" (1108-09)—but still the full mutual giving is forbidden them. The lovers kiss, but for the time being this is all they seem to do. Though the "knot is knit that may not be unbound," they still must "Abide awhile," the lady's "honour" and "womanhede" must be respected (1117-1230).

But the courtship is one that most assuredly intends marriage. All through the poem marriage is suggested. There is the repeated demand on the part of Venus (assented to by the lovers) for mutual constancy till "lyues ende" (365, 385, 435, 493, 1071, 1109, 1128, etc.) with a corresponding warning against all "variaunce" and "doubilnes." In the first part of the poem those whom Venus offers as love models for the lady are the faithful *wives* of old: Griselda, Penelope, and Dorigan. Venus promises the lady that she will eventually have "full possession" of her knight, and the knight is promised as much:

> Abide awhile, & than of thi desire
> The time neigheith, that shal the most delite...

(1194-1204)

And in the poem's epithalamic-like concluding stanzas there is ample suggestion that the long, patient, chaste courtship has at last blossomed into the fullness of conjugal joy:

THE CRAFT OF LOVE

> For he hath wonne hir that he loueth best,
> And she to grace hath take him of pite;
> And thus her hertis bethe bothe set in rest,   (their) (be)
> With-outen chaunge or mutabilite,
> And Venus hath, of hir benygnete,
> Confermed all—what I lenger tarie?
> This tweyn in oon, and neuere forto varie   (These two)
>
> (1292-98)

   C. S. Lewis and, more recently, J. Norton-Smith have considered that the lady of the *Temple of Glass* is a married woman: her heart is set upon the knight but her body is bound to another man.[7] The tell-tale stanzas, they claim, are stanzas 3-7 (11. 335-69) of the lady's complaint to Venus. "For I am bound," she mourns, "to thing that I would not." She lacks liberty "freely to choose." "The body is knit, although my heart is free." She laments that she should "be deprived of choice against all justice, both of God and nature," and instead "be knit under subjection, far from which are both wit and mind." Norton-Smith regards the following passage as especially revealing:

> Deuoide of ioie, of wo I haue plente;
> What I desire, that mai I not possede;
> For that I nold, is redi aye to me,   (will not)
> And that I loue, forto swe I drede,   (pursue)
> To my desire contrarie is me mede.   (reward)
>
> (349-53)

   However, both critics realize the difficulty involved in trying to reconcile the lady's "implied" marriage (to someone other than the knight) with the high moral tone of the rest of the poem. The best they can do is suggest that the lovers were intended to live in the sure hope that some chance event (the death of the husband is proposed as a possibility) will eventually make their own longed-for marriage possible.

   For those used to and expecting precise realistic detail, the passages in question may well be confusing; and if Norton-Smith's theory of the genesis of the poem is correct, perhaps Lydgate himself was aware of the confusion and tried to eliminate it as he revised his poem.[8] But

LYDGATE — LOVE-GOOD LOVE-BAD

might not these passages be merely conventional, intended simply to convey the idea that *some* obstacle was in the way of the lovers? Perhaps the lady was already betrothed (not yet married but promised to another), perhaps she was too high-born for the knight in a society where class was respected, perhaps her parents or guardians had plans for her that did not include the knight, or the respective families were feuding, a la *Romeo and Juliet*.

Norton-Smith himself allows that Lydgate's meaning here may have been intentionally imprecise. With reference to the allusion to the oppresion of Venus by Vulcan in the third stanza of the unrevised version of our poem, he writes: "The simile refers to the distress of the lovers ('we ben oppressed'); but in what way does it so refer? Is the reference imprecise, the simile simply intensifying *oppressed* generally, or does it mean precisely that the lady and the knight are *oppressed* by the husband? There is no doubt that Lydgate meant only a general imprecise emphasis."[9]

Still Norton-Smith inclines toward the husband as oppressor. He reconciles such a reading with the "high moral tone" of the poem generally, by suggesting that the "guaranteed hope" (of the husband's demise) in which the lovers bide their time "is not meant by Lydgate to engage the reader's philosophical [moral?] interests. It is merely the result of an allegorical organization which gives the poem satisfactory shape."[10] But how do we suspend our "philosophical interests" when the moral and aesthetic unity of the poem is so radically disrupted? How can the love between lady and knight, now and in the future, be considered "honorable" when the lady is in violation of love from the beginning (her heart going to one, her body to another) and both lady and knight are hoping, praying for the death of her present husband? Such a reading of the poem renders it absurd.

As I have already suggested, there are simpler interpretations of the passages in question more in tune with the poem as a whole. For dramatic purposes Lydgate suggests that there are obstacles to be overcome before the lovers can unreservedly be united, but these, also for dramatic effect and more universal appeal, are deliberately left vague and unspecified: the mystery surrounding the lovers is intensified and readers may read into the situation their own particular

THE CRAFT OF LOVE

difficulties in the fulfillment of their particular loves. So interpreted the poem remains one that is concerned with a completely honorable love that has to be worked at and suffered for, but is eventually realized to the full within the bond of marriage.

There is not in Lydgate's poetry as detailed an expression of love doctrine as in the poetry of Chaucer and Gower, and so we may not expect satisfactory answers to several of the questions we have been asking. Yet if we consider the incomplete *Reason and Sensuality* together with its original and the *Temple of Glass,* some answers will emerge, in part clear and definite, in part merely suggestive.

1. Sexual love is natural and from God

As wisdom (Pallas) sees it, the world is large and various in things, people, institutions, thoughts and actions. Within this immensity, human sexual love is found as one variety of love. It is of nature and nature of God, and therefore such love also is of God; it is, in Lydgate's word, "divine." For human love to remain good and holy it must be subject to reason, which is not meant to be a limitation of love but an expansion and preservation of it. Passion and pleasure are very much involved, and in fact tend to be uppermost in the consideration of lovers, especially if they are young. But the specifically sexual appetite looks beyond itself for fulfillment, and reason (wisdom) would direct it into a love that looks to the *other* in gentleness, courtesy, lasting fidelity, and fruitfulness. This is the love of marriage, "the most perfect of terrestrial loves." Marriage intends the begetting of children and the mutual support and help of husband and wife, but fundamentally it is husband and wife "sharing each other's company" (Pallas's way of expressing the *sacramentum?).* The "very first concern" of spouses is to love each other "fully from the heart."

2. Justice is rooted in love

The concepts of love and justice are complementary, and justice is seen as rooted in love. In both *Reason and Sensuality* and *Temple of Glass*— in the one as illustrated by the speech of Diana on the honest love of olden times, and in the other as repeatedly declared by Venus and lovers alike—constancy, or fidelity, and love are regarded as inseparable. In the *Temple of Glass* it is especially clear that constancy is a matter of justice over and above love, for, as says Venus, even if a new love should tempt the lovers they must still keep truth with one another:

    if the spirit of nvfangilness   (novelty)
    In any wise youre hertis would assaile,
    To meve or stir to bring in doubilnes   (infidelity)
    Vpon your trouthe to giuen a bataile,
    Late not youre corage ne youre force fail,
    Ne non assautes yov flitten or remeve: (change)
    For vn-assaied men may no trouthe preue.
                                       (1243-49)

Yet it is love that is creative of the justice. Even prior to marriage, once love is seriously proposed, justice enters in. As the theology also claimed and the liturgy reinforced: the sponsalia formed a bond that could not lightly be severed. The principle is clearly formulated by the Pallas of the *Les Echecs Amoureux* as she speaks specifically of conjugal love: "There is not proper friendship *(bonne amistie)* where neither faith nor loyalty are preserved." It is a slight variation of the principle used by St. Thomas Aquinas in his harmonization of love and justice with marriage: "The greater the friendship the more firm and lasting marriage is."

3. Sexual love is restrained by reason to marriage

Nothing is expressly said in either of our poems concerning the act of love. In *Temple of Glass* it is implied that the act is reserved for marriage. The lady is to keep inviolate her honor and her "womanhed," i.e. her sexual integrity, even after she has been knit by Venus to her lover; another step in love is required before "full possession" may be had. But there is the further implication that this full possession is something highly desireable, a pleasure to look forward to: "The time approaches that shall most delight thee," says Venus to the expectant knight. It is the "love feast" of Gower's *Confessio Amantis* that seems to be echoed here, and perhaps also the *delectatio intensissima* of St. Thomas's theology: the pure and innocent joy of conjugal love-making. The act of love seems also to be indirectly commended in *Reason and*

THE CRAFT OF LOVE

Sensuality: in the gracious appearance of Dame Nature "to whom all things incline," and who, as the Pallas of the *Les Echecs Amoureux* declares, inclines to generation; and perhaps also in the description of the ever fresh fruitfulness of the forest of chastity and "honest love paramours." The commendation is less indirect in the description of sad loves in Venus's temple where young May, coupled, "contrary to all nature," to old January, is pitied, for "old age may not long endure to fulfill the desire of *love's play."* (181).

But some measure, some restraint is required, in love in general and therefore, we must suppose, in the act of love. Love must not be exclusively sensual, i.e. *only* for delight. In Lydgate's poetry, as in that of Gower and Chaucer, it is not pleasure or delight in love-making that is banned but "false delight" and "false pleasure" *(Reason* 3231-32). The lover must not surrender desire and physical joy, but must simply "let reason bridle desire by obedience" *(Temple* 878). Both in *Reason and Sensuality* and in *Temple of Glass* courtesy and mutual respect are required of lovers, and in the counsels of Pallas in the *Les Echecs Amoureux* we learn that this courtesy and respect were meant to be carried over into marriage and, presumably, into the act of marriage: the husband was to moderate his desire, was to be chaste and loyal, clean and amiable in his speech with his wife, and was to treat her according to her particular disposition.

4. Woman is free to choose her state in life

That a woman should be free to choose her state in life, and her partner in love and marriage, is written large in Lydgate's poetry. His women give themselves to a particular suitor not through external compulsion but when they choose and of their "mercy" or "pity" or "grace." That this liberty on the part of the woman is meant to be real and not simply a fictional convention of *courtoise* is forcefully evidenced in *Temple of Glass.* The want of liberty experienced by the lady at the beginning of the poem is presented as pitiable, an evil to be overcome that she might have in love and marriage the man of her choice. Within Venus's temple there is depicted the sorry plight of "maidens young of age":

LYDGATE — LOVE-GOOD LOVE-BAD

> That pleined sore with weping & with rage,
> That thei were coupled, againes al nature,
> With croked elde...
>
> (179-81)

Others appear:

> That were constrayned in hir tender youth,
> And in childhode, as it is ofte couthe,   (known)
> Yentred were into religioun,   (relgious life)
> Or thei hade yeris of discresioun,   (before)
> That al her life cannot but complein.
>
> (199-203)

Still others are depicted as "in great rage"

> That thei were maried in her tendir age,
> With-oute fredom of eleccioun,
> Wher loue, at laarge & at liberte,
> Would freli chese, & not with such trete.
>
> (209-14)

The belief—almost a preaching—expressed in this poem is clear and forceful enough:

1. the woman must be free to choose her state in life, at least whether it is to be marriage or the convent;

2. she must have "freedom of election," that is she is to have the partner of her choosing (supposing, of course, he also chooses her);

3. within marriage, love, not force, should have the "domynacioun" or rule; and

4. love and liberty go together, "For love... would freely choose."

5. Premarital love is a fragile thing

As is clear from all of his love poems, Lydgate more than Chaucer and certainly more than Gower is occupied with premarital love or the love conquest, though his conquests are honorable and intend a lifelong fidelity.[11] It is recognized (as in *Reason*) that premarital love can go wrong: it can be double, faithless, merely sensual. But there is also the awareness that such love, precisely as love paramours in *Temple of Glass* confirmed by a chaste kiss and longing for the eventual full possession within marriage, can be, as the chaste Diana is made to tell us in *Reason and Sensuality*, "so pure and free, grounded in all honesty," and can make men "to be virtuous." But care must be taken, for love is a fragile thing so easily marred and broken—perhaps the reason why Venus's temple is said to be made of *glass* and why Lydgate incorporates this word into the very title of his poem.

6. Husband and wife owe mutual obedience

The question of the social relationship between husband and wife does not arise in Lydgate's love poetry as we have it because, as noted, his interest is centered upon courtship rather than marriage. In the courtship it is the woman who holds the first place: she rules her lover and he is but her humble and obedient servant. The extremes of the *Kult der Dame*, however, do not appear, or if they do they are mocked—as in the case of the young lover of *Reason and Sensuality*. Here the poet patently intended not the truth but the naievete of the lover to shine through when, for instance, besotted with love in the forbidden garden, he declares:

> Women be cause of al swetnesse;
> For who hem serveth eve and morwe,
> Hath neuer cause for to sorwe.

(6288-90)

This is simply Chaucer's foolish Januarius in a younger skin. But a certain reasonable worship and subjection on the part of the man toward his beloved does seem to have had the poet's blessing. In *Temple of Glass* at any rate there is no suggestion that the knight's worship of his lady may have been a bad thing, perhaps because the love between them was honest and mutual, thereby excluding the excesses of woman-worship. And in *Reason and Sensuality* Diana looks back with nostalgia on days when knights served their ladies, but again approval seems to be contingent on the fact that excesses were avoided through "honesty" and "mutuality of love" (3190-93).

However, had he finished his translation of the *Les Echecs Amoureux*, Lydgate would have left us a treatment of the specifically conjugal relationship. He would, then, most probably have introduced and commended, as did his original, the traditional ideal of the headship of the man in marriage; but the twin doctrine of the male *servitude in love* even within the marriage bond would have remained. Pallas, as we have seen, taught that the wife was to obey her husband in all that was reasonable. But she added that she was not to be her husband's servant but his companion *(sa compaigne)* and his equal *(sa pareille)*. And if the husband is lord in the marriage, he also appears, more than the woman, as servant: he is to respect and teach his wife, his are to be the heaviest duties, he is to be the first up in the morning and last to bed at night, etc. The end product of *Reason and Sensuality*, then, would have been much the same as what we have seen throughout our study: though the husband was the social superior of his wife, she was nevertheless to be placed beside him in honor and dignity of person, and he was to exercise his authority in love, reverence, and service.

7. Contemplative and active lives

If we consider *Reason and Sensuality* in conjunction with its original, we find that the state of virginity or celibacy is preferred to that of marriage, though the latter, whether as initiated in the honest love of courtship or as consummated within the conjugal bond, is always treated with esteem. We have seen how Pallas, the most notable figure in the *Echecs Amoureux* next to the lover himself, recommends the contemplative life above the active of which marriage is a part. It is only when she understands that the lover is incapable of supporting the burdens of a life of contemplation that she agrees to lecture him on the active life, specifically on marriage. But she teaches that the active life is good and necessary, that no reasonable criticism can be made of marriage, and that in fact marriage is divine and the best of earthly loves. Her attitude in this respect is foreshadowed by Diana of *Reason and Sensuality:* she appears to represent the virginal life, yet (or therefore?) she extols the goodness of honest sexual love.

But if virginity is preferred to marriage, it is with the proviso that it is voluntary and devoted. There is no indication that it is thought to be deserving simply because it is a state of sexual abstinence. Pallas of the *Les Echecs Amoureux* esteems it because she sees it as necessary for a life devoted to contemplation, which she identifies with a life of study. And

THE CRAFT OF LOVE

in *Temple of Glass* the sad story of those who had been forced into religious life seems to carry the moral that a life of celibacy is praiseworthy only if it is voluntary and therefore with purpose. Our monk-poet was apparently well aware of the possible evils of the religious, celibate life as well as of its virtues, just as he was aware of the possibilities for both good and evil of sexual love. Thus, though he may have regarded celibacy, in the abstract and in general, as superior to marriage, his poetry tells us that best of all was for each individual man and woman "freely to choose" his or her own way of life, and faithfully live it.

CHAPTER 12

OTHER POETS OF THE FOURTEENTH CENTURY

"Alias," quath he, "forlorn icham!	(I am)
Whider wiltow go and to wham?	(will you) (whom)
Whider thou gost, ichill with thee,	(I shall)
And whider I go, thou shalt with me...	
Lever me were to lete my lif	(I'd rather) (lose)
Than thus to lese the Quen, my wif!"[1]	(lose)

Sir Orfeo (early 14th c.) ll. 103-106, 153-54

Gawain's Poet

A sensitive appreciation of "honeste" love and the "faire cheine of mariage" lies behind and within other of the best English poetry of our period. It forms part of the moral presuppositions that prove necessary for the dramatic tensions of the late fourteenth-century poem *Sir Gawain and the Green Knight*.[2]

"The poem is fairly and squarely Christian. Pride is the great sin, the Virgin Mary helps humanity, and the characters are continually going to Mass and confessing ..."[3] And it may be added that these beliefs and practices do not appear in the poem as mere conventions; they are the expressions of a genuine and fervent Christian piety. In this genuinely Christian and respectfully orthodox poem sexual attraction appears natural and harmless in itself; but its consummation, in fact and in desire, is reserved for marriage.

Between his arrival at the castle of Bercilak and his testing in the forest of the Green Knight, Gawain is three times tempted by Bercilak's seductive wife. Each time he remains exemplarily courteous towards her, treating her desire for his love, not with prudishness, but with the best of tact and humor. Yet he is fully resolved not to violate her marriage bond. In their first solitary meeting, the wife tells him that if

THE CRAFT OF LOVE

she might choose a lord for her loving, she would choose Gawain. The knight immediately replies by amiably reminding her of the worth of her husband: "Thank God," said Gawain, "your choice was better. But I'm proud to be priced so high in your eyes. For you are my queen and I your servant, and your knight: may Christ repay you, lady." (1276-79)

He graciously accepts her parting kiss but allows nothing more to transpire between them. At their next meeting, the poet tells us that though the wife "tested him, pushed and probed,/ Trying to tempt him..." Gawain "was so graciously evasive that he seemed/ Always polite, and nothing happened but happiness" (1549-51). And in their final meeting we are expressly told that Gawain's restraint was due to no churlishness or want of sentiment or sexual sensibility (the lady "warmed his heart"), but to his sense of justice and honor, which he prized even above his courtesy:

> That beautiful princess pressed him so hard,
> Urged him so near to the limit, he needed.
> Either to take her love or boorishly
> Turn her away. To offend like a boor
> Was bad enough; to fall into sin
> Would be worse, betraying the lord of that house.
> And "He parried, with a loving laugh [luf-laghyng a lyt], her passionate
> Speeches, her talk of special favor
>
> (1770-78).

Though in each of the meetings the wife comes dangerously close to Gawain, there is not the slightest suggestion of the prurience we find, for instance, in the *De Amore* of Andreas Capellanus, which has been regarded as the manifesto of courtly love. Here we have, rather, an enactment of courtly conduct more in tune with the nostalgic longings of the goddess Diana in Lydgate's *Reason and Sensuality*. This is due to the general high spiritual and moral tone of the poem and to the humor the poet has injected into his description of the meetings. But it is also because Gawain is set on keeping even his desire clean: he intends in no way to sin or betray his host. And if in the end there is some slight fault that tarnishes, and humbles, him, it is not because of any misdeed with or unchaste thought about the wife.

OTHER POETS OF THE FOURTEENTH CENTURY

A far more direct presentation of love doctrine appears in another of the Gawain poet's masterpieces, *Purity* or *Cleanness*.[4] The entire poem aims at promoting chastity by reminding the reader of the terrible punishments attached to its opposites. Sins of adultery, fornication, sins against "kind" are condemned with unrelenting severity. But in the midst of all this somber jeremiad, conjugal sexual love emerges unscathed, as God himself speaks and explains its rationale:

> I set them a natural power and secretly taught them its use,
> And held it in mine ordinance singularly dear,
> And placed love therein, the sweetest of joys,
> And the play of passion I depicted myself,
> And made thereto a manner merrier than any other,
> When two true ones had tied them together:
> Between a man and his mate such mirth should come
> Well nigh pure paradise might prove no better;
> Providing they hold each other in honest wise.
>
> (697-705)

Here in a few masterly lines, imbued with enthusiastic conviction, our poet presents even the details of the doctrine found in the theology, liturgy, and other poetry of his time:

1. Sexual love has its origin from God and has God's blessing (it is "oddely dere" to Him);

2. It is a work of nature, "a kynde craft";

3. The sexual act is definitely a matter of love: it involves the "play of paramorez," there is "drwry therinne";

4. It holds, and is divinely intended to hold, the greatest of pleasures, "doole alther swettest," and its joy is almost the joy of Paradise;

5. Such love and joy in love is reserved for the married; and

6. The married must conduct themselves "honestly" toward each other.

THE CRAFT OF LOVE

It should be noted that sexual love is here praised precisely as it involves the lovers themselves. No mention of the generative purpose of sex is made. It is probably implied in the *proviso* that husband and wife love each other "honestly," and certainly its implication is present in the poet's condemnation of unnatural sin. But here, as in the liturgy of the day, all the emphasis is upon the lovers themselves, the "two true togeder" who "had tyghed hem seluen."

William Langland

William Langland's allegorical *Piers Plowman* is yet another of the great fourteenth-century English poems that shares the view of love and marriage that we have been describing.[5] Here, as in *Purity*, lechery appears as a grave sin. Those who after glutting themselves as swine "and bed themselves easily" are liable to be damned (II, 92-105), and "comfortable" confessors who are lenient with lords "who haunt lechery" and with ladies "who love well the same" are satirized (III, 43-58). But it is Wit (wisdom) who affirms and extols love when set on marriage:

> True wedded living folk in this world are Do Well;
> For they must work and earn and the world sustain...
> And thus was wedlock made and God himself it made;
> On earth it is heaven, [God] himself was the witness.
>
> (IX, 109-115)

Marriage is for the begetting of confessors, kings, and knights, kaisers and laborers, maidens and martyrs (IX, 109-10), but it must also be made through and grounded upon love: "For no lands, but for love," says Wit, "look you be wedded" (171-76). The marriage-for-love theme, again as deliberately and pointedly contrasted with marriage "through brokerage," is repeated as Patience offers it as an analogue for the love that leaves all things for the love of God:

OTHER POETS OF THE FOURTEENTH CENTURY

> As a maid for a man's love leaves mother,
> Her father and all her friends, and follows her mate,
> So is such a maid to be loved by him who takes her
> More than a maiden is who is married through brokerage
> As by the consent of various parties with silver to boot,
> More for greed of goods than for natural love.
>
> (XIV, 264-69)

Two other features of the contemporary ecclesiastical doctrine emerge in a brief passage: the wife as helpmate to her husband, and marriage through liberty of choice. The worth of counsel in the formation of a marriage is appreciated, but, adds Wit, the ultimate decision must rest with the couple themselves:

> The wife was made for to be a help in the work,
> And thus was wedlock wrought by means of a third person;
> First by the father's will and the counsel of friends,
> And then by their mutual consent as the two of them might accord.
>
> (IX, 112-15)

Within the marriage bond the sexual act has an honorable place. This is the implication of the declaration that marriage is for the begetting of kings, knights, etc. It is also implied in the poet's whimsical description of himself being mauled by "Elde." He loses his hearing, his teeth are knocked out, he is struck with the gout, and finally he is rendered impotent. And, he adds:

> ... my wife was grieved,
> And wished full well that I was in heaven.
> For the limb that she loved me for and was glad to feel
> Especially at night when we were naked,
> I might in no way make it to her liking
> So Old Age and she had truly laid it waste.
>
> (XX, 192-97)

There is nothing in the text to suggest that the wife's desires for sexual play were wrong. On the contrary, the poet sympathizes with her for her loss and regrets that he can no longer satisfy her. A still

THE CRAFT OF LOVE

further indication that the conjugal act is regarded as morally justified we find in another passage which, like the lines quoted above from *Purity*, repeats in considerable details the ecclesiastical teaching. Again, it is Wit who speaks:

> And every secular person who may not continue [as virgin]
> Wisely go wed and beware of sin;
> For lecherous longing is a measuring rod of hell.
> Whilest thou art young, and thy weapon keen,
> Work it with a wife, if thou wouldst be excused...
> When you have been wedded, beware and respect the times,
> Not as Adam and Eve when Cain was begot.
> For in undue season, truly, between a man and a woman
> There should be no play [Bourde] in bed; except they both be clean
> Both of life and soul, and in perfect charity,
> That secret act [derne dede] no one should do.
> And if they lead thus their life it pleases almighty God;
> For He made wedlock first and himself said:
> It is good that each have his wife to avoid fornication
>
> (IX, 177-91)

Marriage as made by God, and made first (before the other sacraments); marriage as a refuge from lechery, as justifying or "excusing" the sexual act; the sexual act as pleasing to God when performed by those who are clean and in charity; and respect for the times of abstinence—these are common truths in the theology of the time, repeated here by our poet. The higher value of celibacy is hinted at but not insisted upon. Rather, the emphasis is upon the worth of marriage: men are urged that while they are young and their "wepne kene" they should "Wysly go wedde." As in the theology the term "excused" is used relative to the conjugal act, but used broadly: not just the goods of marriage but marriage itself excuses its use.

It would almost seem that, like Duns Scotus before him, Langland had qualms over the use of the word, feeling perhaps that it distorted rather than expressed the truth. For in the C-text, Langland's final revision of his poem, line 181 above has been altered to: "Work it with a

250

OTHER POETS OF THE FOURTEENTH CENTURY

wife for God's work I hold it (C-text, XI, 288). But whatever the reason for the change the C-text makes explicit what is already implicit in this passage from the B-version: the conjugal act is fully justified, "being God's own work." Also in the above passage the belief is expressed that not only is the act of marriage compatible with charity but also it should be rooted in perfect charity and should not be performed unless it is. As in the theology, here too nature and grace are meant to work together, making of the act a divine as well as human deed. In this text, therefore, so obviously reflective of Church teaching, there is not the least suggestion that that teaching appeared to our poet as a threat to love, sex, or marriage. On the contrary, it is seen as an encouragement for the young to marry while they are sexually vigorous and as a command to love and make love out of love's plenty (*caritas*).

As suggested at the beginning of the passage quoted above, virginity or celibacy is recognized in the present poem as a higher state than that of marriage. But, again as in the ecclesastical teaching we have examined, and also in Chaucer and Gower, celibacy is esteemed not for what is surrendered but for what it intends: serious prayer and the works of charity. So at the beginning of the poem Holy Church declares: "Chastity without charity is chained in hell; it is as useless [*lewed*] as a lamp with no light therein" (I, 187-88).

Langland offers still further qualification of the worth of celibacy, revealing, in the matter of vocation, the balanced judgment found elsewhere in the time and place of our study. Like the best of his contemporaries he ranges in his thought through the whole of the universe, personifying each of its elements: Nature, Reason, Wisdom (Wit), Imagination, Scripture, Holy Church, the vices and virtues... are all given their say in the poem, and Love as caritas appears as the "Leche [physician] of lyf and nexte owre lorde selue" (I, 202). In this broad context the institutions and vocations of humankind are viewed. They are hierarchical, parts of an ordered universe—the great "chain of love" of Chaucer's godlike Theseus\—and though "some be clenner [better] than some" (XIX, 244), all are necessary both for each other and for the whole. Thus the good-counseling Imagination is not so much interested in which vocation is better than another as in how each person fulfills his/her proper gift, whatever it might be:

THE CRAFT OF LOVE

> ... if thou be married, love thy mate,
> And continue to live as the law demands, while you both
>   shall live.
> The same if thou be a religious: run thou never more
> To Rome nor Rochemadour than thy rule teacheth,
> And hold thee under obedience, that is highway to heaven.
> And if thou be maid ripe for marriage [mayden to marye]
>   and might well continue [as maid, i.e. virgin],
> Seek thou no distant shrines, for thy soul's health.
>
> (XII, 34-40)

And holy Grace adds that there is place neither for envy, when one is in a lowly position, nor for pride when one's "crafte" is "Fairest." Rather, each must love the other, and the highest in rank must be "mildest of bearing" (XIX, 244-50)

The King's Book

Chaucer, Gower, Langland, and the author of *Sir Gawain* and *Purity* are four of the greatest of the fourteenth-century English poets, and all share a doctrine of love and marriage prominent, if not dominant, in the teaching and practice of their Church. This tradition of "honest love" is carried into the English fifteenth-century poetry in the romances of John Lydgate. It is also shared and perpetuated by Lydgate's worthy contemporary, the author of *The Kingis Quair* (The King's Book, c. 1423).[6] In his edition of this poem W. Mackay MacKenzie quotes with approval the opinion of C. S. Lewis that in the *The Kingis Quair* "the poetry of marriage at last emerges from the traditional poetry of adultery."[7] MacKenzie thinks that "Lydgate had got as far as recognizing the 'unhappy cases' of the feudal loveless marriage and the forced vow of celibacy, but he believes that it was only in the *The Kingis Quair* that "the reconciliation of love and marriage is achieved."[8] It should be obvious by now that such reconciliation was achieved long before the writing of the *The Kingis Quair,* both in the theology and poetry.

However, such love, that is love that is set upon and fulfilled within marriage, is this poem's unambiguous theme. Even aside from the evidence of authorship and historical fact—it is at least probable that

OTHER POETS OF THE FOURTEENTH CENTURY

the poem was written by James I of Scotland in celebration of his love for, and marriage to Joan Beaufort[9]—the poem in and of itself attests to the goodness and beauty of faithful conjugal love. There is the imprisoned poet's vigorous condemnation of marital infidelity: as he gazes upon his beloved from his prison window he begs Philomela (the nightingale) to "Chide thir husbandis that are fals... And bid thame mend" (st. 56). Minerva (Lydgate's Pallas), to whom Venus herself sends the poet for direction in love, repeats the condemnation: "Fy on all swich! fy on thair doubilness!/ Fy on thair lust and bestly appetite!" (136).

The Venus of the poem is definitely the good Venus. There is nothing wild or lustful about her. She is the "goddesse of delyte" (96), but she lies upon her bed modestly, with "A mantill cast ouer hir shuldris quhite"; and the poet addresses her as "in the huge weltering wawis [waves] fell/ Off luftis [love's] rage, blisful havin and sure" (100). Modest in her appearance, she is likewise modest and gracious in her conduct: "Benignely sche turnyt has hir face/ Towardis me full plesantly..." (104). Like Gower's Venus, she directs the poet beyond herself to the one who embodies wisdom, the goddess Minerva: the poet is to abide by her commands (112). As Venus sees herself to be at one with Minerva so Minerva is in conscious accord with Venus. She will not have the poet's love "be sett all-uterly/ Of nyce [foolish] lust" (129), but she definitely sanctions both love and desire; only she would have them "ground and set in Cristen wis" (130, 142).

The poet is docile to all the advice he has received, and eventually wins his love. And it is the fullness of love that is his in the end, which in the genuinely Christian context of the poem can only mean marriage. "Now sufficiente," he says, "is my felicitee" (183). He is now "In perfyte joy, that nevir may remufe/ Bot only deth" (188), echoing, it would seem, the "tyl dethe us departe" in the contemporary nuptial liturgy. At any rate the whole of this line would have suggested to the medieval reader the sureness of the endurance of love that only marriage could bring. Again, the poet-lover's final words before he sends his "litill tretis" on its way may also contain a reference to the nuptial rite. Being "In lufis yok, that esy is and sure [secure]," he declares that his love "from day to day,/ Flourith *ay newe*." Such, as we have seen, was the express hope of the Church as the bride's dowry was presented: "in the clear sonority of silver is symbolized the internal love that must always be new *(semper recens)* between them [spouses]." But whatever the echoes of current theology and liturgy, the entire mood and drift of the poem—the condemnation of marital infidelity, the express desire for fullness of love and the declared achievement of it, the insistence that love be grounded "in Christian wise," the pointed harmonization of Venus and Minerva (love and reason, love *subject to* reason), the presentation of Venus as not just the "blissful haven" against love's rage but the "sure" haven, and the poet's final corresponding rest under not just the "easy" yoke of love but under love's "secure" yoke—all of this leaves little room for doubt that the happy romantic love being celebrated here is one that is set upon and eventually realized within marriage.

The act of love is not specifically mentioned in the *The Kingis Quair*. But implicit is the doctrine on conjugal intercourse that we have seen operative in the theology and in our other poetry. As with Gower and Lydgate (and the author of the Echecs) Venus, "the goddess of delight," is reconciled with Minerva, representative, as always, of reason and wisdom and, in the *The Kingis Quair*, of Christian wisdom. And Minerva declares that she does not deny desire, but simply requires it to be "set in Christian wise" and be not "only" (alluterly) for pleasure. Having abided by this teaching, our lover-poet has in the end the fullness, the completion of his joy, which can only mean that both his body and spirit were satisfied.

In much the same way as Lydgate's *Temple of Glass* our present poem inculcates the need for liberty to choose one's state of life and one's partner in marriage. Those who in their youth were forced into the cloister come before Venus filled with sorrow and complain against those who had beguiled them" (90). Also before Venus, equally distressed and sad, are those who "by maistry were fro thair chos [choice] dryve" and "Were coplit with othir that could noght accord" (92). These stand in dreary contrast to the joyous liberty of the poet-lover who gave his heart "For ever of free wyll" (41) and received his lady's heart in return "onely of hir grace" (193).

There is nothing in the poem concerning the social relationship of husband and wife, because, as in the poems of Lydgate, courtship rather than marriage is central. The woman is called the man's "hertis sovereyne" (183), but this, as we have argued, does not seem to have been incompatible in medieval literature with the social sovereignty of the male. Also, there is no comparison drawn between celibacy and marriage. The celibate state is mentioned but only as forced (82, 90) and in its failures (81, 88-89), and the consequences in both cases are presented as tragic. But there is no implied condemnation of celibacy as such. It is not because the "folk of religioun" had surrendered love that they are shamed, but because "thay first forsuke him [Love] opynly,/ And efter that therof had repenting" (89). The implication is that they should not have repented their original choice but kept their vow in good spirit. The vow of celibacy, like that of marriage, must be freely made and faithfully kept. The *The Kingis Quair* seems here to be saying nothing more, nor less, than this.

CHAPTER 13

CONCLUSIONS

Needless to say (yet again!), the conclusions that may be drawn from this study must be read within the limits of the ecclesiastical teaching and the poetry that have been actually considered. As argued in our Prologue, and also throughout our text and notes, in the later medieval world there were theological and canonical statements still effectual of an earlier period that would seem to be irreconcilable with a moral appreciation of sexual love even when set upon or grounded in marriage. There are yet other ecclesiastical considerations of marriage that are suspiciously silent concerning the mutual love of spouses or that seem to accord it only minor importance. Even in the theology that we have observed we might isolate passages that seem to hold little sympathy for a love paramours within as well as outside of marriage.

Further, there must have been individual churchmen and preachers who knew dangerously little theology and expressed only their own bias, fears, and scruples. As for the poetry, we must remember that little enough medieval English secular verse has survived to tell the whole tale. And much of what does remain sings of loves more at home within the dusky temple of Venus/Priapus than out under the warm and joyous sun of Dame Nature, "Vicar of the Almighty Lord."

However, the ecclesiastical teaching that has been presented—and presented in full context this side (I hope!) of tedium—represents a strong and prominent current in the thinking and practice of the late medieval Church. And if there were churchmen who thought and preached their own Manichaean propensities, there were surely others who learned from the theologies, liturgies, and preaching we have considered, taught and preached what they learned therein, and had enough tact and good sense to follow that telling rubric at the end of

THE CRAFT OF LOVE

the nuptial liturgy and leave spouses, precisely as they reclined on their bed, "in peace."

Likewise, the poetry we have considered is the finest English poetry of its time, and much of it was regarded as such by its contemporaries. And, as instanced in Lydgate and the author of the *The Kingis Quair* relative to Chaucer and Gower, it was early and widely imitated not only stylistically but also in its "doctrine" of "honeste love." Whatever contrary beliefs, therefore, may have been present in the England of the time, the one that has appeared throughout this study was common enough and enjoyed more than adequate sanction. Both Church and poet seem to have been at home in it.

The following summary and generalized conclusions as to shared doctrine of Church and poet of late fourteenth- and early fifteenth-century England would seem to be reasonable:

1. Human sexual love appears as a continuous part of a larger cosmic love that originates from God, and also as a natural urge that is fundamentally good. But its goodness depends on whether or not in a given instance it is subject to nature and reason (spirit, wisdom), both of which require that it be fulfilled within the indissoluble or life-long fidelity of marriage. When it is so fulfilled, it is not just good but holy.

2. Such love may and should have its beginnings prior to marriage in courtship and engagement, for marriage must be rooted in the free choice of the partners and must be motivated, fundamentally, by their love for one another, which requires time for discovery and development. But the specifically sexual expression and consummation of this love are reserved for marriage itself.

3. The ultimate or "natural" aim of marriage is the begetting and rearing of children. But most essential to marriage, and most important within it, is the faithful love bond between husband and wife—the *sacramentum*—and of all the loves under God that between spouses is meant to be the greatest. Marriage is also—and partly because of the love therein—a bond of justice: husband and wife have definite rights before God and society over each other's body and goods.

4. All love principally intends a union of hearts or affection, and this is a greater good than is the physical intimacy of love. But within

CONCLUSIONS

marriage the latter, including the delight—the most intense delight—that may issue from it, is likewise good and holy and is continuous with the deeper, more essential union. However, the physical act of love must be properly motivated and fulfilled. And, generally, it is such when husband and wife, grounded in the charity that embraces God and society as well as one another, are intent upon procreation and/or are each graciously (courteously) concerned for the needs of the other as well as self.

When, however, conjugal love-making is "unnatural" or brutish, or when one uses the other only for private, self-centered satisfaction, then the act, together with its pleasure, is vitiated. The principle operative throughout seems to be that of organic totality. Not this or that aspect or goal of marriage in isolation from the others, not one spouse exclusive of the other, or marriage itself apart from society as a whole or the God who made it. But all of it together in vital mutuality and harmony, each element sustaining and sustained by the other. Not all need be in the conscious intent of the lovers but all must be respected.

5. Husband and wife must bear themselves toward each other in mutual love and obedience. The husband is lord in the marriage, head of the household, but in dignity of person his wife is his equal, and is to be regarded as such within the home and before society. While she must obey him in all things reasonable he must seek and respect her counsel. And he must exercise his lordship not tyranically but in the service of love.

6. Celibacy, as a way of life allowing for a fuller and more direct service of God and humankind, is higher in dignity and merit than is marriage. The latter, however, if faithfully lived has its own nobility and holiness and may in truth be considered a religious order on a par with the various orders of celibates. And if in theory celibacy is a higher state than marriage, in point of fact many of the married may well earn a higher place in heaven than many a celibate. Celibates and the married, therefore, are not to envy each other. Rather, all must seek to serve the common good in and through their proper gifts and calling. Again, it is the principle of totality, the great chain of love that is at work.

THE CRAFT OF LOVE

These, I must repeat, are only generalized conclusions, and are offered more to focus attention on a common attitude and tendency than on the specifics of agreement. Not all of these points are expressed in all of the poetry and ecclesiastical teaching examined, though in some cases—as in the theologies of Aquinas and "Brother Alexander" and in the poetry of Chaucer and Gower—they are.

But in all of the doctrine considered, whether of poetry or theology, the desirability of a full, courteous, physically and spiritually romantic and joyous love between husband and wife is amply in evidence. Also in evidence is the undesirability of bestial or extra-marital or contra-marital love and a love that grows old and dies. There was, therefore, no conflict between the ecclesiastical teaching on human love as it appears in the Church's liturgy and the best of its theologians, and the love themes of the greatest English poetry of our period. And a concrete, living instance of the harmony between the two may be found in the person of one who was both priest and monk of apparently irreproachable conduct and a poet of considerable reputation and influence in his time—John Lydgate. Lydgate could write as easily of love *paramours* as of the love of God or of the Virgin. And as far as is known, none of his contemporaries, whether cleric or lay, took scandal and reproved him for it.

Nor need we search beneath the letter of our poems to find the spirit of the *caritas* taught by the Church. Charity is very much to the fore in much of the poetry. Not necessarily the pure or "elicited" charity that seems to be the only kind recognized by some critics of the medieval scene; but the charity that welcomes and perfects one's natural graces and virtues and loves. Almost all the love celebrated by our poets is an honorable love grounded "in Cristen wis," and therefore it is—or at least was for the medieval poet and theologian—part of the universal love or charity that looks to God directly and to the whole of humankind.

Finally, if, as some have theorized, the Church's attitude toward love and marriage was "softened" at an earlier stage by the "new love" philosophy of Troubadour and kindred poetry; by the late fourteenth century the influence, if influence there was, would have been in the opposite direction. The poets of our period, unlike those of the twelfth

CONCLUSIONS

and early thirtheenth centuries, were born into a Church where doctrine on marriage was already shaped in considerable detail—by an Alexander of Hales, a Thomas Aquinas, a Bonaventure, a Duns Scotus—and was all but finalized. They were, therefore, in the position of receivers only.

This is not to suggest that the poets of the late fourteenth century simply parroted the theologians and preachers. True, there are, as we have seen, unmistakable reflections of theology, sermon, and liturgy in the poetry. But these inherited materials of doctrine and practice the poets viewed from their own perspective, shaped into their own philosophy of life, and used toward the ends of their art. They found in their Church a doctrine of love that was to their liking, and they made the most of it.

Notes

Chapter 1 Prologue

[1] F. Schlosser, *The Art of CourtlyLove, by Andreas Capellanus*, with introduction, translation, and notes by John Jay Parry (New York: Columbia University Press, 1941), vi.

[2] Henri Davenson, *Les Troubadours [par] Henri Davenson* (Paris: Éditions du Seuil, 1961), 96 and 101.

[3] See Rene Descartes's, *Dscourse on Method and his Meditations on First Philosophy*.

[4] Thomas Cahill, *How the Irish Saved Civilization* (New York: Anchor Books, 1996).

[5] John Noonan, *Contraception:A History of its Treatment by Catholic Theologians and Canonists* (Cambridge: Harvard University Press, 1965).

[6] Ursala King, *The Tablet*, 7 July, 1990, pp. 858-59. For Ranke-Heinemann, See *Eunuchen fur das Himmelreich*.

[7] Cahill, *How the Irish*.

[8] Saint Augustine, *On Continence*, ch. 9 PL 40:364, trans. Sr. Mary McDonald, O.P., *The Fathers of the Church*, ed. Roy J. Deferrari, vol. 16, p. 216.

[9] Henry Charles Lea, *History of Sacerdotal Celibacy in the Christian Church* (London:Ballantyne & Co., 1907). His indictments as instanced in many studies to the present day including a 4th ed. of Lea's original work (1966).

[10] Edvard Westermarck, *The History of Human Marriage* (New York: The Allerton Book Company, 1922), Vol. I: 414-15.

[11] Stuart Alfred Queen, *The Family in Various Cultures* (Philadelphia: Lippincott, 1952), 156.

[12] Philip Sherrard, *Christianity and Eros: Eessays on the Theme of Sexual Love* (London: S.P.C.K., 1976), 10-12.

[13] Uta Ranke-Heinemann, *Eunuchs for the Kingdom of Heaven: Women, Sexuality, and the Catholic Church*, trans. Peter Heinegg (New York : Doubleday, 1990).

[14] Uta Ranke-Heinemann's, *Eunuchs*. passim.

[15] Margaret Miles, *Carnal Knowing: Female Nakedness and Religious Meaning in the Christian West* (Boston, Mass.: Beacon Press, 1989).

[16] James Brundage, *Law, Sex, and Christian Society in Medieval Europe* (Chicago: University of Chicago Press, 1987), 5, 81, 85, 154.

[17] Peter Lamont Brown, *Body and Society: Men, Women and Sexual Renunciation in Early Christianity* (New York: Columbia University Press, 1988), xviii and 425.

[18] R. W. Southern, *Western Society and the Church in the Middle Ages* (New York: Penguin Books, 1982).

THE CRAFT OF LOVE

[19] W. A. Pantin, *The English Church of the Fourteenth Century* (Notre Dame, Ind.: University of Notre Dame Press, 1962), 253.

[20] Beryl Smalley, *English Friars and Antiquity in the Early XIV Century* (New York: Barnes & Noble, 1961), 28-29.

[21] George H. Joyce, *Christian Marriage* (London and New York: Sheed and Ward, 1933), 48 ff.

[22] Driver and Massey, "Comparative Studies of North American Indians" in *Transactions of the American Philosophical, Society*, New Series, Vol. 47, part 2, p. 394. For many other examples of the legal and contractual aspects of marriage see Westermarck's *History of Human Marriage, passim*.

[23] See Smalley *passim*, and J. B. Allen, *The Friar as Critic: Literary Attitudes in the Later Middle Ages* (Nashville: Vanderbilt University Press, 1971), 40-41 and *passim*. See also D. W. Robertson on almost any page of his many writings.

Chapter 2 Priests and Poets

[1] C. S. Lewis, *The Allegory of Love* (Oxford: The Clarendon Press, 1936), 17-18.

[2] D. W. Robertson, *A preface to Chaucer; studies in medieval perspectives* (Princeton, N.J.: Princeton University Press, 1962), 6-31 and *passim*. See also the same author's essay, "Some Medieval Literary Terminology," S.P., 48: 669-92.

[3] See Maxwell Luria's review in *Studies in the Age of Chaucer* (Knoxville: New Chaucer Society, the University of Tennessee, Knoxville, c1985), 4: 181-89.

[4] D. S. Brewer, "Love and Marriage in Chaucer's Poetry" in *The Modern Language Review*, 49 (1954), 461.

[5] Jack A. W. Bennett, *The Parlement of Foules, an interpretation* (Oxford: Clarendon Press, 1957), 10-11: The argument is developed, with special reference to Thomas Aquinas, on 144-45, 191-92. See also Professor Bennett's article, "Gower's 'Honeste Love'" in *Patterns of Love and Courtesy*, 121, where he concludes on the *Confessio*: "'Honeste love' in wedlock, caritas in the commonwealth, are wholly compatible ideals", and it is Gower's distinctive achievement to have harmonized them in a single poem, while still setting forth the graces and 'gentilesse' of coutoisie."

[6] Gervase Matthew, *The Court of Richard II* (London: Murray, 1968), especially Ch. XIV, "The Heroine and Marriage," where examples are given of earlier English or Anglo-Norman romance still popular in Richard's day, which preview *amour courtois* within marriage. See also Matthew's essay, "Marriage and Amour Courtoise in Late Fourteenth Century England," in *Essays Presented to Charles Williams* (London: New York: Oxford Univ. Press, 1947), 128-35.

NOTES

[7] Gervase Matthews, "Ideals of Friendship," in *Patterns of love and courtesy: essays in memory of C. S. Lewis* (London: Edward Arnold, 1966), 45-53.

[8] T. P. Dunning, "Chaucer's Icarus-Complex," *BST* (1962), 89-106.

[9] Henry A. Kelly, *Love and Marriage in the Age of Chaucer* (Ithaca, NY: Cornell University Press, 1975), *passim*.

[10] Dorothy Bethurum, "Chaucer's Point of View as Narrator in the Love Poems," *PMLA*, lxxiv, 511-20.

[11] Henry A. Kelly, 245-85.

[12] Eamon Duffy, The Stripping of the Altars: Traditional Religion in England, c.1400-c.1580 (New Haven, CT: Yale University Press, 1992), 11.

[13] See Romans 12, 1 Cor. 12-14, Col. 1:24, etc. for St. Paul's conception of the Mystical Body of Church Universal. St. Thomas further details the teaching when he discusses the question of Christ as head of the Church or Mystical Body in S.T., III, q. 8, aa. 1-8.

[14] H. C. Lea, *History*, I: 36-37 (p. 25 in the abbreviated 1966 edition.)

[15] For an altogether different reading in the 1990's of the tradition behind clerical celibacy see Christian Cochini, *Apostolic Origins of Priestly Celibacy* (San Francisco: Ignatius Press, 1990), *passim*.

[16] See John R. Connery, S.J., "The Role of Love in Christian Marriage: A Historical Overview," *Communio* 11:3 (Fall 1984), pp. 244-57.

[17] As quoted by Janet Smith in her *Humanae Vitae: A Generation Later* (Washington DC: Catholic University of America Press, 1991), 59.

[18] S.T. I, q. 1, a. 8, ad 2

[19] Eric Fuchs, Sexual Desire and Love: Origins and History of the Christian Ethic of Sexuality and Marriage (Cambridge: J. Clarke; New York: Seabury Press, 1983), 86-92, 104-108.

[20] Tertullian, *Ad Uxorem*, ii, 9, EL, t. i, cols. 1302-1304. from *Ancient Christian Writers: Tertullian Marriage and Remarriage*, ed. and trans. William P. LeSaint, S.J. (Westminster, Md.: Newman Press, 1951), 35-36.

[21] Tertullian *De exhortatione castitatis*, x, 11, EL, t. ii, col. 926; and Per Monogamia, i, EL, t. ii, col. 931. trans. 59, 70.

[22] Tertullian, 151, note 2.

[23] A chronological list of Tertullian's extant works, together with the division and dating of his life according to his Catholic, Semi-Montanist, and Montanist periods, can be found in D'Ales, *La Theologie de Tertullien*, p. xiii.

That the older Tertullian was recognized in his own time as a heretic is amply evidenced in other early Christian writers.

[24] St. Jerome, Epistle xlviii, 8 ff, PL, t. xxii, cols. 498-501.

[25] See Peter Brown.

[26] The ante-Nicene fathers. *Translations of the Writings of the Fathers Down to A. D. 325* (New York: C. Scribner's sons, 1899-1900), 7: 5.

[27] *pivin. Instit.* vi, 16, EL, t. vi, cols. 692-93, trans. William Fletcher. Rather than "lawful object" for *legitimum torum*, as Fletcher translates, I have more accurately translated it as in the text.

[28] *A history of the councils of the church, from the original documents*, by Charles Joseph Hefele, trans. and ed. William R. Clark (New York: AMS Press, 1972), 1: 479.

[29] Peter Brown, 429.

[30] Hefele as rendered by Clark, vol. ii, pp. 326-336. Thus Clark's translation of the original Greek as "married intercourse" and 'as "seemly." But "married intercourse" should read "the state of marriage," and "honorable" is a more accurate translation than "seemly." For the original texts, French translations, comments and glosses on Gangra as of all the councils, See C. J. Hefele, *A History of the Christian Councils*, trans. and ed. by William R. Clark (Edinburgh: 1883), 1: 1029-1045.

[31] Margaret Miles, *Carnal*, 66-70.

[32] See G. LeBras, "Vacant" (*DTC*), vol. 9 (2), cols. 2177-78.

[33] A letter to *The Tablet*, 21 Aug. 1993, p. 1072.

[34] Kahlil Gibran, The *Prophet*, "On Marriage" (New York: Alfred Knopf, 1952).

[35] Etienne Gilson, *History*. 325.

Chapter 3 Aristotelian Thomism

[1] Thomas Gilby, *St. Thomas Aquinas: Philosophical Texts* (Oxford: Oxford University Press, 1960), xvii.

[2] Gilby, xvii.

[3] W. Kasper, *Theology of Christian Marriage* (New York: Seabury Press, 1980), 7-8.

[4] The text of the condemnation in systematic order may be found in P. Mandonnet's *Siger de Brabant . . . lime partie*, 175-88. Andreas is not mentioned by name (neither is Thomas Aquinas) but the book "De amore, sive De Deo amoris, qui sic incipit: 'Cogit me multum, etc.'..." is condemned in the

NOTES

prologue of the condemnation. For a list of the philosophical propositions which may be traced to St. Thomas. See E. Gilson *History*, 728.

[5] Etienne Gilson, History. 356. See also William Hinnebusch, The History of the Dominican Order (Staten Island, N.Y.: Alba House, 1966), 2: 149-161.

[6] F. Roensch, *Early Thomistic School* (Dubuque, Iowa: Priory Press, 1964), 28-83.

[7] Vernon J. Burke, *Aquinas' Search for Wisdom* (Milwaukee: Bruce Pub. Co., 1965), 225. Citation from the *Fontes Vitae S. Thomae Aquinatis*, VI, 656.

[8] Roensch, 18. For Thomas's early title of "doctor communis." See K. Foster's *The Life of Saint Thomas Aquinas: Biographical Documents* (London: Longmans, Green; Baltimore, Helicon Press, 1959), 134, citing the *Historia Ecclesiastica* (c. 1317) by Tolomeo of Lucca: "And let me say here [writes Tolomeo] that this man is supreme among modern teachers of philosophy and theology, and indeed in every subject. And such is the common view and opinion, so that nowadays in the University of Paris they call him the *doctor communis* because of the outstanding clarity of this teaching."

[9] For an impression of St. Thomas's contemporary impact see the biographical documents cited in Kenelm Foster.

[10] Angelus Walz, *Saint Thomas Aquinas, a biographical study*. trans. Fr. Sebastian Bullough (Westminster, Md.: Newman Press, 1951), 188.

[11] M. D. Chenu, *St. Thomas D'Aquin et la theologie* (Paris: Éditions du Seuil, 1959), e.g. 116.

[12] D. W. Robertson, *A preface to Chaucer*, 304, 311-14, 323, 360.

[13] See B. Smalley, "The Biblical Scholar," in *Robert Grosseteste: scholar and bishop. Essays in commemoration of the seventh centenary of his death*. ed. Callus, Daniel and Angelo, Philip (Oxford: Clarendon Press, 1955), 86.

[14] Thomas Aquinas *Commentary on the Sentences of Peter Lombard*, Book IV, dists. xxvi-xlii.

[15] For a list and the dates of St. Thomas's various works, see. Chenu, *St. Thomas*, 186-87; also Walz, 178-85. For a full and critical discussion of all Thomas's works in the context of the scholastic methods of the time, see. Chenu's *Toward understanding Saint Thomas*, tr. with authorized corrections and bibliographical additions by A. M. Landry and D. Hughes (Chicago: H. Regnery Co., 1964).

[16] D. Knowles, *The Evolution of Medieval Thought* (Baltimore: Helicon Press, 1962), 143.

THE CRAFT OF LOVE

[17] James Brundage, 423-425,

[18] S.T., Ia, 20, 1.

[19] Ia, 45, 7.

[20] Ia, 2ae, 1, 6. Also for instances in both medieval philosophy and literature generally of "cosmic love," i.e. of the *primum movens* moving all "by being loved," See P. Dronke's article, "L'amor the move it sole e l'altre stelle," in *Studi Medievali*, serie terza, 1965, 389-422.

[21] S.T., Ia, 6, 4.

[22] 2ae, 2ae, 23, 2.

[23] *Nature and grace; selections from the Summa theologica of Thomas Aquinas.* Translated and edited by A. M. Fairweather (Philadelphia: Westminster Press,1954), 21.

[24] Thomas treats Original Sin together with personal or actual sin in S.T., Ia2ae, 71-89, after discussing virtue. The vices, of course, outnumber the virtues, since one virtue is the "mean" between two extremes.

[25] S.T., suppl., 41, 1.

[26] See H. A. Kelly, 163-242 for a discussion of clandestine marriage and its relevance to a poem such as Chaucer's *Troilus and Criseyde.*

[27] See Fairweather. The principle of grace presupposing and perfecting nature is enunciated time and again by Aquinas, e.g. S.T.., Ia, 2, 2 ad 1; Ia2ae, 99, 2 ad 1; 3a, 71, 1 ad 1; Ia, 1, 8 ad 2; 2a2ae, 26, 9 obj. 2.

[28] S.T., suppl., 49, 3; suppl., 65, 1.

[29] For Thomas's use of the terminology see S.T., 3a, 66, 1; 73, 6; 84, 1, ad 3.

[30] 4 Sent., dist. 31, q. 1, a. 3.

[31] F. Schlosser, *Andreas Capellanus*, 266.

[32] Kenelm Foster, *God's tree: essays on Dante and other matters* (London: Blackfriars Publications, 1957), 148.

[33] ST Ia2ae, 65, 1.

[34] 3: 123.

[35] Thus T. P. Dunning in the essay "Chaucer's Icarus-Complex", 100 warns that to translate *amicitia* today as "friendship" is to mistranslate it. And S. Pinckaers in "Ce que le Moyen Age pensait du mariage," *Suplement de la Vie Spirituelle*, 430, note 24 remarks that "For St. Thomas, friendship is the most perfect degree of love and therefore can embrace conjugal love."

NOTES

[36] S.T., 1a, 92, 2.

[37] C. S. Lewis, 17: The theologians "are not talking about the same kind of passion as the romantics. The one party means merely an animal intoxication; the other believes, whether rightly or wrongly, in a 'passion' which works a chemical change upon appetite and affection and turns them into a thing different from either. About 'passion' in this sense Thomas Aquinas has naturally nothing to say—as he has nothing to say about the steam-engine. He had not heard of it. It was only coming into existence in his time, and finding its first expression in the poetry of courtly love."

[38] See J. Pieper, *Guide to Thomas Aquinas,* trans. from the German by Richard and Clara Winston (Notre Dame, IN: University of Notre Dame Press, 1962), 118. "... almost as soon as Thomas awoke to critical consciousness he recognized that it was his life's task to join these two extremes; "Aristotle" and the "Bible"; "nature" and the "supernatural" which seemed inevitably to be pulling away from one another."

[39] la 2ae, 26-28.

[40] For a discussion of the use of mystical language and the language of love apropos the relationship between human and divine love see Peter Dronke *Medieval Latin and the Rise of European Love-lyric* (Oxford: Clarendon Press, 1965-1966), vol. I, ch. 2, especially pp. 59-78 where Gerard de Liege, Bernard of Clairvaux, Richard of St. Victor, and Hildegard of Bingen are instanced, and their respective attitudes distinguished. See also Jean LeClercq, *Monks on marriage, a twelfth-century view,* (New York: Seabury Press, 1982), *passim.*

[41] S.T., la 2ae, 28, 5.

[42] S.T., la 2ae, 24, 3.

[43] S.T., 2a2ae, 26, 7.

[44] S.T., 26, 11.

[45] S.T., suppl., 41, 3.

[46] See Eric Fuchs, 97, and others noted for their misreading of the *malum poenae* as *malum culpae.* They also, for the most part, share what St. Thomas would regard as an excessively optimistic view of human sexuality.

[47] S.T., suppl., 49, 4, ad 3.

[48] S.T., Suppl., 41, 4.

[49] S.T., suppl., 49, 6.

[50] C. S. Lewis, p. 15.

[51] S.T., suppl., 49, 5, ad 2.

[52] S.t., suppl., 64, 2.

[53] S.T., suppl., 64, 1, ad 2.

[54] So in St. Albert's *Commentary on Peter Lombard's Sentences*, bk. 4, dist. 32, B, a. 4, ad 1: "dicendum quod licet non requiratur [coitus] ex verecundia, tamen jus praeviae petitionis, scilicet quando contrahit matrimonium, adhuc stat, et tunc in contractu primo semper intelligitur petere nisi reclamet aliquando aliqua de causa."

[55] Ivor Armstrong Richards, *Principles of Literary Criticism* (San Diego: Harcourt Brace Jovanovich, 1985, c1925), 96.

[56] Charles Bruehi, *This Way Happiness; Ethics: the Science of the Good Life* (Milwaukee: The Bruce Publishing Company, 1941), 69.

[57] *Contra Gentiles*, iii, 26, 83.

[58] S.T., suppl., 45, 1.

[59] See Ch. 2 of G. H. Joyce, 73.

[60] See. George E. Howard, *A History of Matrimonial Institutions Chiefly in England and the United States* (Chicago: The University of Chicago Press, Callaghan & company; London: T. F. Unwin, 1904), 310.

[61] S.T., suppl., 47, 1-6.

[62] See Eric Fuchs, p. 143.

[63] See *Liber sententiarum* IV, dist. 27.

[64] See. Ildefonse Schuster, *The Sacramentary (Liber sacramentorum)* (London: Burns, Oates & Washbourne Ltd., 1924-30), 1, part 1: 192-93.

[65] S.T., suppl., 43, 1.

[66] *S.T.*, art. 3, ad 6.

[67] See. S.T., suppl, 43, 2, ad 1

[68] S.T., 2a2ae, 154, 4.

[69] S.T., 2a2ae,152, 2-3.

[70] S.T., 2a2ae,153, 3 ad 3.

[71] S.T., suppl. 64, 5-7.

[72] S.T., suppl, 64, 6, ad 2.

[73] S.T., suppl., 41, 4, ad 2.

[74] S.T., 2a2ae, 152, 2, ad 1.

NOTES

[75] Johan Huizinga, The Waning of the Middle Ages, a Study of the Forms of Life (London: E. Arnold & co., 1924), 55.

[76] S.T., suppl., 41, 4, gicl 3.

Chapter 4 Franciscan Augustinianism

[1] For Alexander See Gilson, *History*, 327-29, 682-85; also *New Catholic Encyclopedia*, 1: 296-97.

[2] Cited by Gilson, *History*, 327. Stewart C. Easton, in his *Roger Bacon and his search for a universal science; a reconsideration of the life and work of Roger Bacon in the light of his own stated purposes* (Westport, CT: Greenwood Press, 1970), 30, 68, remarks of Bacon vis-a-vis Alexander that he "was a person of no particular importance to his contemporaries ... totally unlike Alexander of Hales who, according to Bacon's own account, was treated with such exaggerated respect by the Order [of Franciscans] and whose entry brought it such renown." For a discussion of the composition of Alexander's *Summa* see V. Doucet, "The History of the Problem of the Authenticity of the Summa" (*Franciscan Studies*, 7 1947), 26-41, 274-312.

[3] Gilson, *History*, 327.

[4] Alexander of Hales, *Summa Theologica* (–ad fidem codicum edita- Quaracchi, 1924-48). Tomus II, II lib, 1 pars., Incl. IV, Tract. II, sect. II, quaest. I, Tit. I, mem. I, cap. II.

[5] Alexander, quaest. II, cap. I.

[6] Alexander, cap. II.

[7] Alexander, cap. V.

[8] Margaret Miles, Image as Insight: Visual Understanding in Western Christianity and Secular Culture (Boston: Beacon Press, 1985), and Carnal Knowing.

[9] Margaret Miles, *Carnal*, 12.

[10] Reported by Margaret Hebblethwaite, *The Tablet*, 28 Aug., 1993, 1115.

[11] Chaucer, *Canterbury Tales*, WBT, 711-827.

[12] Margaret Miles, *Image*, 75-80.

[13] Margaret Miles, *Carnal Knowing*.

[14] Margaret Miles, *Image*, 90.

[15] Alexander, *Summa,* Tom. IV, lib. III, p. II. inq. II, q. IV, mem. III, cap. I, art. I.

[16] Alexander, art. IV.

[17] Alexander, Tom. III, lib. II, inq. III, tract. IV, sec. II, q. I, Tit. VII, cap. II, art. IV.

[18] See above, Ch. 2, also S.T., suppl., 49, 5 ad 2.

[19] Tom. IV, lib. III, p. II, inq. III, tract. II, sec. I, q. II, Tit. VI. cap. VIII, a. I.

[20] *Ibid.*, ad 1 and 5.

[21] Etienne Gilson, *The Philosophy of St. Bonaventure*, trans. Dom Illtyd Trethowan (New York: Sheed & Ward, 1938), 1-86.

[22] Saint Bonaventure, *Super Libros Sententiarum* (Quaracchi, 1934ff), Liber 2, dist. 18, art. 1, quest. I (hereafter abreviated as: 2 Dist. 18, a. 1, q. 1.)

[23] Bonaventure, *Opera Omnia*, ed. studio et cura PP. collegii a S. Bonaventura (Quaracchi, 1882-1902). Sermon on Rev. 12: 1, vol. 9 (Quaracchi), ser. 6, p. 704b.

[24] Robert P. Prentice, O.F.M. in *The Psychology of Love According to St. Bonaventure* (St. Bonaventure, NY: Franciscan Institute, 1957), 93, note 18.

[25] 4 Dist. 26, a. 1, q. 2.

[26] 4 Dist. 26, a. 1, q. 3.

[27] 4 Dist. 33, a. 1, q. 2.

[28] 3 Dist. 29, a. 1, q. 5.

[29] 3 Dist. 27, a. 1, q. 1.

[30] 4 Dist. 26, a. 2, q. 3.

[31] 4 Dist. 29, a. unicus, q. 1. In question 3 of this article Bonaventure asks whether one can be forced to marry by one's parent's precept. The answer is no, unless one had previously freely consented to the espousals. Then an exception may be made and the marriage carried out at the command of the parent.

[32] 4 Dist. 26, a. 2, q. 1.

[33] 4 Dist. 26, a. 2, q. 2.

[34] 4 Dist. 31, a. 2, q. 3; Dist. 26, a. 2, q. 3 ad 5.

[35] 4 Dist. 31, a. 2, q. 3; for Thomas See. 5.T. suppl., q. 49, a. 6.

[36] 4 Dist. 26, a. 2, q. 2.

[37] For a summary of Scotus's life, his teaching, and his "school", see Gilson, *History*, 454-71. Also see C. R. S. Harris, *Duns Scotus* (Oxford: The Clarendon press, 1927). For a more complete coverage of Soctus's life, teaching, and works. For this, the first volume of this two volume work is especially

NOTES

valuable. Dorothea E. Sharp in *Franciscan Philosophy at Oxford in the Thirteenth Century* (New York: Russell & Russell, 1964), 277-368, has a briefer but satisfactory coverage of the same material. She concentrates on Scotus's career and influence at the English University. For a more recent treatment of Scotus see B. M. Bonansea, O.F.M., *Man and His Approach to God in John Duns Scotus* (Lanham, MD: University Press of America, c1983). In an appendix Bonansea, in addition to a brief, up-to-date account of Scotus's life and philosophical system, gives a catalogue of Scotus's published authentic works.

[38] Gilson, *History*, 736: "... the text printed by Wadding blends different reportations, but it represents the actual teaching of Duns Scotus." The *Summa Theologica* will be referred to in the following notes simply as *Summa*. References to Scotus's commentary on the *Sentences* as it appears in Wadding's edition will be prefaced by that editor's name.

[39] In his introduction to *Duns Scotus on the Will and Morality*, Allan Wolter, O.F.M. (Washington, D.C.: Catholic University of America Press, 1986), describes Scotus's methodology in moral science and within the text proper gives, in both the original and the translation, examples of it. According to Wolter, Scotus was not a voluntarist, as is often claimed, but was closer to Aquinas in his appreciation of nature and reason in matters moral than history has acknowledged.

[40] Wadding, *Sentences* 4 Dist. 26, q. unica, 4th conclusion.

[41] *Summa*, Tom. 5, pars III, q. XLI, a. II.

[42] Wadding, *Sentences*, 4 Dist. 27.

[43] Wadding, *Sentences* 4 Dist. 27, q. 1.

[44] Wadding, *Sentences* 4 Dist. 31, q. unica.

[45] *Summa*, Tom. V, p. III, q. XLIX, a. III.

[46] Wadding, *Sentences* 4 Dist. 31, q. unica. In offering the sacramentum itself by itself as a completely justifying reason for the marital act, Scotus seems to be saying that simply by being married in Christ, husband and wife may make love. No other reason is necessary. In this he is one with St. Albert the Great, who argues that any one of three reasons renders the conjugal act meritorious:

1) the hope for offspring (*spes prolis*);

2) fidelity in rendering due love (*fides reddendi debiti*);

3) awareness of the sacrament (*in rememoratione boni sacramenti*). See. Albert's commentary on the *Sentences*, 4 Dist. 26, C, a. 11.

[47] *Summa*, Tom. V, p. III, q. XLIX, a. I. Thomas Gilby offers the following admonition: "Be warned... that his respect for traditional usage can make St. Thomas an author difficult to pin down; some of the terms he adopts come to him loaded with implications he does not accept, and sometimes his own meanings are in consequence masked." (*Temperance*, pp. 168-69, note a).

[48] Wadding, *Sentences*, Dist. 31, q. i

[49] (121C, vol. ix [2], col. 2179). As for St. Thomas's retention of the term, one must not suppose he thereby accepts its traditional implications. Thomas's thought, often quietly and subtly, changes the meaning of words he is forced to use.

[50] *Summa*, Tom. V, p. III, q. XLI, a. IV.

Chapter 5 The Mind of Christendom

[1] S.T. suppl., 49, 6 sed contra.

[2] St. Albert the Great, *Commentary on the Sentences*, Lib. 4, Dist. 26, B, a. 7.

[3] C. S. Lewis, *Allegory*, 17.

[4] John Crowe Ransom, *The Equilibrists*, On the conjugal act in the state of innocence, see Scotus, *Summa*, Tom. II, p. I, q. XCVIII, a. II; St. Thomas, S.T., Ia, 98, 2 ad 3; and Albert the Great's *Commentary on the Sentences*, 4 Dist. xxvi, a. 7.

Chapter 6 Praying and Believing

[1] *Manuale et Processionale ad Usum Insignis Ecclesiae Eboracensis*, ed. W.G. Henderson (London: Surtees Society Publications, 1875), vol. LXIII (containing marriage rituals of York, Salisbury, and Hereford, together with extracts from 10 other marriage services from the eitht to the fifteenth century). The *ordo ad facienda sponsalia* of the York manual begins on page 24 and continues, in the order in which it is treated in here. The continental rituals of the same period may be found in *De Antiquis Ecclesiae Ritibus*, ed. Martène, Edmond (Antwerp: 1763-64), 4 Vols in 2 (Lib. I, pars ii, c. ix for continental nuptial ritee). For an account of the formation of the liturgy of marriage in the western Church See E. Schillebeeckx, O.P., *Marriage: Secular Reality and Saving Mystery*, trans. N. D. Smith (London: Sheed and Ward, 1965), 2: 33-149. The reader may also consult the summary of the history of conjugal rites in Kenneth Stevenson's introduction to his and Mark Searle's *Documents of the Marriage Liturgy* (Collegeville, Minn.: Liturgical Press, 1992), 1-19.

NOTES

[2] The ms. of the *York Manual* in the University Library, Cambridge, is one of four mss. used by W. G. Henderson in preparing his edition. It is from the fourteenth century. See Henderson, Preface, xiv.

[3] See below for its expression in the Hereford rite.

[4] See Martène, ordo xvi: ex Graecorum Euchologio.

[5] G. H. Joyce, *Christian Marriage*, 581.

[6] Louis Duchesne, *Christian Worship: its Origin and Evolution; a Study of the Latin Liturgy up to the Time of Charlemagne*, trans. McClure (London: Society for Promoting Christian Knowledge; New York: E. & J.B. Young, 1903), 429.

[7] Also edited by Henderson in the same volume as the York Manual the Sarum nuptial rite begins on p. 17 and continues, again in the order in which it is here taken, through p. 26. Henderson omits those parts which are identical with the York rite.

[8] Ms. no. 47, the one manuscript (along with the printed versions) used by Henderson in preparing his edition. See. his preface, xviii.

[9] Martène, *De Antiquis*, ordo x. Richard Lewinsohn, in his *A History of Sexual Customs*, trans. Alexander Mayce (London: New York: Longmans Green, 1958), 183, reproduces a fifteenth-century woodcut of a bridal pair in bed receiving a blessing from a bishop.

[10] Ed. by Henderson, 115-120. Parts identical with York or Sarum are omitted.

[11] The exact reference in Isidore is: "People first began to wear rings on the fourth finger from the thumb because from it a certain vein reaches to the heart (*eo vena quaedam usgue ad cor Dertingat*)." Saint Isidore, of Seville, *Etymologiarum* (Oxonii: E Typographeo Clarendoniano; New York: Oxford University Press, 1911), lib. XIX, c. 32, P.L.., 82, col. 701.

[12] Henderson, *Manuale*, 163-165.

[13] Léon Gautier *La Chevalerie* (Paris: Féchoz et cie, 1896), 358ff.

[14] Searle and Stevenson's, *Documents*, 269, For the marriage liturgies see Henderson, *Manuale*, vol. LXIII -- containing the rituals of York, Salisbury, and Hereford, together with extracts of ten other marriage services from the eight to the fifteenth century. For continental liturgical rites covering a wide area of medieval Europe I have used Martène *De Antiquis*, liber I, pars ii, cap. ix: de ritibus ad sacramentum Matrimonii pertinentibus.

[15] G. R. Owst, *Literature and Pulpit in Medieval* England (Cambridge: University Press; New York: The Macmillan Company, 1933), 384.

THE CRAFT OF LOVE

---

[16] Owst, 234.

[17] *Middle English Sermons*, ed. from British Museum ms. Royal 18 B. xxiii by Woodburn O. Ross (London: Published for the Early English Text Society by H. Milford, Oxford University Press, 1940), p. lvii, and sermon 24.

[18] Middle English Sermons, 375-404, 488.

[19] Middle English Sermons, 385.

[20] ms. Gg. vi, 16, fol. 28b-31b, entitled *In nupciis sollacio*. The manuscript is in the Cambridge University Library and is dated fifteenth century.

[21] ms. Gg. vi, 16, fol. 32a-33b, entitled *In solemnizatione matrimonii*.

Chapter 7 The Moral Manual

[1] Prosper of Aquitaine *De gratia Dei* "Indiculus", cap. 8,

[2] See Denzinger, *Enchiridion symbolorum* (Friburgi Brisgoviae: Herder & Co., 1937). 139. Also John Miller, *Fundamentals of the Liturgy* (Notre Dame, IN: Fides, 1960), 3. For Prosper of Aquitaine see O. Bardenhewer, *Patrology, the Lives and Works of the Fathers of the Church*, trans. from the sec. ed. by Thomas J. Shanhan (Freiburg im Breisgau: St. Louis, MO: B. Herder, 1908), 511-14.

[3] See G. R. Owst, Literature, 71-547.

[4] W. A. Pantin, *The English Church*, 189 ff.

[5] Fr. Lorens O.P., *The Book of Vices and Virtues, a Fourteenth-Century English Translation of the Somme le roi of Lorens d'Orléans*, ed. from the three extant manuscripts by W. Nelson Francis (London: Pub. for the Early English Text Society by H. Milford, Oxford University Press, 1942), ix. See also *Concilia Magnae Britanniae et Hiberniae*, ed. David Wilkins (Londini: Sumptibus R. Gosling, [etc] 1737), 2: 54.

[6] G. R. Owst, *Preaching in Medieval England; an Introduction to Sermon Manuscripts of the Period, c. 1350-1450* (New York: Russell & Russell, 1965), 279, 308.

[7] G. R. Owst *Preaching*, 289.

[8] Maistre Nicole Oresme: *Le Livre de Yconomique d'Aristote*, ed. A. D. Menut (Philadelphia: Transactions of the American Philosophical Society, 1957), N.S., 47: 5, and 783-853.

[9] John Noonan, *Contraception*.

[10] In *New Blackfriars* Sept., 1995.

[11] Menut, 799.

[12] Menut, 792

NOTES

[13] No page or folio references will be given in our discussion of Oresme's treatise. References and quotations simply follow the treatise as given in Menut. For the most part, the pseudo-Aristotelian text will be given followed by Oresme's *gloss* or commentary. It is sufficient to note here that the text had mistakenly been introduced into the Aristotelian corpus before the twelfth century and throughout the thirteenth and fourteenth centuries was regarded as authentically the work of Aristotle and valued as such.

[14] As Duns Scotus seems to have taught when he says that even though venial sin should enter the conjugal act, still its meritorious character may be preserved.

[15] See. M. Haureau, *Nova et Vetra,* vol. i: 188-202.

[16] Menut, 791.

[17] See. G. Le Bras in *DTC,* vol. 9 (2), col. 2180.

[18] *Sermones in Epistolas et Evangelia Dominicalia* (Anvers, 1575), cited by Le Bras.

[19] Cited by A. Lecoy de la Marche, La Chaire Française au Moyen Age, spécialement au XIIIe siècle, d'après les manuscrits contemporains (Paris: Renouard, H. Laurens, successeur, 1886), 429.

[20] William Peraldus, *Summae virtutum ac vitiorum* (Antverpiae, 1588). lib. I, par. 3, tract. 3, c. xv

[21] de La March, *La chaire,* 429.

[22] Hugh of St. Victor *Summa Sententiarum,* Tract. VII, c. 4, P.L. 176, col. 157. See also Duns Scotus, *Summa,* Tom. V, par. III, q. xlviii, a. II.

[23] Peraldus, *Summae,* c. xvi.

[24] *Summae,* c. xvii, for Peraldus's discussion of the marriage act with regard to sin. The three cases in which the marriage act can be performed

[25] *Summae,* c. xvii, for Peraldus's discussion of the marriage act re sin.

[26] Quotations from *The Book of Vices and Virtues* are as they appear in W. Nelson Francis's EETS edition, 245 ff.

[27] St. Thomas himself, who argued that the "mixed life", where action was the *overflow* of contemplation, was to be preferred to contemplation alone, could provide nine reasons for the superiority of the contemplative life above the active, the former being *simpliciter* better, the latter being better only *secundum quid,* that is where necessity required it. (*S.T.,* 2a2ae, 182, 1.)

[28] For a discussion of the penitentials and for English translations of several of Irish, Welsh, Anglo-Saxon and continental origin, see J. T. McNeill and Helena M. Gamer, *Medieval Handbooks of Penance; a Translation of the Principal Libri Poenitentiales and Selections from Related Documents* (New York: Octagon Books, 1965), *passim*.

For their specific relevance to marriage and to sexuality in general, see Pierre Payer, *Sex and the Penitentials: the Development of a Sexual Code, 550-1150* (Toronto: Buffalo: University of Toronto Press, 1984), *passim*, and J. Noonan, *Contraception*, 190-212.

[29] J. Brundage, *Law*, for instance, with regard to marriage, 154-64.

Chapter 8 Love in Secular Manuals and Poetry

[1] Geoffroy de la Tour *The Book of the Knight of La Tour-Landry*, ed. T. Wright (London: Published for the Early English Text Soc. 33, 1868). Wright says in his introduction, the earlier, anonymous translation, which he edited, is, though incomplete as we have it, to be preferred from a literary standpoint.

[2] The French original was later translated and published by William Caxton; reputed to be the first English printer.

[3] Wright's edition, 1. See Ch. 4, note 12 above for dating and provenance. All the following references are to chapters and pages in Wright's edition.

[4] *The Book*, Prologue, 4.

[5] *The Book*, ch. 1, 4

[6] *The Book*, ch. 13, 18.

[7] J. T. Noonan, *Contraception*, 309.

[8] *The Book*, ch. 118, p. 162. None of the ecclesiastics we have examined mentions the existence of such a law or advocates its existence. Perhaps the pious layman felt he had much more to lose through adultery than the celibate was able to envision — perhaps!

[9] *The Book*, ch. 22 (Caxton), 171.

[10] *The Book*, ch. 29 (Caxton), 180.

[11] *The Book*, ch. 34, (Caxton), 48.

[12] *The Book*, ch. 25 (Caxton), 176.

[13] Nevill Coghill, in "Love and 'Foul Delight'...".

[14] *The Book*, the last two quotations are from ch. 17, 24.

[15] *The Book*, ch. 36-37, p. 52; ch. 114-15, 156.

NOTES

[16] See Eileen Power's chapter on "The Menagier's Wife" in her *Medieval People* (London: Methuen & Co., 1924), 96-119. The summary here of *Le Menagier*, is that of Miss Power as is also the quotation.

[17] *Dante's lyric poetry*, edited and translated from the Italian by K. Foster and P. Boyde (Oxford: Clarendon P., 1967).

[18] *Dante's lyric poetry*, xv.

[19] For St. Thomas see S.T., la, 1, 10.

[20] Judson Allen, *The Friar*, 54.

[21] D. W. Robertson. *A Preface*, 243.

[22] Judson Allen, *The Friar*, p. 130, note 21. For a further critique of the extremes of Robertsonian allegorism see my review of Robertson's *A Preface to Chaucer*, in *Medium Aevum*, xxxv.3, JAM, 273-279.

Chapter 9 Chaucer's Craft of Love

[1] *The Riverside Chaucer*, 3rd ed., gen. ed., Larry D. Benson; revision of *The Works of Geoffrey Chaucer*, ed. by F. N. Robinson (Boston: Houghton Mifflin Co., 1987). All quotations from Chaucer in the following pages are from *The Riverside Chaucer*. Abbreviations of Chaucer's works are also as therein.

[2] George Kittredge, "Chaucer's Discussion of Marriage," *Chaucer Criticism: An Anthology*, edited by Richard J. Schoeck and Jerome Taylor (Notre Dame, Ind.: University of Notre Dame Press, 1960); Jiro Takimoto "Re-examination of the marriage group in The Canterbury Tales"; Donald Howard, *Chaucer: His Life, His Works, His World* (New York: Dutton, 1987), 428-435.

[3] Kittredge, *Chauser Criticism*, 1: 157.

[4] Donald Howard, *Chaucer*, 434-435

[5] See D. S. Brewer, *Chaucer*, 63-87; J. A. W. Bennett, *Parlement, passim*; P. G. Ruggiers, "The Unity of Chaucer's House of Fame," in Edward Wagenknecht's *Chaucer: Modern Essays in Criticism* (New York: Oxford University Press, 1959), 295-308; Kumiko Shikii, "A Religious Approach to the Canterbury Tales," in *Sella* (March 10, 1980), pp. 28-32.

[6] Judson Allen, *The Friar*, 129.

[7] William F. Bryan and Germaine Dempster eds., *Sources and Analogues of Chaucer's Canterbury Tales* (Chicago, IL: The University of Chicago Press, 1941), 89.

[8] J. A. W. Bennett, Chaucer's 'Book of Fame': An Exposition of 'The House of Fame,' (Oxford: Clarendon Press, 1968), 187.

THE CRAFT OF LOVE

⁹ C. McDonald, "An Interpretation of Chaucer's Parlement of Foules," in Wagenknecht, *Modern Essays*, 316.

¹⁰ See Bennett, *Parlement*, 92-93; also D. S. Brewer, *Chaucer*, 81: "Her [Venus's] temple, in contrast to the freshness outside, is filled with sighs and rich with a thousand sweet odours. Priapus, the lustful god, stands "in sovereyn place," shameful, ludicrous, obscene..."

¹¹ Bennett, *Parlement*, 116, 118: "Is it fanciful to see in this shading of one scene into another the suggestion that the realms of Nature and of Love march together, that however different their climates may be, no sharp impenetrable boundary divides them?... The outskirts of the temple merge on the one side with the park and on the other with Nature's 'launde'..."

¹² *Troilus*, V, 1835-48.

¹³ For example, *Troilus*, V, 1744-50; *BD*, 618 ff; KnT, 1238ff. For Chaucer's use of Fortune generally, and his specifically Christian conception of it, see Howard R. Patch, *The Goddess Fortuna in Mediaeval Literature* (Cambridge: Harvard University Press, 1927), 30-32 and *passim*.

¹⁴ Bennett, Chaucer's Book of Fame, 38.

¹⁵ See "The Book of the Duchess Re-Opened," in Wagenknecht, 276.

¹⁶ A. Denomy, "The Two Moralities of Chaucer's Troilus..." in *TRSC*, XLIV, III, 2: 36-43. For a more recent though similar judgment see Ian Robinson, *Chaucer and the English Tradition* (Cambridge, England: University Press, 1972), 73-85: "There is no way to make the end of the poem... follow from its beginning" (p. 73). Reservedly, and with respect, I beg to differ, for reasons given in the text.

¹⁷ See 368-71, 386-89, 400-11, 416-18, 620-23, 627-30.

¹⁸ Burke Severs (in Bryan and Dempster, 288 ff) notes Chaucer's additions to his source for the CT, the most notable of which have to do with Griselda's tender relationship with her children. Chaucer, says Severs, makes "the sergeant who takes away the children more darkly sinister." "Griselda's plea to the sergeant that she be allowed to say goodbye to her baby girl before it is borne away to its fate" is also Chaucer's innovation. And Griselda's long speech and double swoon in the reconciliation scene ("o tendre, o deere, o yonge children myne...") constitute "by all odds... Chaucer's longest single expansion in the whole poem."

¹⁹ English translation of Boccaccio as in R. K. Gordon, The Story of Troilus: As Told by Benoît de Sainte-Maure, Giovanni Boccacio (translated into English prose), Geoffrey Chaucer and Robert Henryson (London: Dent, 1934), 90.

NOTES

[20] Chaucer allows Griselda "even to pass judgment upon her husband's actions in a speech which has more than a hint of implied reproach in it," one of the "emphases which are original with Chaucer and not to be found in either the Latin or French source." See B. Severs, 290.

[21] For example, W. H. Clawson in "The Framework of *The Canterbury Tales*," in Wagenknecht, 16.

[22] D. W. Robertson, *Preface*, 319.

[23] St. Jerome in his *Adversus Jovinianum*, i., 36, P.L. 23, col. 260.

[24] The poem may be found in Bryan and Dempster, *Sources and Analogues of Chaucer's Canterbury Tales*, 24264

[25] C. H. Holman remarks in "Courtly Love in the Merchant's and Franklin's Tales," in Wagenknecht, 241: "[The Merchant's] long celebration of the joys and felicities of marriage... is so excellent a paean that it would probably be regarded as one of Chaucer's most profound statements on marriage were it not embedded in a story of such dark cynicism as the *Merchant's*." Still, what is said therein concerning marriage may be dissociated from the exaggerations and cynicism of the characters, from their dark and sinister motivation, and viewed in the context of an honest motivation, as, for instance, in *The Franklin's Tale*, and as such may indeed stand as Chaucer's praise of marriage, one of his "most profound statements" on it.

[26] The agreement of both was absolutely necessary before the marriage and, if celibacy was desired after the marriage, both must also agree to refrain from intercourse. The instance of the fourteenth-century English mystic Margery Kempe may be cited. For all her desire to live as a virgin, and all her weeping and pleading before her husband, she realized that before God and the Church she had to continue to have sexual intercourse with him for as long as he wished, which, apparently, was for a very long time. And even in her "visions" she received no dispensation from the Lord. See *The Book of Margery Kempe*, ed. Meech and Allen, ch. 3, 34 ff (p. 11); ch. 11, 1 ff (p. 24); ch. 21, 29 ff (p. 48).

[27] See the "explanatory notes" in *The Riverside Chaucer*, 956-957. See also Lee W. Patterson, "The 'Parson's Tale' and the Quitting of the Canterbury Tales," *Traditio* 34 (1978), 331-80. Patterson compares the tale to contemporary penitential manuals, but notes Chaucer's structuring of the tale and reflections back upon other tales (thus its late date) and his withdrawal from fiction (thus his retractions).

THE CRAFT OF LOVE

Chapter 10 Gower's Confession of a Lover

[1] *Middle English Verse Romances*, ed. Donald Sands (New York: Holt, Rinehart and Winston, 1966), 128-29.

[2] For the life and works of Gower, see Macaulay's introduction of the poet's writings, *The Works of John Gower*, ed. George C. Macaulay (Oxford: 1899-1902), 4 vols. see also John Fisher's, *John Gower, Moral Philosopher and Friend of Chaucer*, John Fisher ed. (New York: New York University Press, 1964). Citations of Gower in the following pages are from *Confessio Amantis*, ed. Geroge C. Macauley (London: Early English Texts Society Extra Series 81 and 82, 1901-1903). All emphases within my quotations from Gower are mine.

[3] C. S. Lewis in *Allegory*, 198-222, considered the *Confessio Amantis* to be a poem about love. John Fisher in *John Gower*, 187 is careful "not to deny that the matter [of the poem] is courtly love," but views the love theme more as a means used by Gower to illustrate his primary interests in politics and law. J. A. W. Bennett in "Gower's 'Honeste Love'" in *Patterns of Love and Courtesy: Essays in Memory of C. S. Lewis*, ed. John Lawlor (London: Arnold, 1966), 107-21, inclines to Lewis's emphasis, claiming that the genre of the *Confessio Amantis* is not political philosophy, but, as its title indicates, the doctrine of love. But unlike Lewis, Bennett sees the doctrine expressed in the body of the poem as continuous with that of the prologue and epilogue, the "specifically Christian *caritas*" being "threaded through the whole poem." Paul Strohm in "Form and Social Statement in *Confessio Amantis*...," *Studies in the Age of Chaucer* (Norman, OK: New Chaucer Society, University of Oklahoma, c1979), 17-40, treats of the political, hierarchical aspects of the poem, noting "Gower's success in connecting those sections of the poem which deal with ethical disorder in love and with political disorder in the state," but he insists that the poem "is literally about what it says it is about—the shriving and reordering of the unruly passions of a representative lover ..." (pp. 28-29).

[4] S.T., 2a2ae, 143, *unicus*.

[5] S.T., 2a2ae, 145, 1.

[6] Fisher, *John Gower*, pp. 177-79:

[7] Fisher, 187-203.

[8] J.A.W. Bennett, "Gower's 'Honeste Love'", in *Patterns...*, 120.

[9] J.A.W. Bennett, Preface, 376.

[10] Alan Gunn, The Mirror of Love; A Reinterpretation of "The Romance of the Rose" (Lubbock, TX: Tech Press, 1951), 278, note.

NOTES

[11] Leon Gautier, *Le Chevalerie* (1895), 358-59.

Chapter 11 Lydgate — Love-Good Love-Bad

[1] *Medieval English Lyrics: A Critical Anthology*, ed. R. T. Davies (London: Faber and Faber, 1963), 99.

[2] See Walter F. Schirmer's *John Lydgate; A Study in the Culture of the XVth Century*, trans. Ann E. Keep (Berkeley, University of California Press, 1961) for an account of Lydgate's life, work, and times. Schirmer sees nothing incongruous about the monk's secular interests (including the writing of love poetry) and finds no contradiction between them and the genuine piety evidenced in Lydgate's life and works in general. "On the whole it can be said that his secular tendencies helped to counterbalance his spiritual meditations...," 9. See also Derek Pearsall's *John Lydgate* (London, Routledge & K. Paul, 1970), 115-20, 104-105 for brief treatments of *Reason and Sensuality* and *Temple of Glass* respectively.

[3] *Reson and Sensuallyte*, ed. Ernst Sieper (London: Early English Texts Society Extra Series 84, 89, 1901-1903), 2 vols. All references to *Reason and Sensuality* are to Sieper's edition.

[4] *Les Echecs Amoureux* is an anonymous allegorical poem written in imitation of the Roman de la Rose and dates from the last third of the fourteenth century. Sieper in his edition of Reason and Sensuality gives a synopsis of folios 1 to 53 of the Dresden MS (lost with the levelling of the city in WW II). A complete synopsis of the poem is given by Stanley L. Galpin, "Les Echecs Amoureux: A Complete Synopsis with unpublished estracts," in *RR* vol XI, 1920, pp. 283-307. Hans Hofler, "*Les Echecs Amoureux*" in *RF*, t. xxvii, 1910, pp. 625-89, quotes generously from the section devoted to marriage. The following synopsis of Pallas's instructions concerning marriage is wholly dependent upon Galpin and Höfler.

[5] Höfler, p. 631.

[6] *Lydgate's temple of glass*, ed. J. Schick (Millwood, N.Y.: Kraus Reprint, 1987). References are to the poem as it appears in Schick's edition, with some modifications in orthography. The poem also appears with detailed notes in *John Lydgate Poems; with an introduction, notes, and glossary*, by John Norton-Smith (Oxford: Clarendon P., 1966).

[7] Lewis, *Allegory*, p. 241; Norton-Smith, *Poems*, pp. 178, 183.

[8] Norton-Smith, "Lydgate's Changes in the Temple of Glass," *Med. Aev.*, xxvii, 1958, pp. 166 ff. Norton-Smith presents the case that they represent Lydgate's own literary development of the poem. J. Schick had regarded the

changes appearing in the several versions of the poem as merely mechanical and scribal.

[9] Norton-Smith, "Lydgate," p. 169.

[10] Norton-Smith, p. 178.

[11] For Lydgate's minor love pieces, see H. N. MacCracken, ed. *The minor poems of John Lydgate, edited from all available mss., with an attempt to establish the Lydgate canon, by Henry Noble MacCracken* (London: Pub. for the Early English Text Society by K. Paul, Trench, Trübner & Co., Ltd. 1910). Eight poems of "courtly love" are given. Seven of them are of love-longing, and one, *The Servant of Cupyde Forsaken*, is a comedy piece against the "doubleness" of women. There are no adulterous insinuations in any of the poems. At the conclusion of the *Complaint of the Black Knight*, the poet alludes to "jealousy" that seems to be in the way of all lovers, but there is no mention of a husband, and the lovers are counselled that they "in al honeste ... to-gedre speke" (st. 95); and in *The Floure of Curtesye* the poet-lover praises his lady who has "euermore her trewe aduertence/Alway to reason; so that her desyre/ Is brideled aye by wytte and prouydence" (st. 20).

Chapter 12 Other Poets of the 14th Century

[1] Donald Sands, *Middle English verse romances*, ed.Donald B. Sands (New York: Holt, Rinehart and Winston, 1966), pp. 189-90.

[2] References are to the poem as it appears in *Sir Gawain and the Green Knight*, ed. J. R. R. Tolkien and E. V. Gordon, 2nd ed. revised by Norman Davis (Oxford: Clarendon Press, 1967). For the most part, I have chosen to use translations (modernizations) of the poets cited in this chapter because, unlike our inherited London dialect of a Chaucer and Gower, their language is not so easily understood. In each instance, however, the translation has been carefully compared with the original and the original words and phrases more crucial to the argument at hand have been noted in the text.

[3] Norton W. Bloomfield, "Sir Gawain and the Green Knight..." *PMLA*, LXXVI (1961), 15. See also the introduction to Tolkien's and Gordon's first edition of the poem, xix: "The homiletic character of *Patience* and *Purity* [two other poems attributed to the Gawain poet], the theology of *Pearl* [also by our poet], the moral earnestness of Sir Gawain, all suggest that the author might have been a priest. Certainly he had an ecclesiastical education, but his familiarity with courtly life, and his delight in it, make it doubtful whether he was a priest." But what of John Lydgate, priest and courtier and courtly poet? Though in that age of "the devout and literate layman" the author

NOTES

might also have been of the laity, knowing his theology and familiar with court and courtoisie, much as were Chaucer, Gower, and (perhaps) Langland.

[4] *Purity, a Middle English poem*, ed.with introd., notes, and glossary by Robert J. Menner (Hamden, CT: Archon Books, 1970).

[5] Except where indicated references are to the B-Text, as it appears in *The vision of William concerning Piers Plowman, together with Vita de Dowel, Dobet, et Dobest, and Richard the Redeles*, by William Langland, ed. from numerous manuscripts, with prefaces, notes, and indexes by Walter W. Skeat. Part IV, section I, Notes to texts A, B, and C. (Millwood, N.Y.: Kraus Reprint, 1987). For a survey of recent studies on the poem see Mary Clemente Davlin, O.P., "The Spirituaity of Piers Plowman: A New Look," *New Blackfriars*, March, 2000, pp. 124-128. Davlin quotes Fr. Conrad Pepler in his 1939 study of the poem (*Blackfriars*, pp. 846-854) as finding "a truly English and liturgical type of spirituality that must have been characteristic of the devout members of the Church, both ecclesiastical and lay." Supported by such further studies as M. T. Tavormina's *Kindly Similitude: Marriage and Family in Piers Plowman*, Davlin herself comments: "The poem's focus upon lay life, its positive valuation of marriage, sexuality, and the body, its profoundly Biblical character, its strong teaching on social justice, are all aspects of spirituality particularly attractive and relevant to *twenty-first-century needs*." (Emphasis mine.)

[6] References to the *Quair* are as it is in *The Kingis Quair*, ed. from the manuscript with introduction, notes, and glossary by W. Mackay Mackenzie (London: Faber and Faber Limited, 1939).

[7] MacKenzie, 38. For Lewis, see *Allegory*, 237.

[8] MacKenzie, 38

[9] See MacKenzie's introduction for a summary of James's life and facts concerning his marriage with Joan Beaufort and for discussion of problems relating to James's authorship of the poem.

SELECTED BIBLIOGRAPHY

Alexander of Hales. *Summa Theologica.*
    Glossa in quatuor libros Sententiarum Petri Lombardi.
Allen, J. P. *The Friar as Critic: Literary Attitudes in the Later Middle Ages.* Nashville: Vanderbilt University Press, 1971.
Bennett, Jack A. W. "Gower's 'Honeste Love,'" *Patterns of Love and Courtesy: Essays in Memory of C. S. Lewis* ed. John Lawlor. London: Arnold, 1966.
---------*Chaucer's 'Book of Fame': An Exposition of 'The House of Fame.* Oxford: Clarendon Press, 1968.
--------- *The Parlement of Foules: An Interpretation.* Oxford: Clarendon Press, 1957.
Bethurum, Dorothy. "Chaucer's Point of View as Narrator in the Love Poems," *PMLA,* 74 (19--): 511-20.
Bonansea, B. M., O.F.M. *Man and His Approach to God in John Duns Scotus.* Lanham, MD: University Press of America, 1983.
Bonaventure, Saint. *Opera Omnia.* ed. studio et cura PP. collegii a S. Bonaventura. Quaracchi, 1882-1902.
---------*Super Libros Sententiarum.* Quaracchi, 1934ff.
Brewer, D. S. "Love and Marriage in Chaucer's Poetry," *The Modern Language Review.* 49 (1954).
Brown, Peter Lamont. *Body and Society: Men, Women and Sexual Renunciation in Early Christianity.* New York: Columbia University Press, 1988.
Bruehi, Charles. *This Way Happiness; Ethics: the Science of the Good Life.* Milwaukee: The Bruce Publishing Company, 1941.
Brundage, James. *Law, Sex, and Christian Society in Medieval Europe.* Chicago: University of Chicago Press, 1987.
Burke, Vernon J. *Aquinas' Search for Wisdom.* Milwaukee: Bruce Publishing, 1965.

SELECTED BIBLIOGRAPHY

Cahill, Thomas. *How the Irish Saved Civilization*. New York: Anchor Books, 1996.

Capellanus, Andreas. *The art of courtly love, by Andreas Capellanus, with introduction, translation, and notes by John Jay Parry*. New York: Columbia University Press, 1941.

Chaucer, Geoffrey. *The Riverside Chaucer*, 3rd ed., gen. ed., Larry D. Benson; revision of *The Works of Geoffrey Chaucer*, ed. by F.N. Robinson. Boston: Houghton Mifflin Co., 1987.

Chenu, M. D. *St. Thomas D'Aquin et la theologie*. Paris: Éditions du Seuil, 1959.

--------- *Toward Understanding Saint Thomas by M. D. Chenu*, trans. with authorized corrections and bibliographical additions by A. M. Landry and D. Hughes. Chicago: H. Regnery Co., 1964.

Cochini, Christian. *Apostolic Origins of Priestly Celibacy*. San Francisco: Ignatius Press, 1990.

Connery, John R., S.J. "The Role of Love in Christian Marriage: A Historical Overview." *Communio* 11:3 (Fall 1984).

D'Ales. *La Theologie de Tertullien*.

Davenson, Henri. *Les troubadours [par] Henri Davenson*. Paris: Éditions du Seuil, 1961.

Davies, R. T., ed. *Medieval English Lyrics: A Critical Anthology*. London: Faber and Faber, 1963.

Davlin, R. T., O.P. "The Spirituaity of *Piers Plowman*: A New Look." *New Blackfriars* (March, 2000).

de la Marche, A. Lecoy. *La chaire française au moyen âge, spécialement au XIIIe siècle, d'après les manuscrits contemporains*. Paris: Renouard, H. Laurens, successeur, 1886.

Denzinger, *Enchiridion Symbolorum*. Friburgi Brisgoviae: Herder & Co., 1937.

Decartes, Rene. *Meditations on First Philosophy*.

---------- *Dscourse on Method*.

Doucet, V. *The History of the Problem of the Authenticity of the Summa*. Franciscan Studies, 7 (1947).

Driver and Massey. "Comparative Studies of North American Indians." *Transactions of the American Philosophical,Society*, New Series, vol. 47.

Dronke, Peter. "L'amor sole e l'altre stelle," *Studi Medievali*, serie terza, (1965).

---------- *Medieval Latin and the Rise of European Love-Lyric*. Oxford: Clarendon Press, 1965-1966.

Duchesne, Louis. *Christian Worship: Its Origin and Evolution; A Study of the Latin Liturgy Up To the Time of Charlemagne*. trans. McClure. London: Society for Promoting Christian Knowledge, New York: E. & J.B. Young, 1903.

Duffy, Eamon. *The Stripping of the Altars: Traditional Religion in England, c.1400-c.1580*. New Haven, CT: Yale University Press, 1992.

Dunning, T. P. "Chaucer's Icarus-Complex," *BST* 1962.

Duns Scotus, John. *Summa Theologica*.

Easton, Stewart C. *Roger Bacon and His Search for A Universal Science; A Reconsideration of the Life and Work of Roger Bacon in the Light of His Own Stated Purposes*. Westport, CT: Greenwood Press, 1970.

Fairweather, A. M., ed., trans,. *Nature and Grace; Selections from the Summa Theologica of Thomas Aquinas*. Philadelphia: Westminster Press, 1954.

Fisher, John, ed. *John Gower, Moral Philosopher and Friend of Chaucer*. New York: New York University Press, 1964.

Foster, Kenelm. *God's Tree: Essays on Dante and Other Matters*. London: Blackfriars Publications, 1957.

---------- *The Life of Saint Thomas Aquinas: Biographical Documents*. London: Longmans Green; Baltimore: Helicon Press, 1959.

Foster K. and Boyde, P., eds., trans. *Dante's lyric poetry*. Oxford: Clarendon Press, 1967.

Francis, W. Nelson, ed. *Somme le Roi* of Lorens d'Orléans. London: Published for the Early English Text Society by H. Milford, Oxford University Press, 1942.

Fuchs, Eric. *Sexual Desire and Love: Origins and History of the Christian Ethic of Sexuality and Marriage*. Cambridge: J. Clarke; New York: Seabury Press, 1983.

Galpin, Stanley L. "*Les Echecs Amoureux*: A Complete Synopsis with Unpublished Extracts." *RR* 11 (1920).

Gilby, Thomas. *St. Thomas Aquinas: Philosophical Texts*. Oxford: Oxford University Press, 1960.

SELECTED BIBLIOGRAPHY

Gilson, Etienne. *History of Christian philosophy in the Middle Ages.* New York: Random House, 1955.

--------- *The philosophy of St. Bonaventure.* trans. Dom Illtyd Trethowan. New York: Sheed & Ward, 1938.

Gordon, R. K., trans.*The Story of Troilus: as Told by Benoît de Sainte-Maure, Giovanni Boccacio,* introduction by R. K. Gordon. London: Dent, 1934.

Gower, John. *Confessio Amantis.* ed. G. C. Mcaulay. Oxford:Early English Texts Society, 1957-69.

Gunn, Alan. *The Mirror of Love: A Reinterpretation of "The Romance of the Rose."* Lubbock, Texas: Tech. Press, 1951.

Harris, C. R. S. *Duns Scotus.* Oxford: The Clarendon press, 1927.

Hefele, Charles Joseph. *A history of the councils of the church, from the original documents.* trans. and ed. William R. Clark. New York: AMS Press, 1972.

Hinnebusch, William. *The History of the Dominican Order.* Staten Island, NY: Alba House, 1966.

Höfler, Hans. "*Les Echecs Amoureux*". RF, t. 27, 1910.

Howard, Donald. *Chaucer: His Life, His Works, His Wworld.* New York: Dutton, 1987.

Howard, George E. *A history of Matrimonial Institutions Chiefly in England and the United States.* Chicago: The University of Chicago Press, Callaghan & Co. London: T. F. Unwin, 1904.

Huizinga, Johan. *The Waning of the Middle Ages, A Study of the Forms of Life.* London: E. Arnold & Co., 1924.

Isidore of Seville, Saint. *Etymologiarum.* Oxonii: E Typographeo Clarendoniano. New York: Oxford University Press, 1911.

James I King of Scotland. *The Kingis Quair,* ed. W. Mackay Mackenzie. London: Faber and Faber, 1939.

Jerome, Saint. *Epistle xlviii.*

Joyce, George H. *Christian Marriage.* London: New York: Sheed and Ward, 1933.

Kasper, W. *Theology of Christian Marriage.* New York: Seabury Press, 1980.

Kelly, Henry A. *Love and Marriage in the Age of Chaucer.* Ithaca, NY: Cornell University Press, 1975.

THE CRAFT OF LOVE

Kittredge, George. "Chaucer's Discussion of Marriage," *Chaucer Criticism: An Anthology*, ed. Richard J. Schoeck and Jerome Taylor. Notre Dame, IN: University of Notre Dame Press, 1960.

Knowles, D. *The Evolution of Medieval Thought*. Baltimore: Helicon Press, 1962.

Lea, Henry Charles. *History of Sacerdotal Celibacy in the Christian Church*. London: Ballantyne & Co., 1907.

LeClercq, Jean. *Monks on Marriage, a Twelfth-Century View*. New York: Seabury Press, 1982.

LeSaint, William P. S., S.J., ed., trans. *Ancient Christian Writers: Tertullian Marriage and Remarriage*. Westminster, MD: Newman Press, 1951.

Lewinsohn, Richard. *A History of Sexual Customs.* trans. Alexander Mayce. London: New York: Longmans Green, 1958.

Lewis, C. S. *The Allegory of Love*. Oxford: The Clarendon Press, 1936.

Lorens, Fr., O.P. *The Book of Vices and Virtue*. See also W. Francis Nelson

Luria, Maxwell. *Studies in the Age of Chaucer*. Knoxville: New Chaucer Society, The University of Tennessee, Knoxville, 1985.

Lydgate John. *Poems*. with an introduction, notes, and glossary by Norton-Smith. Oxford: Clarendon Press, 1966.

Mackenzie, W McKay, ed. *The Kingis Quair*. London: Faber and Faber Limited, 1939.

MacCraken, Henry. *The Minor Poems of John Lydgate*, ed. from all available mss., with an attempt to establish the Lydgate canon. London: Early English Text Society by K. Paul Trench, Trübner & Co., 1910.

Macaulay, George C., ed. *The Works of John Gower*. Oxford: 1899-1902. 4 vols.

Martène, Edmond, ed. *De Antiquis Ecclesiae Ritibus.* Antwerp: 1763-64. 4 vols in 2 parts. (Lib. I, pars ii, c. ix for continental nuptial rites).

Matthew, Gervase. *The Court of Richard II*. London: Murray, 1968.

---------"Marriage and Amour Courtoise in Late-fourteenth Century England," in *Essays Presented to Charles Williams*. London: New York: Oxford University Press, 1947.

--------"Ideals of Friendship." *Patterns of Love and Courtesy: Essays in Memory of C.S. Lewis*. London: Edward Arnold, 1966.

Menner, Robert, ed. *Purity, a Middle English Poem*. ed. with introd., notes, and glossary. Hamden, CT: Archon Books, 1970.

SELECTED BIBLIOGRAPHY

Miles, Margaret. *Carnal Knowing: Female Nakedness and Religious Meaning in the Christian West*. Boston: Beacon Press, 1989.

--------- *Image as Insight: Visual Understanding in Western Christianity and Secular Culture*. Boston: Beacon Press, 1985.

Miller, John. *Fundamentals of the Liturgy*. Notre Dame, IN: Fides, 1960.

Noonan, John. *Contraception: A History of its Treatment by Catholic Theologians and Canonists*. Cambridge: Harvard University Press, 1965.

Norton-Smith, John, ed. [John Lydgate] *Poems*; with an introduction, notes, and glossary by Norton-Smith. Oxford: Clarendon P., 1966.

--------- "Lydgate's Changes in the *Temple of Glass*," *Med. Aev.*, 27, 1958,

Orsme, Maistre Nicole. *Le Livre de Yconomique d'Aristote*, ed. A. D. Menut. *Transactions of the American Philosophical Society*. Philadelphia, (1957).

Owst, G. R., *Literature and Pulpit in Medieval England*. Cambridge: University Press; New York: The Macmillan Company, 1933.

Pantin, W. R. *The English Church of the Fourteenth Century*. Notre Dame, IN: University of Notre Dame Press, 1962.

Patch, Howard R. *The Goddess Fortuna in Mediaeval Literature*. Cambridge: Harvard University Press, 1927.

Pearsall, Derek. *John Lydgate*. London: Routledge & K. Paul, 1970.

Peraldus, William. *Summae virtutum ac vitiorum*. Antverpiae: 1588.

Pieper, Joseph. *Guide to Thomas Aquinas by Josef Pieper*. trans. from the German by Richard and Clara Winston. Notre Dame, IN: University of Notre Dame Press, 1962.

Pinckaers, C. K. "Ce que le Moyen Age pensait du mariage," *Suplement de la Vie Spirituelle* (1967).

Power, Eileen. *Medieval People*. London: Methuen & Co., 1924.

Prentice, Robert P., O.F.M. *The Psychology of Love According to St. Bonaventure*. St. Bonaventure, NY: Franciscan Institute, 1957.

Queen, Stuart Alfred. *The Family in Various Cultures*. Philadelphia: Lippincott, 1952.

Ranke-Heinemann, Uta. *Eunuchs for the Kingdom of Heaven: Women, Sexuality, and the Catholic Church*, tr. Peter Heinegg. New York: Doubleday, 1990.

Richards, Ivor A. *Principles of Literary Criticism*. San Diego: Harcourt Brace Jovanovich, 1985.

Robertson, D. W. *A Preface to Chaucer; Studies in Medieval Perspectives*. Princeton, NJ: Princeton University Press, 1962.

---------"Some Medieval Literary Terminology." *S.P*, vol. 48.

Roensch, Fredrick J. *Early Thomistic School*. Dubuque, IA: Priory Press, 1964.

Ross. Woodburn O., ed. *Middle English sermons,* from British Museum ms. Royal 18 B. xxiii. London: Early English Text Society H. Milford, Oxford University Press, 1940.

Sands, Donald, ed. *Middle English Verse Romances*. New York: Holt, Rinehart and Winston, 1966.

Schick, J., ed. *Lydgate's Temple of Glas*. Millwood, NY: Kraus Reprint, 1987.

Schirmer, Walter F. *John Lydgate; a study in the culture of the XVth century,* trans. Ann E. Keep. Berkeley: University of California Press, 1961.

Schlosser, F. *The Art of Courtly Love, by Andreas Capellanus,* with intro., trans., and notes by John Jay Parry. New York: Columbia University Press, 1941.

Schuster, Ildefonse, *The Sacramentary (Liber sacramentorum)*. London: Burns, Oates & Washbourne, 1924-30.

Searle, Mark and Stevens, Kenneth. *Documents of the Marriage Liturgy*. Collegeville, MN: Liturgical Press, 1992.

Sharp, Dorothea. *Franciscan Philosophy at Oxford in the Thirteenth Century*. New York: Russell & Russell, 1964.

Sherard, Philip. *Christianity and Eros: Essays on the Theme of Sexual Love*. London: S.P.C.K., 1976.

Sieper, Ernst, ed. *Reson and Sensuallyte*. London: Early English Text Society extra series 84, 89, 1901-1903.

Skeat, Walter W., ed. *The Vision of William Concerning Piers Plowman etc. by William Langland*. Millwood, NY: Kraus Reprint, 1987.

SELECTED BIBLIOGRAPHY

Smalley, Beryl. *English Friars and Antiquity in the Early XIV Century.* New York: Barnes & Noble, 1961.

---------- "The Biblical Scholar," in *Robert Grosseteste: Scholar and Bishop: Essays in Commemoration of the Seventh Centenary of His Death*, ed. Daniel Angelo Philip Callus. Oxford: Clarendon Press, 1955.

Southern, R. W. *Western Society and the Church in the Middle Ages.* Penguin Books, 1982.

Tertullian. *Ad Uxorem*, ii, 9, EL, t. i, cols. 1302-1304, *Ancient Christian Writers: Tertullian Marriage and Remarriage*, ed. and trans. William P. LeSaint, S.J. Westminster, MD: Newman Press, 1951.

Wagenknecht, Edward. *Chaucer: Modern Essays in Criticism.* New York: Oxford University Press, 1959.

---------- *Chaucer's 'Book of fame': an exposition of 'The House of Fame.'* Oxford: Clarendon Press, 1968.

Walz, Angelus. *Saint Thomas Aquinas, a Biographical StudY*, trans. Fr. Sebastian Bullough. Westminster, MD: Newman Press, 1951.

Westermarck, Edward. "J. A. W. Bennett in 'Gower's Honeste Love,'" *Patterns of Love and Courtesy: Essays in Memory of C. S. Lewis*, ed. John Lawlor. London: Arnold, 1966.

---------- *The History of Human Marriage.* New York: The Allerton Book Co, 1922.

INDEX

A

abortion   6, 132, 193
abstinence   30, 59, 127, 138, 216, 222, 243, 250
Adam   72, 79, 80, 93, 99, 112, 113, 114, 117, 133, 195, 220, 250
adultery   6, 13, 53, 69, 77, 128, 133, 135, 144, 162, 163, 167, 172, 194, 209, 247, 252
affection   25, 76, 115, 117, 163, 187, 258
Albert the Great   33, 54, 92, 93, 151
Alexander of Hales   63, 64, 65, 66, 67, 68, 75, 76, 77, 78, 81, 83, 86, 88, 93, 95, 125, 130, 206, 260, 261
Allen, Judson   153, 157
Ambrose, Saint   78
amorous   189, 190, 197, 205
Andreas Capellanus   2, 13, 34, 148, 246, 263
Anthony and Cleopatra   162, 173
Arabic   33
Aristotle   27, 28, 33, 34, 36, 40, 63, 94, 95, 122, 123, 124, 126, 128, 130
Augustinianism   35, 63, 94
authority   6, 20, 21, 22, 23, 26, 28, 29, 40, 54, 59, 91, 119, 149, 178, 179, 180, 182, 187, 196, 203, 219, 220, 231, 243
Averroes   33

B

Beaufort, Joan   253
Being   3, 112, 113, 115, 253
belief   1, 13, 14, 23, 24, 38, 70, 72, 75, 91, 140, 146, 170, 184, 185, 187, 192, 220, 221, 241, 251
Bennett, Jack A.W.   15, 16, 159, 205
Bernard of Clairvaux   46
betrothal   11, 57, 58, 109
Bible   21, 143, 153
Boccaccio   158, 176, 178
body   3, 5, 6, 8, 9, 21, 23, 27, 28, 30, 40, 44, 55, 58, 67, 68, 70, 74, 84, 93, 94, 97, 99, 105, 106, 107, 112, 113, 127, 128, 135, 137, 138, 139, 145, 150, 164, 172, 173, 187, 188, 193, 194, 195, 196, 203, 204, 212, 213, 214, 215, 236, 237, 254, 258
Bonaventure, Saint   37, 63, 64, 78, 79, 80, 81, 82, 83, 84, 86, 95, 130, 147, 148, 261
Boyde, Patrick   151
Brewer, D. S.   15
bride   11, 80, 82, 98, 99, 100, 101, 102, 103, 104, 106, 107, 108, 109, 117, 143, 169, 189, 191, 210, 213, 226, 232, 253
Bridget of Sweden   74
Bronson, B. H.   165
Brown, Peter Lamont   4, 8, 27, 28, 263

INDEX

Bruehi, Charles 55
Brundage, James 7, 21, 29, 37, 140, 263

C

Cahill, Thomas 3, 5, 263
Cambridge University 10, 98, 111, 123, 263
Cana 131, 132, 134, 135, 195
canonical 21, 23, 35, 119, 257
Canterbury 34, 121, 155, 157, 175, 181, 192, 197, 225
Capellanus, Andreas 2, 13, 34, 148, 246, 263
carnal 25, 59, 64, 65, 66, 69, 82, 86, 87, 95, 117, 126, 127, 138, 148, 206, 213, 215, 228, 232, 234, 263
Catharite 134
Catherine of Siena 74
celibate 3, 4, 7, 21, 28, 29, 58, 85, 92, 168, 183, 188, 222, 243, 244, 250, 251, 252, 255, 259, 263
ceremony 3, 41, 57, 58, 98, 100, 102, 103, 105, 106, 107, 108, 109, 110, 117, 140, 170, 190
charity 15, 36, 38, 43, 48, 51, 66, 80, 81, 89, 94, 101, 106, 108, 201, 202, 203, 204, 205, 206, 211, 212, 225, 250, 251, 259, 260
chastity 17, 53, 58, 77, 101, 107, 125, 129, 136, 137, 183, 188, 195, 196, 204, 222, 227, 231, 232, 233, 235, 240, 242, 246, 247, 251
Chaucer, Geoffrey 5, 10, 14, 15, 16, 18, 20, 27, 72, 103, 123, 133, 153, 155, 156, 157, 158, 159, 160, 161, 162, 163, 164, 165, 166, 167, 169, 170, 173, 174, 175, 176, 177, 178, 180, 181, 182, 183, 184, 185, 186, 187, 188, 189, 190, 191, 192, 193, 197, 199, 206, 212, 215, 216, 220, 225, 234, 238, 240, 241, 242, 251, 252, 258, 260
Chaucerian 175, 176

Chenu, Jean-Charles 32
children 3, 6, 17, 42, 48, 49, 51, 56, 67, 73, 77, 81, 86, 87, 88, 89, 95, 101, 110, 124, 132, 134, 135, 156, 160, 173, 174, 188, 196, 199, 210, 215, 230, 238, 258
Chretien de Troyes 13
Christ 6, 11, 22, 24, 41, 65, 66, 67, 70, 75, 76, 79, 83, 86, 87, 95, 99, 100, 120, 135, 166, 168, 179, 192, 194, 197, 204, 246
Christ (Crist) 187, 194, 196, 222
Christendom 9, 91, 121, 131, 194
Christian 1, 3, 4, 5, 7, 8, 9, 11, 13, 19, 20, 24, 27, 33, 35, 39, 41, 42, 43, 46, 48, 52, 67, 69, 70, 75, 84, 85, 89, 92, 95, 97, 104, 119, 120, 121, 127, 132, 136, 138, 140, 144, 151, 157, 158, 166, 169, 178, 193, 200, 212, 221, 223, 245, 253, 254, 263
Cleopatra 162, 173
clergy 10, 19, 27, 31, 120, 123, 136, 141, 182, 202, 222, 230
clerk 141, 143, 147, 164, 169, 180, 192, 219
Coghill, N 148
cohabitation 2, 57
coitus 6, 17
conception 60
concubinage 57
concupiscence 125, 216, 228
concupiscense 52, 77, 83, 147, 169, 188
confession 139, 149, 199, 200, 248
conjugal 2, 7, 16, 17, 27, 30, 39, 40, 42, 43, 45, 48, 49, 50, 51, 53, 54, 63, 76, 77, 78, 81, 82, 83, 84, 85, 86, 87, 88, 91, 92, 106, 107, 110, 117, 122, 123, 127, 128, 132, 134, 135, 138, 145, 148, 155, 164, 166, 168, 169, 170, 172, 179, 183, 184, 185, 189, 194, 196, 197, 209,

215, 216, 218, 219, 220, 235, 239, 242, 243, 247, 250, 251, 253, 254, 259
Connery, John R.   22
conscience   83, 218
consent   11, 24, 55, 56, 57, 58, 80, 81, 82, 86, 98, 146, 249
consummated   57, 89, 95, 161, 166, 243
contemplative   49, 136, 227, 230, 243
continence   29, 30, 78, 188, 195
contraception   6, 134, 193
copulate   6, 99, 138
courtesy   54, 176, 177, 212, 219, 238, 240, 246
courtesy (*courtoisie*)   1, 2, 15, 16, 161
courtship   144, 221, 235, 242, 243, 254, 258
Creator   30, 37, 99, 161
Cupid   166, 228, 230, 232

D

Dante   5, 35, 152, 158, 227
Davenson, Henri   2, 263
de Beauvoir, Simone   68
de la Marche, A. Lecoy   132
de la Tour-Landry, Geoffroy   141, 142
de Lorris, Guillaume   13
de Meun, Jeun   220
de Sorbon, Robert   110, 128, 132, 133
de Vitry, Jacques   131
de Wulf, Maurice   32
death   31, 33, 41, 44, 58, 74, 107, 142, 156, 158, 168, 170, 171, 175, 176, 179, 180, 212, 234, 236, 237
debt (*debitum*)   17, 51, 52, 53, 59, 128, 172, 184, 185, 216, 217, 218
debt (*redditio*)   51, 52, 53, 89, 107, 128, 172, 184, 188, 216, 217, 218

delight   16, 50, 59, 92, 125, 126, 176, 178, 185, 196, 197, 200, 209, 221, 226, 239, 240, 254, 259
delight (*dilectionis*)   67, 99, 106
Demomy, A.   166
Descartes, René   3, 92, 263
desire   5, 14, 24, 25, 27, 37, 38, 43, 47, 52, 53, 54, 55, 83, 89, 124, 126, 127, 134, 135, 138, 139, 143, 144, 147, 150, 156, 176, 193, 196, 203, 204, 206, 212, 218, 229, 231, 233, 234, 235, 236, 240, 245, 246, 253, 254
dignity   29, 34, 60, 67, 70, 72, 74, 94, 106, 117, 131, 132, 136, 202, 213, 234, 243, 259
divine   8, 17, 30, 38, 39, 46, 60, 70, 75, 80, 85, 120, 125, 157, 161, 226, 230, 231, 238, 243, 251
divorce   2
doctrine   2, 9, 15, 16, 18, 19, 20, 23, 27, 35, 36, 39, 40, 50, 51, 57, 63, 84, 91, 95, 109, 118, 119, 120, 123, 125, 130, 137, 138, 141, 145, 152, 155, 170, 172, 178, 179, 181, 185, 186, 189, 192, 197, 206, 216, 218, 220, 231, 238, 243, 247, 249, 252, 254, 258, 260, 261
Dominican   33, 34, 35, 36, 82, 122, 131, 134, 135
dowry   11, 57, 98, 99, 102, 170, 253
dualism   3, 8, 39, 161
Duffy, Eamon   19
Dunning, T. P.   16, 17
Duns Scotus   63, 84, 88, 119, 130, 151, 250, 261

E

ecclesiastical   7, 10, 13, 16, 18, 19, 20, 25, 55, 57, 58, 59, 70, 91, 102, 110, 119, 130, 141, 142, 144, 150, 152, 155, 169, 172, 173, 178, 181, 183, 186, 187, 192, 193, 197, 216, 217, 220, 249, 250, 257, 260

INDEX

ecumenical 3, 119
Eliot, T. S. 28
Ellis, Alice 31
engagement 13, 57, 89, 144, 235, 258
England 9, 10, 11, 12, 14, 18, 20, 34, 35, 91, 94, 106, 110, 121, 123, 131, 139, 142, 144, 149, 258
English 10, 14, 27, 64, 66, 97, 98, 102, 104, 105, 108, 110, 111, 118, 121, 123, 131, 135, 141, 163, 178, 199, 245, 248, 252, 257, 258, 260
equality 7, 45, 66, 67, 68, 69, 72, 74, 79, 108, 117, 129, 133, 178, 179, 180, 181, 185, 220
eternal 1, 24, 41, 99, 101, 157, 158, 161, 174, 221, 226
ethics 7, 8
European 2, 7, 69
Eve 66, 72, 73, 79, 80, 93, 99, 110, 113, 117, 195, 220, 250
evidence 2, 8, 10, 18, 26, 29, 36, 101, 106, 145, 155, 180, 197, 219, 252, 260
evil 2, 5, 8, 21, 24, 56, 57, 93, 128, 132, 134, 135, 184, 187, 231, 240, 244

F

faith 23, 27, 65, 67, 120, 121, 129, 149, 194, 207, 239
faith (fidei) 37, 42
family 1, 133, 191
father 3, 44, 55, 126, 129, 135, 143, 146, 147, 168, 170, 208, 210, 249
Fathers of the Church 5, 7, 8, 21, 22, 23, 24, 25, 26, 27, 28, 29, 34, 43, 59, 120, 203, 263
female 28, 45, 66, 67, 69, 71, 126, 127
feminine 3, 8, 70, 79

fidelity 24, 34, 40, 41, 42, 43, 44, 49, 58, 77, 83, 84, 88, 89, 104, 107, 109, 128, 129, 138, 142, 150, 162, 216, 238, 241, 258
Fisher, John 203, 204
flesh 3, 6, 24, 25, 47, 48, 59, 65, 66, 67, 76, 77, 93, 99, 100, 103, 104, 107, 117, 194, 211, 213, 222
Fletcher, William 27
fornication 6, 53, 58, 77, 100, 108, 112, 135, 138, 144, 160, 162, 169, 188, 195, 217, 218, 231, 247, 250
Foster, Kenelm 43
Franciscan 37, 63, 64, 75, 82, 121
free 17, 45, 55, 56, 58, 60, 80, 81, 92, 106, 108, 111, 169, 178, 220, 236, 240, 241, 242, 254, 258
freedom 19, 55, 56, 80, 94, 104, 108, 125, 144, 169, 220, 221, 241
friendship 1, 16, 44, 45, 46, 48, 52, 54, 78, 125, 126, 127, 216, 230, 239
friendship, love (*amicitia*) 44, 45
Fuchs, Eric 7
Fukuyama, Francis 2
fulfillment 1, 50, 95, 138, 149, 168, 173, 176, 183, 205, 207, 208, 209, 221, 228, 229, 232, 238
Fulgentius 12

G

Gangra, Council of 29, 59
Gautier, L 109, 220
Gerard de Liege 46
Gervase Mathew 16
Gibran, Kahlil 31
Gilson, Etienne 33, 34, 63, 78
gnosticism 29
goddess 159, 160, 200, 205, 226, 229, 231, 233, 234, 246, 253, 254
good, the (*bonum*) 41, 42, 82, 87, 112

Gower, John 14, 18, 20, 117, 123, 163, 175, 199, 200, 202, 203, 205, 206, 211, 215, 216, 218, 219, 220, 221, 228, 234, 238, 239, 240, 241, 251, 252, 253, 254, 258, 260
grace 8, 27, 38, 39, 40, 41, 43, 48, 49, 51, 61, 64, 65, 75, 76, 81, 84, 85, 88, 89, 92, 95, 99, 107, 114, 116, 147, 160, 162, 169, 174, 196, 236, 240, 251, 254
Greek 33, 69, 100, 130
Gregory of Nyssa 29, 57
groom 11, 82, 98, 99, 101, 102, 103, 104, 106, 109, 117, 191, 210
Guillaume de Lorris 13
Gunn, Alan 220

H

Hanley rite 105
hate 25, 159
heart 32, 47, 53, 68, 73, 92, 99, 103, 105, 107, 117, 120, 125, 134, 137, 142, 145, 168, 169, 176, 196, 211, 213, 220, 227, 231, 236, 237, 238, 246, 254
heaven 47, 61, 78, 106, 136, 158, 160, 162, 226, 248, 249, 252, 259, 263
heaven (heven) 112, 113
Hedwig of Bavaria 74
hell 31, 93, 250, 251
Hereford rite 104, 105, 108, 150
heretics 30
hierarchy 61, 195, 203, 251
Hilda of Whitby 74
Hildegard of Bingen 74
history 3, 4, 8, 9, 10, 28, 43, 74, 132, 182, 183
holiness 23, 29, 76, 85, 102, 106, 132, 186, 259
holy 24, 35, 38, 39, 59, 83, 85, 89, 92, 94, 97, 101, 102, 103, 104, 106, 107, 114, 115, 116, 117, 119, 136, 139, 146, 164, 166, 171, 172, 186, 188, 190, 192, 194, 195, 205, 225, 231, 238, 251, 252, 258, 259
Howard, Donald 10, 156
Howard, G. E. 56
human 3, 6, 8, 9, 11, 13, 14, 15, 16, 17, 30, 34, 36, 38, 39, 40, 41, 43, 45, 46, 47, 48, 50, 68, 69, 79, 80, 88, 94, 95, 99, 106, 125, 126, 127, 131, 156, 157, 158, 159, 161, 162, 166, 175, 199, 200, 201, 204, 206, 207, 211, 217, 225, 226, 238, 251, 260
humility 29, 66, 228

I

Icarus-Complex 16
iconography 7, 35
image 68, 71, 72, 73, 74, 151
Indians, North American 11
indissolubility 41, 44, 85, 86, 87, 258
infidelity 53, 77, 162, 163, 172, 173, 216, 239, 253, 254
influenced 4, 18
innocent 101, 145, 150, 173, 185, 218, 239
inseparability 76, 103
intention 2, 21, 41, 54, 58, 142, 143, 151, 159, 166, 176, 184, 185, 195, 199, 201, 206
intercourse 4, 6, 29, 30, 44, 49, 50, 54, 59, 73, 76, 77, 82, 83, 123, 127, 135, 193, 197, 215, 254
intimate 1, 48, 58, 66, 85, 95, 101, 117, 127, 150, 187, 211
Isidore, Saint 105
Islam 9, 69

J

James I of Scotland 253
jealousy 147, 148
Jerome, Saint 23, 25, 26, 27, 28, 29, 184, 194

INDEX

Jerusalem 112, 157, 162, 197
Jesus 3, 79, 103, 192
Jeun de Meun 13
John Paul II 8
joy 25, 47, 50, 79, 84, 93, 95, 100, 106, 109, 110, 113, 150, 161, 171, 173, 210, 211, 213, 214, 215, 216, 235, 239, 240, 247, 253, 254
Joyce, G. H. 11, 56, 100
Julian of Norwich 10, 74
Julian, Bishop 5
justice 5, 7, 17, 36, 39, 42, 43, 44, 45, 51, 52, 77, 81, 129, 134, 135, 137, 138, 147, 171, 172, 185, 200, 203, 216, 218, 236, 238, 239, 246, 258
justification 49, 78, 87, 250, 251

K

Kasper, W. 34
Kelly, Henry A. 17
Kilwardby, Archbishop 34
King, Ursala 263
kiss 93, 101, 102, 103, 107, 109, 235, 242, 246
kissing 58, 147, 194
Kittredge, George 155, 156, 165
Knapwell, Richard 34
Knowles, D. 37

L

Lactantius 27, 40
laity 10, 11, 97, 120, 123, 130, 136, 139, 140, 141, 142, 149
Langland, William 248, 250, 251, 252
lascivious 6, 144, 165
law 1, 6, 7, 11, 15, 31, 37, 59, 68, 74, 75, 76, 83, 85, 99, 104, 107, 144, 157, 160, 162, 166, 174, 202, 205, 207, 208, 211, 216, 218, 252
layman 3, 10, 17, 123, 141, 142
le Chantre, Pierre 30

Lea, H. C. 6, 21, 22, 29, 263
lecherous 162, 165, 186, 208, 211, 250
lechery 138, 160, 174, 184, 185, 186, 188, 193, 195, 203, 204, 248, 250
Lewis, C. S. 14, 15, 17, 45, 53, 93, 148, 236, 252
liberty 55, 57, 58, 73, 81, 170, 171, 178, 181, 218, 220, 236, 240, 241, 249, 254
libido 27, 52, 65, 77
liturgy 9, 19, 20, 39, 68, 73, 74, 97, 99, 100, 101, 102, 104, 107, 108, 109, 116, 117, 120, 123, 140, 146, 167, 168, 170, 175, 178, 183, 215, 219, 239, 247, 248, 253, 258, 260, 261
lollardry 192, 196
Lorens, Friar 16, 121, 122, 135
love 99, 107, 128
love (*amorem*) 81, 99
love (*caritas*) 1, 17, 38, 48, 52, 79, 80, 82, 93, 134, 148, 202, 205, 212, 251, 260
love (*loued*) 142, 145, 146
love-making 17, 30, 46, 47, 53, 76, 83, 84, 89, 91, 93, 95, 128, 138, 150, 184, 189, 197, 218, 239, 240, 259
love-play 83
lover 1, 14, 44, 45, 46, 47, 52, 53, 71, 93, 125, 127, 130, 142, 144, 145, 146, 157, 158, 160, 165, 173, 177, 199, 200, 201, 205, 208, 209, 212, 215, 219, 221, 223, 226, 227, 228, 229, 230, 232, 235, 236, 237, 238, 239, 240, 242, 243, 248, 253, 254, 259
love-union 107, 176, 215
lust 5, 6, 16, 55, 58, 65, 77, 134, 138, 160, 163, 164, 174, 183, 185, 186, 189, 190, 191, 193, 194, 203,

205, 206, 207, 208, 209, 210, 213,
214, 215, 216, 219, 222, 233, 253
Luther, Martin 57
Lydgate, John 14, 18, 225, 228,
229, 231, 234, 236, 237, 238, 240,
241, 242, 246, 252, 253, 254, 258,
260

M

Macclesfield, William 34
male 28, 45, 53, 66, 67, 68, 69,
70, 71, 72, 73, 74, 100, 126, 129,
174, 179, 180, 214, 219, 220, 243,
255
Manichaean 5, 7, 8, 21, 22, 23, 27,
30, 39, 48, 51, 161, 257
manualists 122, 123, 130, 139, 148
manuals 110, 117, 120, 121,
122, 135, 139, 140, 141, 142
Marian 72
marital 4, 8, 22, 25, 30, 49, 52,
58, 84, 85, 91, 95, 125, 164, 165,
166, 193, 196, 209, 211, 216, 253,
254, 260
marriage-act 5, 6, 14, 17, 21, 44,
47, 48, 49, 50, 51, 52, 53, 54, 57,
58, 59, 60, 61, 76, 77, 80, 81, 82,
83, 84, 86, 87, 88, 91, 92, 95, 107,
125, 127, 128, 132, 134, 135, 137,
138, 144, 148, 150, 160, 172, 183,
189, 193, 196, 203, 216, 239, 240,
247, 249, 250, 251, 254, 259
married 3, 5, 7, 16, 29, 30, 41,
55, 57, 58, 74, 77, 85, 92, 95, 118,
124, 126, 130, 131, 132, 136, 139,
140, 143, 145, 146, 164, 165, 194,
195, 197, 223, 236, 237, 241, 247,
249, 252, 259
marry 2, 49, 55, 56, 57, 100,
104, 107, 108, 126, 133, 143, 148,
166, 169, 186, 187, 221, 231, 251
Martini, Simone 35
Mass 99, 101, 103, 105, 106,
108, 117, 120, 132, 149, 245

masturbation 6
Matfre Ermengau 37
mating 165, 170, 174
matrimony 42, 60, 84, 111,
115, 116, 117, 133, 194, 217
maturity 36, 40
McDonald, C. 160
McDonald, Mary 263
medieval 1, 2, 3, 6, 7, 9, 12,
13, 14, 15, 16, 17, 18, 19, 20, 21,
22, 27, 30, 31, 32, 36, 37, 39, 40,
41, 42, 43, 44, 45, 54, 55, 56, 57,
60, 63, 68, 69, 70, 72, 73, 74, 82,
92, 104, 108, 109, 110, 111, 119,
120, 130, 132, 133, 136, 139, 142,
143, 148, 151, 153, 158, 161, 178,
183, 202, 203, 220, 223, 253, 255,
257, 260, 263
medievalists 13
men 6, 8, 15, 16, 18, 40, 56, 66,
68, 69, 70, 71, 72, 73, 74, 75, 78,
126, 127, 131, 133, 135, 136, 137,
138, 147, 157, 164, 172, 174, 178,
181, 182, 183, 194, 195, 202, 206,
209, 220, 222, 223, 226, 230, 239,
242, 250, 263
merit 51, 52, 53, 60, 61, 76, 77, 83,
85, 87, 88, 95, 134, 138, 196, 202,
218, 259
Middle Ages 1, 7, 9, 14, 20, 21, 22,
28, 40, 44, 60, 70, 71, 75, 85, 91,
92, 94, 119, 120, 124, 140, 141,
156
Miles, Margaret 7, 21, 29, 68,
69, 72, 73, 74, 263
mistress 205
modesty 25, 53, 108, 127, 253
Mohammed 69
monk 18, 106, 133, 225, 244, 260
monogamy 45, 195, 230
moral 12, 39, 47, 49, 50, 56,
66, 117, 118, 121, 122, 125, 130,
133, 134, 139, 140, 141, 143, 149,
151, 152, 153, 165, 166, 176, 177,

INDEX

178, 191, 197, 199, 212, 234, 236, 237, 244, 245, 246, 257
mother 2, 44, 73, 79, 104, 105, 126, 129, 135, 146, 249
Muslim 69
mutual 16, 40, 41, 42, 54, 55, 56, 57, 58, 64, 66, 79, 86, 106, 107, 108, 109, 124, 144, 150, 156, 162, 177, 178, 181, 185, 188, 219, 220, 230, 231, 235, 238, 240, 242, 249, 257, 259
mutuality 5, 242, 259
mystics 10, 17, 46

N

naked 31, 215, 249
Naples, University of 33
natural 5, 11, 28, 37, 38, 39, 43, 46, 48, 51, 56, 64, 65, 75, 76, 79, 81, 82, 94, 95, 108, 124, 125, 160, 161, 173, 174, 175, 201, 205, 208, 213, 215, 238, 245, 247, 249, 258, 260
nature 2, 3, 8, 9, 14, 37, 40, 45, 48, 49, 52, 56, 57, 66, 75, 76, 80, 81, 82, 85, 95, 106, 107, 108, 109, 126, 155, 156, 157, 160, 161, 165, 174, 178, 201, 205, 206, 207, 208, 211, 213, 216, 223, 226, 227, 228, 229, 230, 232, 236, 238, 240, 241, 247, 251, 257, 258
newly-weds 103, 107, 132
Noonan, John 3, 123, 143, 263
Norton-Smith, J 236, 237
nuptial 19, 41, 56, 101, 102, 104, 105, 108, 109, 117, 130, 146, 147, 167, 168, 170, 178, 190, 215, 253, 258

O

obedience 40, 128, 150, 176, 185, 219, 240, 242, 252, 259

obedience (obsequium) 40, 42, 178, 188
Oresme, Nicole 16, 122, 123, 124, 125, 127, 128, 129, 130, 137, 231
Orfeo, Sir 245
Orford, Robert 34
orthodox 13, 21, 25, 30, 149, 196, 245
Ovid 12, 16, 125, 164, 175
Owst G. R. 72, 110, 121, 122
Oxford University 9, 10, 34, 35, 63, 102, 123

P

pantheism 38, 39
Pantin, W. A. 10, 120
Paradise 80, 92, 93, 131, 132, 133, 195, 247
paramours 166, 209, 232, 233, 240, 242, 257, 260
parents 6, 11, 48, 56, 80, 81, 110, 166, 169, 237
Paris, Gaston 2
passion 1, 2, 13, 14, 15, 16, 17, 21, 27, 28, 36, 44, 45, 46, 47, 50, 51, 52, 53, 75, 92, 93, 94, 95, 134, 148, 161, 176, 190, 246, 247
Paul, Apostle 2, 25, 49, 59, 78, 108, 126, 187
peace 24, 79, 98, 101, 102, 103, 105, 107, 108, 109, 132, 133, 149, 159, 191, 195, 200, 202, 203, 204, 205, 206, 223, 258
penance 139, 180, 193
Peraldus, Guillaume 121, 122, 131, 132, 133, 134, 135, 137, 138, 148, 191
Peter Lombard 36, 38, 53, 57, 85, 88
philosophy 34, 86, 175, 182, 183, 200, 260, 261, 263
Phyrinus 221, 222
physical 17, 22, 25, 45, 46, 48, 56, 65, 70, 74, 84, 92, 93, 161, 176,

211, 213, 215, 228, 229, 234, 240, 258
pleasure   25, 30, 47, 50, 51, 52, 53, 54, 55, 59, 76, 83, 84, 85, 89, 91, 92, 93, 95, 126, 127, 134, 138, 148, 150, 177, 185, 188, 189, 190, 191, 197, 213, 215, 222, 227, 228, 229, 230, 233, 234, 238, 239, 240, 254, 259
pleasure (plesure)   115
pleasure-seeking   77, 91
polygamy   195
Pope   8, 27, 35, 57, 101, 119
pornography   31
Pratt, R. A.   158
prayer   25, 59, 68, 73, 77, 86, 99, 100, 101, 102, 103, 105, 106, 109, 120, 147, 149, 150, 202, 215, 216, 251
preachers   12, 20, 74, 110, 117, 132, 133, 145, 148, 257, 261
preaching   11, 30, 49, 63, 68, 72, 75, 110, 116, 117, 120, 121, 146, 182, 187, 234, 241, 257
pre-Christian   8, 11
pregnant   73, 126
Prentice, Robert P.   80
prestige   28, 59
priest   12, 13, 15, 18, 20, 28, 31, 97, 98, 99, 100, 101, 102, 103, 104, 105, 106, 107, 108, 109, 110, 114, 123, 146, 178, 191, 192, 199, 200, 209, 216, 234, 260
procreation   2, 7, 21, 23, 41, 77, 79, 83, 84, 86, 87, 106, 107, 123, 127, 150, 165, 173, 174, 175, 176, 184, 188, 193, 214, 259
promiscuous   84, 129, 144
psychological   47, 54, 93
public   49, 57, 78, 108, 119, 139, 140, 157, 203
pure   2, 31, 32, 47, 92, 101, 116, 233, 239, 242, 247, 260
Purity   247, 248, 250, 252

R

Ranke-Heinemann, Uta   4, 7, 21, 263
Ransom, John Crowe   93
rape   91, 216, 219
reason   9, 10, 17, 18, 24, 39, 47, 48, 50, 51, 54, 55, 56, 58, 59, 63, 67, 82, 84, 85, 87, 88, 91, 92, 121, 124, 125, 127, 128, 129, 138, 167, 177, 178, 181, 184, 185, 195, 201, 204, 205, 206, 207, 211, 216, 225, 226, 230, 231, 238, 239, 246, 251, 254, 258
Reformation   7, 19, 110, 121
relationship   2, 7, 13, 40, 48, 57, 79, 91, 123, 124, 125, 127, 134, 152, 153, 166, 175, 179, 193, 208, 218, 231, 242, 243, 254
religion   19, 24, 192, 204
revelation, Christian   23, 70, 85
ring   57, 58, 98, 99, 103, 105, 107, 109, 117, 133, 170
rite   19, 57, 97, 101, 102, 103, 104, 105, 106, 107, 108, 109, 110, 117, 120, 130, 144, 147, 150, 167, 190, 253
ritual   19, 41, 102, 104, 110, 190, 191
Robertson, D. W.   14, 35, 153, 182, 220
Roger Bacon   63
romance   1, 2, 4, 11, 16, 130, 143, 144, 157, 161, 174, 175, 252
romantic   1, 2, 9, 17, 24, 31, 44, 85, 142, 145, 161, 175, 233, 254, 260
Ross, W. O.   110
rubric   99, 100, 102, 105, 108, 257

S

Sacerdotal   21, 263
sacrament   22, 34, 41, 56, 57, 75, 80, 82, 84, 87, 88, 94, 100, 101, 111, 112, 113, 114, 115, 116, 117,

303

INDEX

132, 137, 139, 145, 169, 182, 187, 188, 194, 195, 220, 250
sacrament (sacramentum)   22, 37, 41, 42, 81, 82, 86, 87, 95, 100, 107, 133, 150, 169, 211, 238, 258
sacramental   8, 11, 41, 56, 100, 120, 169
sacrilegious   5, 190
Saint Augustine   3, 5, 6, 7, 8, 23, 34, 35, 36, 42, 76, 78, 91, 119, 120, 151, 263
salvation   99, 110
sanctify   75, 99, 106
Sarum rite   102, 103, 104, 105, 110, 170, 191
Schlosser, F.   42, 263
scholastic   16, 32, 36, 37, 38, 41, 86, 91, 93, 124, 134, 137, 138, 151, 229
scholasticism   32
science   32, 33, 124, 130
Scripture   6, 15, 23, 48, 65, 77, 119, 120, 126, 127, 153, 183, 251
Searle, Mark   109
secular   10, 31, 47, 55, 70, 130, 142, 149, 151, 250, 257
seduction   144
self-love   52
Sensualists   25
sensuality   23, 25, 93, 226, 227
sermon   10, 19, 68, 72, 79, 80, 81, 97, 109, 110, 111, 116, 117, 128, 131, 132, 134, 145, 192, 261
sex   2, 3, 4, 5, 6, 8, 24, 27, 30, 37, 49, 50, 51, 59, 72, 73, 79, 83, 84, 91, 93, 94, 97, 132, 166, 197, 208, 248, 251, 263
sexology   7, 17, 28, 54, 73
sexual   1, 3, 4, 6, 7, 8, 14, 17, 21, 27, 30, 36, 37, 48, 49, 50, 53, 54, 55, 57, 59, 64, 65, 69, 72, 73, 75, 77, 79, 84, 87, 93, 94, 95, 107, 123, 125, 126, 127, 128, 132, 138, 144, 145, 148, 156, 158, 159, 160, 161, 162, 164, 167, 168, 172, 173, 175, 176, 183, 184, 194, 200, 201, 202, 203, 204, 205, 206, 207, 216, 218, 221, 222, 225, 226, 232, 233, 238, 239, 243, 245, 246, 247, 248, 249, 250, 251, 257, 258, 263
sexuality   4, 6, 31, 51, 53, 93, 127
shame   6, 8, 24, 26, 49, 50, 53, 135, 139, 177, 179
Sherrard, Philip   6, 263
sickness   104, 138, 163
sin   6, 9, 14, 17, 21, 23, 37, 39, 49, 50, 52, 53, 57, 58, 59, 60, 65, 72, 73, 76, 78, 83, 84, 89, 91, 93, 95, 100, 101, 110, 118, 125, 128, 132, 134, 135, 138, 139, 140, 184, 185, 188, 189, 193, 194, 195, 196, 197, 200, 208, 209, 216, 218, 221, 234, 245, 246, 247, 248, 250
sin (peccatum)   132
sinner   164, 199
Smalley, Beryl   10
society   1, 2, 3, 7, 9, 20, 28, 40, 42, 44, 53, 54, 60, 68, 69, 75, 79, 84, 95, 97, 107, 143, 188, 200, 208, 216, 222, 237, 258, 259
soul   25, 66, 68, 81, 82, 83, 137, 138, 139, 140, 194, 250, 252
Southern, R. W.   9
sovereignty   178, 179, 180, 185, 220, 255
spirit   3, 6, 12, 23, 24, 25, 26, 27, 28, 30, 38, 47, 59, 64, 65, 66, 67, 68, 70, 76, 92, 93, 94, 107, 117, 127, 150, 153, 178, 197, 211, 212, 213, 214, 215, 227, 239, 254, 255, 258, 260
spiritual   22, 24, 25, 39, 45, 46, 59, 64, 65, 74, 87, 99, 117, 139, 140, 152, 153, 176, 192, 213, 215, 246
spouses   22, 23, 42, 44, 51, 75, 76, 77, 86, 87, 99, 100, 107, 130,

133, 134, 150, 165, 188, 195, 213, 215, 238, 254, 257, 258
Suetonius 93
supernatural 38, 43, 48, 51, 66, 82, 107
Sutton, Thomas 34

T

Takimoto, Jiro 155
Tempier, Etienne 33, 34, 35
Temple 225, 234, 235, 236, 238, 239, 240, 242, 244, 254
terrestrial 230, 238
Tertullian 24, 25, 28, 29
theologian 3, 4, 6, 7, 8, 9, 12, 14, 17, 18, 19, 20, 22, 26, 27, 30, 31, 32, 33, 34, 37, 38, 41, 42, 43, 45, 50, 52, 55, 57, 63, 64, 66, 67, 68, 69, 73, 74, 75, 78, 80, 82, 83, 85, 87, 88, 91, 92, 94, 95, 97, 109, 117, 119, 123, 124, 130, 133, 134, 137, 138, 139, 144, 148, 151, 178, 182, 188, 189, 192, 196, 197, 202, 218, 260, 261
theological 6, 17, 32, 36, 37, 38, 63, 77, 109, 120, 148, 151, 152, 155, 156, 182, 190, 197, 257
theology 10, 15, 16, 17, 18, 21, 22, 23, 26, 27, 32, 34, 36, 37, 41, 42, 44, 51, 56, 63, 64, 70, 71, 72, 73, 75, 79, 82, 91, 94, 97, 106, 107, 109, 116, 117, 119, 120, 123, 138, 140, 142, 144, 146, 147, 148, 155, 161, 168, 175, 176, 178, 182, 183, 189, 190, 191, 194, 197, 200, 202, 211, 215, 216, 221, 222, 223, 225, 234, 239, 247, 250, 251, 252, 254, 257, 260, 261
Thomas Aquinas 16, 23, 28, 33, 34, 35, 36, 37, 38, 39, 41, 43, 44, 45, 47, 48, 51, 52, 53, 54, 55, 57, 58, 60, 63, 64, 75, 76, 77, 78, 79, 80, 81, 86, 87, 88, 91, 92, 93, 117, 119,
130, 131, 134, 152, 162, 183, 195, 201, 206, 216, 239, 261
Thomas Cahill 3, 5, 263
Thomas of Ireland 33
Thomism 33, 34, 35, 39, 40, 45, 51, 63, 94, 95
Tiberius 93
traditional 8, 35, 72, 80, 94, 107, 138, 190, 195, 211, 243, 252
Trinity 36, 38, 99, 105, 106, 109, 117, 200, 223
Troubadours 2, 5, 13, 15, 260, 263
truth 6, 9, 10, 18, 19, 22, 24, 74, 129, 146, 148, 151, 166, 177, 178, 182, 192, 193, 207, 208, 214, 228, 239, 242, 250, 259
Tuchman, Barbara 10

U

Umberto Eco 10
union 3, 5, 7, 38, 40, 41, 42, 43, 45, 49, 55, 66, 67, 75, 79, 82, 84, 85, 86, 87, 91, 94, 95, 100, 101, 106, 107, 124, 126, 127, 137, 157, 158, 169, 173, 174, 176, 177, 187, 213, 215, 258
University of Paris 3, 35, 63, 64, 123

V

venial 17, 52, 59, 76, 83, 84, 89, 91, 132, 138, 185, 193, 195, 196
Virgil (Publius Vergilius Maro) 12, 163
Virgin Mary 72, 73, 79, 245
virginal 72, 243
virginity 6, 17, 21, 22, 25, 26, 27, 28, 29, 58, 59, 60, 61, 73, 78, 85, 131, 132, 136, 183, 184, 221, 222, 231, 232, 233, 234, 243, 251
virtue 4, 7, 26, 29, 31, 39, 43, 49, 50, 51, 52, 67, 81, 86, 88, 117,

118, 121, 126, 129, 130, 135, 143, 148, 176, 177, 178, 179, 185, 190, 199, 200, 201, 202, 203, 204, 212, 226, 228, 231, 232, 233, 234, 244, 251, 260
virtuous   51, 59, 88, 89, 126, 127, 129, 165, 172, 177, 187, 193, 201, 202, 203, 207, 221, 228, 234, 242
virtuous (virtutum)   121, 131
vocation   136, 183, 251

W

wedded   97, 98, 100, 104, 146, 165, 168, 181, 191, 194, 195, 210, 215, 217, 248, 250
wedding   3, 41, 58, 100, 109, 133, 164, 174, 176, 189, 190
wedlock   21, 28, 29, 138, 187, 189, 248, 249, 250
Westermarck, E.   6, 263
Western   2, 31, 36, 101, 121
widowhood   136
widows   101, 136, 166, 195
William of Moerbeke   33
wisdom   12, 31, 78, 110, 133, 226, 229, 231, 234, 238, 248, 253, 254, 258
woman   1, 2, 3, 7, 11, 13, 29, 31, 40, 41, 44, 45, 49, 52, 53, 55, 57, 65, 66, 67, 68, 69, 70, 72, 73, 74, 78, 79, 80, 82, 84, 85, 94, 97, 98, 99, 100, 101, 102, 103, 104, 107, 109, 110, 111, 112, 113, 115, 116, 117, 124, 126, 127, 129, 132, 133, 134, 135, 142, 143, 145, 146, 148, 149, 163, 164, 169, 179, 180, 184, 187, 193, 194, 195, 197, 217, 220, 233, 236, 240, 241, 242, 243, 244, 250, 255
Worcestershire rite   105, 108, 130
worship   19, 24, 59, 107, 108, 139, 143, 146, 147, 177, 185, 242
Wycliffite reform   192

Y

Yeats, W. B.   28
York rite   78, 97, 99, 102, 103, 104, 105, 110

www.ingramcontent.com/pod-product-compliance
Lightning Source LLC
Chambersburg PA
CBHW021053080526
44587CB00010B/231